JavaScript and HTML 4.0 User's Resource

William H. Murray
Chris H. Pappas

Prentice Hall PTR
Upper Saddle River, NJ 07458
http://www.phptr.com

ISBN 0-13-977422-X

9 780139 774225

90000

Library of Congress Cataloging-in-Publication Data

Murray, William H.

    JavaScript and HTML 4.0 user's resource / William H. Murray, Chris
H. Pappas.

       p.   cm.

    Includes bibliographical references and index.

    ISBN 0-13-977422-X

    1. JavaScript (Computer program language)   2. HTML (Document
markup language)   I. Pappas, Chris H., 1953-   II. Title.

QA76.73.J39M87   1998

005.7'2--dc21

                                       98-39484

                                          CIP

Editorial/Production Supervision: Nick Radhuber
Acquisitions Editor: Jeffrey Pepper
Editorial Assistant: Linda Ramagnano
Manufacturing Manager: Alexis Heydt
Cover Design: Design Source
Cover Design Director: Jerry Votta

© 1999 Prentice Hall PTR
Prentice-Hall, Inc.
A Simon & Schuster Company
Upper Saddle River, NJ 07458

Prentice Hall books are widely used by corporations and government agencies
for training, marketing, and resale.

The publisher offers discounts on this book when ordered in bulk quantities.
For more information, contact

    Corporate Sales Department, Phone 800-382-3419;
    FAX: 201-236-714; e-mail: `corpsales@prenhall.com`
    Or write:
    Prentice Hall PTR, Corp. Sales Dept., One Lake Street, Upper Saddle River, NJ 07458

Printed in the United States of America

10 9 8 7 6 5 4 3

ISBN 0-13-977422-X

Prentice-Hall International (UK) Limited, *London*
Prentice-Hall of Australia Pty. Limited, *Sydney*
Prentice-Hall Canada Inc., *Toronto*
Prentice-Hall Hispanoamericana, S.A., *Mexico*
Prentice-Hall of India Private Limited, *New Delhi*
Prentice-Hall of Japan, Inc., *Tokyo*
Simon & Schuster Asia Pte. Ltd., *Singapore*
Editora Prentice-Hall do Brasil, Ltda., *Rio de Janeiro*

Dedicated to
Dr. Joseph M. Newmark

CONTENTS

Chapter 16   Math in JavaScript   341

Chapter 17   Date and Time   353

 # PREFACE

This book instructs the reader on how to incorporate the power of the JavaScript programming language in ordinary HTML documents. Through four, well-defined sections you will review HTML fundamentals and get a taste of what a programming language can offer good Web page design. You'll then learn valuable new information related to HTML 4.0, such as image maps, forms, and style sheets. Another section is devoted to JavaScript fundamentals. In this section you'll learn the terms and definitions of the JavaScript language and investigate simple applications that reinforce these concepts. Finally, a section of the book is devoted to the specific integration of HTML and JavaScript. Here you will get a taste of the real power of JavaScript combined with HTML 4.0.

WHOM THIS BOOK IS FOR

This book was designed for people actively creating HTML documents who are ready to incorporate the power of a programming language in their projects. We do not make the assumption that you are a programmer by trade. However, we do assume you know the fundamentals of creating HTML documents and have probably worked with a programming language such as BASIC, Pascal, or even C/C++.

Perhaps you have not developed a Web page for some time, or dabbled in the mysteries of HTML 4.0 cascading style sheets. If that is the case, you'll learn that Web page designers now have new power at their fingertips. An entire section of this book is designed to bring you up to speed on the powerful new features of HTML 4.0.

This book will teach you the terms and definitions used in the JavaScript programming language and show you how to integrate JavaScript into your HTML documents.

If you are serious about using HTML 4.0 and JavaScript in your Web projects, this book is for you.

WHAT YOU'LL NEED

Working in the HTML 4.0 environment with JavaScript is relatively inexpensive and easy to do. In terms of materials, you will need a computer with a current browser, such as Microsoft's Internet Explorer 4.0 (or later) or Netscape (version 4.0 or later). In most cases, these are available free of charge from the Web or provided with your operating system.

In terms of knowledge, we assume you have been working on the Web for some time and have actually used some version of HTML to create simple documents. Somewhere in your background, you have also learned some programming fundamentals from the BASIC, Pascal, or C/C++ programming languages. You'll find concepts such as constants, variables, conditional statements, loops, and so on transfer immediately to the JavaScript language. For example, with minor variations in syntax, you'll see that a loop in JavaScript is very similar to a loop in C/C++ or even BASIC.

Armed with this material and knowledge, you'll very quickly learn the advantages of the JavaScript language and how to incorporate it within an HTML 4.0 document.

HOW THIS BOOK IS ORGANIZED

This book is divided into four major sections. Part One, "Getting Started," deals with the essentials of HTML and JavaScript. In this section you learn terms and definitions and investigate some relative simple HTML documents that use simple JavaScript code to illustrate the power of adding a programming language to HTML documents.

Part Two, "HTML 4.0 Fundamentals," provides a quick review of HTML fundamentals and at the same time introduces you to many of the new HTML 4.0 concepts. If you are familiar with HTML, you'll find this section a snap to master. You'll quickly grasp concepts, such as image maps, forms, style sheets, and scripting.

In Part Three, "JavaScript Fundamentals," you'll learn the keys to JavaScript. If you have programmed in BASIC, Pascal, or C/C++, you'll find many familiar programming concepts are similar in the JavaScript language. JavaScript, however, goes one step beyond traditional procedure-oriented languages. With JavaScript you'll also learn object-oriented programming fundamentals. For example, new terms like objects, events, methods, and so on are introduced at a pace which you can master as you move from chapter to chapter.

Part Four, "HTML and JavaScript," covers the specific features in the integration of HTML 4.0 and JavaScript. You'll work with frames and layers, cookies, history lists, and various JavaScript objects. In the final chapter, you'll even learn how to create a custom JavaScript object.

Appendixes A through C are an added bonus. In these appendixes, you'll be treated to three easy-to-read tables that provide a comprehensive list of HTML 4.0 elements and colors, as well as a list of attributes and related elements.

PART ONE

Getting Started

This part is devoted to those topics necessary for getting started with HTML and JavaScript. Here you will learn terms and definitions and investigate some relatively simple HTML documents that used simple JavaScript code. You may find many of the topics discussed are a reinforcement to knowledge you have already gained. Simple examples will show you the early stages in bridging the JavaScript language to your HTML document.

CHAPTER 1

INTRODUCTION TO HTML AND JAVASCRIPT

- Tools You Need to Get Started

- What You Need to Know to Get Started

- JavaScript the Language

Good news! You are going to *love* JavaScript. Why? Because, except for HTML, it's the easiest thing a state-of-the-art programmer can learn. If you have been around programming languages for a while, you are very aware that high-level language compilers have exploded from their single floppy editions (i.e., Borland International's original Turbo Pascal) to 200+-megabyte monsters like Microsoft's Visual C++.

Programming fundamentals also have escalated from simple procedural, top-down, structured programming to object-oriented, event-driven, multitasking, multimedia, multimigraine formulas. Unfortunately, *you* cannot increase your mental storage capacity as easily as adding a terabyte hard disk! Well, good news. JavaScript is *easy* to master and is fun and powerful.

Introduction

If you are reading this, then you have already discovered that HTML provides little more than sophisticated Web page formatting. While HTML pages can be as exciting to view as today's state-of-the-art $3-million Hollywood production, in all honesty, to a serious programmer, they are little more than monitor-sized flashy billboards.

You have purchased this book because you need to go beyond a "pretty face" and need to have your Web page meaningfully interact with the user.

JavaScript allows you to use Web page accessories such as counters, catalogs, calendars, maps, scrolling messages, and games. With JavaScript you can control your system's audio, video, and virtual reality plug-ins. By the time you finish this book, you'll have a thorough understanding of the JavaScript language and how to design effective scripts for input validation, forms, searches, calculations, games, and more.

Plug-ins

Allow program modules to dynamically extend the capabilities of most state-of-the-art browsers. These extensions include the handling of new data types and information, along with Java and JavaScript that facilitate actual Web page programming.

Tools You Need to Get Started

You basically need two tools to begin writing and testing JavaScript programs. The first is a good source code editor, such as Microsoft

WordPad. The second is a copy of the latest version of Netscape or Internet Explorer. The latter is necessary in order for you to develop and test program code. If you need to download a current version of Netscape, you can get it from Netscape's home page at http://home.netscape.com, or from Netscape's FTP (File Transfer Protocol) server at ftp://ftp.netscape.com. For the latest at Microsoft, surf on over to http://www.microsoft.com.

What You Need to Know to Get Started

If one were to equate HTML (HyperText Markup Language) to the shell of an automobile, then JavaScript would be the vehicle's engine. One without the other is useless. While this text is not a comprehensive manual on HTML, Chapters 1 through 13 discuss the fundamental HTML terms and methodology necessary to author in-depth Web pages with sophisticated front ends. Chapters 10 through 23 will then teach you how to add programmable functionality.

JavaScript Ancestry

JavaScript is not a totally *new* programming language but instead could be considered a dialect, just as C++ is not a totally new language but an evolution of C. JavaScript's ancestry begins at Netscape, which originally developed a language called LiveScript. LiveScript provided a basic scripting capability to both Netscape Navigator and Internet Explorer.

Starting With Netscape 2.0, LiveScript was given the new name JavaScript.

JavaScript supports both Web browser and Web server scripting. Browser scripts are used to create dynamic Web pages that are more interactive, more responsive, and more tightly integrated with plug-ins and Java applets. JavaScript supports these features by providing special programming capabilities, such as the ability to dynamically generate HTML and to define custom event-handling functions.

You incorporate a JavaScript into an HTML document via the HTML <SCRIPT> tag element. When a JavaScript-enabled browser loads an HTML document containing scripts, it evaluates the scripts as they are encountered. The scripts may be used to create HTML elements that are added to the displayed document or to define functions, called *event handlers*, that respond to user actions, such as mouse clicks and keyboard entries. JavaScript also controls Java applets and plug-ins.

From a Web server viewpoint, JavaScripts can process form data, perform database searches, and implement custom Web applications. Server-side JavaScripts are more tightly integrated with the Web server than traditional Common Graphical Interface (CGI) programs.

JavaScript the Language

In late November 1995, Netscape's LiveScript officially became JavaScript in a joint announcement by Netscape and Sun Microsystems, Inc. With such a symbiotic relationship, there is little doubt that JavaScript will continue to resemble Java and that it will become the choice tool for gluing Java applets into Web pages (at least from Netscape's point of view).

If you compare the number of Netscape Navigator (Internet Explorer) users versus those Navigator users who actually write JavaScripts, you'll soon discover that JavaScript is one of the least-used components of Netscape's suite of interactivity tools. Yet the ease of using JavaScript, by simply inserting the appropriate code into an HTML document with the benefits of quick access to browser properties, makes for an enticing programming scenario.

Navigator or Internet Explorer can report back to a JavaScript meaningful information such as history lists, currently loaded documents, frames, forms, and links to the programmer. Capturing user events such as changing form values or pointing at links are second nature for JavaScript.

Unlike many current state-of-the-art languages, such as C and C++ which are compiled languages, and the unique niche created by the Java language, which is both compiled and interpreted, JavaScript is an interpreted language. This means that your JavaScript source code is executed directly at runtime. Interpreted languages offer several advantages as well as several disadvantages.

Interpreted languages are generally simpler than compiled languages and are easy to learn. Frequently, it is easier to develop, change, and trouble-shoot programs because the need to recompile with each change is removed. On the down side, the need to interpret commands as the program is run can produce a performance hit with some interpreted languages. JavaScripts are precompiled to *bytecode* format, similar to Java source code, as the script is downloaded and interpreted.

JavaScript is similar in syntax, basic structure, flow constructs, and security validation checking. Note however, that Netscape Navigator, Dynamic HTML 4.0, and JavaScript are all under intense development and are constantly evolving. For all intents and purposes, this means you are trying to hit a moving target.

What Is a Scripting Language?

Scripting languages have been around for a long time, predating the Web. UNIX used scripts to perform repetitive system administration tasks and to automate many tasks for less computer-literate users. Scripting languages are the fundamental building block for much of the CGI programming that is currently used to add a limited form of interactivity to Web pages (for example the Perl language). JavaScript makes it possible to program responses to user events such as mouse clicks and data entry in forms because of the way in which JavaScript is integrated into the browser and its direct interaction with HTML documents.

JavaScript Is Object-Oriented

The simplest way to define an object to a procedural programmer is to say that an object is a syntactic bundling of data members with functions that work exclusively on those data members. Therefore, when you pass "data" around, you also pass the "horsepower" that works on that data, all in one neat tidy code package. Note, however, that the object doesn't give you any additional capabilities, just a new protected syntax. And so that you understand object-oriented terminology, in a procedural language one would say, "I'm declaring a variable," but in an object-oriented language one would say, "I'm instantiating an object." Also, an object-oriented programmer uses the term *method* or *member function* to distinguish a subroutine syntactically bundled to a specific object, from regular standalone functions *not* specific to *any* object.

JavaScript provides several built-in objects that report back information about currently loaded Web pages and contents. A sample object hierarchy would look like Window, Location, History, Document-Forms/Anchors. Other built-in objects, such as the strings Math and Date, allow you to manipulate strings, perform trigonometric calculations, and retrieve current date information.

JavaScript Is Platform-Independent

Since you have no way of knowing an end-user's system configuration, any program you write, distributed across the Web, must necessarily be hardware- or platform-independent, in order to execute properly. JavaScript is platform-independent. The same program code can be used on any platform for which Netscape Navigator or Internet Explorer is available.

Source Code Plagiarism

From a code security point of view, the one downside to JavaScript is that *there is no code security!* Since an entire JavaScript is embedded within an HTML document, it is visible to all who care to view. This means that any signature-specific algorithm you design necessarily becomes public domain.

Quick Get Me Started –
What Is HTML?

Since JavaScripts are hosted by HTML documents, it is necessary for you to understand HTML. The beginning chapters of this book review the necessary fundamentals. If you are already thoroughly familiar with HTML tag elements, you can skip directly to Part Three, "JavaScript Fundamentals." Note, however, that HTML is also a moving target. By skipping Parts One and Two you may inadvertently miss discussions of the newer dynamic HTML 4.0 features.

From IBM to grandmothers, everybody's getting into WWW (World Wide Web, a hypertext-based system of presenting information over the Internet) page development, the visually exciting way to say to the world, "I've arrived!" Undoubtedly the most exciting aspect of Web page construction is the easy to learn protocol of HTML. But let's not put the cart before the horse. HTML has a very interesting history.

HTML Ancestry

You see, it all began at the high-energy physics laboratory in Geneva, Switzerland, named CERN. The simple problem encountered by the scientists involved the time delay in disseminating research papers and other documents. And this time delay wasn't restricted to the nucleus of buildings on the CERN campus, since their vital statistics were shared throughout the world. It is *Tim Berners-Lee* who is credited with designing the system that would allow scientists to share fairly complex materials easily, using a simple set of protocols over the Internet (the term used to describe all the worldwide interconnected TCP/IP networks).

Tim broke his solution down into two parts: HTTP, the HyperText Transfer Protocol definition, which provided a simple way for users to request and receives files over the Internet, and the more familiar HTML or HyperText Markup Language. Unlike HTTP, which defines how information is sent or received, HTML defines the visual presentation of the material on the receiving end.

TCP/IP

An abbreviation for Transport Control Protocol/Internet Protocol, a set of protocols that applications use for communicating across networks or over the Internet. These protocols specify how packets of data should be constructed, addressed, checked for errors, and so on.

Needless to say, as originally designed, HTML was never intended to be used for the variety of display potentials presented by today's multitasking object-oriented operating systems like UNIX and Microsoft Windows. Nor was it ever designed to create wild multimedia sites that incorporated graphics and animation. The fledgling Internet was seen more as a library than as a Virtual Reality Mall. As such, the original definition of HTML included as much output display control as would be needed by the typical scientific journal article.

Because HTML's protocols were succinct and complete, they were immediately accepted by the scientific community which adopted it as its electronic typesetter. Scientists were particularly excited about HTML's ability to create links to other pages of information, making the documents much more alive than a static piece of paper. Unfortunately, this forward-only hotlink capability left something to be desired.

SGML

Actually, HTML is a subset of an even larger page display protocol definition known as SGML, or Standard Generalized Markup Language. The scientists at CERN used SGML for highly technical and legal documentation. SGML is still used by large organizations that maintain libraries of frequently referenced documentation.

SGML flavoring lingers to this day within the formal HTML standard with its insistence on document structure, the separation of content from formatting, and the use of logical tags (tags are the special control characters that separate HTML markup from ordinary text, namely the left and right angle brackets: < >).

DTD

All documents that can be marked up with the same hierarchy of elements are said to belong to a certain *document type*. Rather than describe a set of tools to mark up documents, SGML defines the structure of a particular type of document in what is called Document Type Definition, or DTD. HTML 4.0, code-named *Cougar*, is an example of an SGML DTD.

SGML in HTML

The most prominent throwbacks to SGML are the <H1> through <H6> tags used to generate a six-level outline format. Today's users employ these tags as a quick way to format headings with varying degrees of emphasis. Some tags like <B> for bold and <EM> for emphasis may appear to be two different ways of saying the same thing, and indeed some *browsers* treat them as such. However, technically, <B> is font-specific, whereas <EM> provides more leeway in formatting the document.

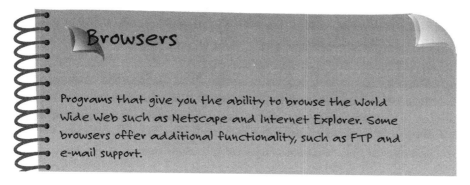

Browsers

Programs that give you the ability to browse the World Wide Web such as Netscape and Internet Explorer. Some browsers offer additional functionality, such as FTP and e-mail support.

With the explosion in popularity of the Internet, the browser market skyrocketed in 1995 and so too did the availability of new HTML tags. However, the SGML throwbacks are still the quickest and easiest way to create tables of contents and indices automatically.

Realizing the tremendous profit potential of this new electronic media, Netscape and Microsoft locked into a perpetual battle over trying to give their customers the de facto standard in Web browser capabilities. Fortunately the W3C (World Wide Web Consortium–http://www.w3.org/–which technically oversees HTML revisions) stepped in to maintain some sort of compatibility across platforms. One of the exciting protocols to come out of these meetings is the cascading style sheet. Cascading style sheets make it possible to specify particular fonts, point sizes, and text placement for a wider variety of HTML elements.

What Is an Element?

An element is any HTML tag or tag pair that is parsed and treated as a unique item on a page. An element differs from an object in that an element is an object only if it is named with an ID attribute. Some examples of elements are headers, paragraphs, lists of items, or tables. Elements can contain plain text, or other elements, or both.

More on Tags

HTML tags, as mentioned earlier, mark the elements of a file for your browser. Tags are usually paired, for example <H1> for a level-one header definition followed by a closing </H1> end tag instruction. End tags look just like beginning tags except for the addition of a forward slash / symbol immediately after the left angle bracket <.

Some elements may include an *attribute*, which is additional information that is included inside the start tag. For example, files in GIF or JPEG format can use top-, middle-, or bottom-edge alignment by including the appropriate attribute with the image source HTML code. One final note. HTML tags are *not* case sensitive so <H1> = <h1> (well most of the time–the few exceptions will be documented throughout the book).

What Is an HTML Document?

Technically, an HTML document is nothing more than a combination of HTML tags placed inside a standard ASCII text file. This means that you can create an HTML file using Windows Notepad, or Emacs or vi on UNIX architectures, and even BBEdit on a Macintosh platform. If you are running the latest editions of many popular software suites such as Corel Office, or Microsoft Professional, then you own a WYSIWYG (What You See Is What You Get) word processor capable of generating and visually displaying HTML documents!

So If It's So Easy, What's the Catch?

There's only one snag to your actually taking a completed HTML document and flashing it on every monitor from here to Moscow—money (unless you are a student). You see, you need someone (a host server, and for students, well, let the institution take it out of your tuition) willing to store your multimedia punched front page, willing to pay for the electricity running the system, willing to pay for the hardware connection to the Internet, and willing to pay a tech support person to keep everything static free and running clean.

The great news is that some communities operate what is called *FreeNet*, a community-based network that provides free Internet access. If all else fails, well, you'll have to subscribe to a service such as AOL (America Online) or a local service provider. These services usually charge two separate rates, one rate for personal and a separate rate for business Web page accounts.

OK, Here's a Quick HTML Document

Whether you are using Assembly Language, Ada, Java, Perl, or C++, every language, beyond its formal description, has an industrywide acceptable list of language-specific dos and don'ts—HTML is no exception. Even a minimal HTML document should contain certain standard HTML tags, mainly a head and body text. The head contains the title, while the body encapsulates the actual text to be displayed. The body can contain multiple paragraphs, lists, tables, graphics, and other elements.

Browsers, similar to compilers, expect an HTML document to be in a certain form. This standard form comes directly from the SGML and its sibling HTML specifications. The simplest, properly formed HTML document you can create looks very similar to the following code listing:

```
<HTML>
<HEAD>
<TITLE>My First HTML Document</TITLE>
</HEAD>
<BODY>
<H1>Hello World!</H1>
<P>This is my first paragraph letting the world
know that I am ready to begin my cottage industry.
<P>OH, and make my first MILLION!
</BODY>
</HTML>
```

<HTML>

The first tag in the listing, <HTML>, flags the browser to the fact that it is parsing an HTML encoded file format. HTML files always contain an *.html* file extension (or for systems using the eight-letter filename, three-letter file extension format, *.htm* extension).

<HEAD>

The <HEAD> tag identifies the first part of your HTML encoded document that contains the document's title. The title is shown as part of your browser's window.

<TITLE>

The <TITLE> tag defines your document's title and broadcasts its content in a global context. Your browser displays the title in an area separate from the document text. Choosing your document's <TITLE> is a little more important than it may initially appear since it is this line of text that is displayed on someone's hotlist or bookmark list. It is your document's title that is referenced when using search engines. For this reason, you should always choose a <TITLE> that is unique, descriptive, and pulls those Web surfers right down onto your Web page.

<BODY>

The largest portion of your HTML document is encapsulated within the <BODY>, </BODY> tag pairs and contains the information displayed by the browser. The following tags are used within the <BODY>, </BODY> tags:

< H 1 > - L E V E L H E A D E R

As mentioned earlier, HTML has a six-level throwback to its SGML proginator. These tags are <H1> through <H6> and </H1> through </H6>, respectively. Each level header is displayed using a larger and/or bolder font than is used by the browser for displaying normal text.

Browsers ignore carriage returns embedded within the <BODY> of an HTML document. This means that you do not have to concern yourself with how long each of your text lines is since any text formatting you want must be accomplished with an appropriate HTML tag. So, for example, the two lines in the source file

```
<P>This is my first paragraph letting the world
know that I am ready to begin my cottage industry.
```

are seen as one continuous line and will be formatted based on the browser's current screen width. From the browser's point of view, the source file could have been entered as follows:

```
<HTML> <HEAD> <TITLE>My First HTML Document</TITLE>
</HEAD> <BODY> <H1>Hello World!</H1> <P>This is my
first paragraph letting the world know that I am ready
to begin my cottage industry. <P>OH, and make my first
MILLION! </BODY> </HTML>
```

with identical visual display interpretations. Browsers also condense multiple spaces embedded within an HTML document down to a single space.

You may be wondering why the sample HTML document contains no </P> end tags. This is because browsers understand that a start <P> tag indirectly indicates that a previous paragraph is terminating.

Note however, there is a </P> end tag, but it is traditionally used only when the encapsulated paragraph (<P>, </P>) requires a certain attribute, such as centering, as in this reworked example:

```
<ALIGN=CENTER>
<P>This is my first paragraph letting the world
know that I am ready to begin my cottage industry.
</P>
```

A Word about HTML Document Formatting

Since browsers ignore carriage returns and extra spaces, you can use these to visually format your HTML document. For example, you should separate headings from their associated bodies with a blank line. Use extra blank lines to separate document sections. All of this will go a long way to streamlining any edits or modifications the document may need over time.

Some Common File Types and Their Extensions

Web pages are never going to be the same with the spectacular multimedia enhancements possible with HTML 4.0. Throughout this book you will learn how to add images in their various formats, sounds, even animation. Table 1.1 enumerates these file types by name and file extension.

Table 1.1: *Common File Types and Their Extensions*

File Type	File Extension
Plain ASCII text	.txt
HTML document	.html or for 8.3 formats, .htm
GIF image	.gif
TIFF image	.tiff or for 8.3 formats, .tif
X Bitmap image	.xbm
JPEG image	.jpeg or for 8.3 formats, .jpg
PostScript file	.ps
AIFF sound file	.aiff or for 8.3 formats, .aif
AU sound file	.au
WAV sound file	.wav
QuickTime movie	.mov
MPEG movie	.mpeg or for 8.3 formats, .mpg

Quick Tell Me—How Does the Web Work?

The World Wide Web (WWW) can be viewed in three parts. The first is the server that is hosting (storing/connecting to the Internet) your HTML document. The second is the surfer or end user viewing your HTML document. The third is the protocol making the bidirectional communication possible.

It Allows Every Type of Computer World Access!

But most importantly, the Web is *platform-independent*. This means that you can access the World Wide Web regardless of whether you're running on a low-end PC, Apple Mac, an expensive Silicon Graphics workstation, a VAX cluster, or a multimillion dollar Cray supercomputer!

Web Browsers—The Electronic Sears Catalog

A Web browser, as mentioned earlier, is a program that you use to view pages on the World Wide Web, sometimes called *Web clients*. A vast diversity of Web browsers are available for just about every type of architecture you can imagine, most importantly Graphical-User-Interface–based systems or GUI systems such as X11, Windows, and Mac platforms. There are even text-only browsers available for simple dial-up UNIX connections.

Full-Color Shopping at Your Fingertips

One of the key features of Web browsers is their ability to display both text and graphics in full color on the same page, and all of this with a simple URL address followed very often by nothing more than consecutive mouse clicks. If you are just jumping onto your Internet surfboard for the first time, you may not be aware that in its fledgling state, the Internet was accessed by nonstandard, confusing, command-line, text-only protocols. Of course today's state-of-the-art rendition incorporates sound, and even streaming video. Even 3D virtual reality simulations are possible with VRML, Virtual Reality Markup Language.

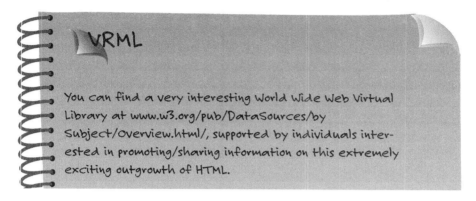

You can find a very interesting World Wide Web Virtual Library at www.w3.org/pub/DataSources/by Subject/Overview.html/, supported by individuals interested in promoting/sharing information on this extremely exciting outgrowth of HTML.

Info, Info Everywhere

Of course the very name, World Wide Web, indicates that the information you are downloading is distributed throughout the entire globe. Since the information you are accessing occupies vast amounts of disk storage, particularly when you include images, multimedia, and streaming video, there hasn't been a computer built to date that could house this bit explosion in one physical location.

Actually, this distributed diversity of data storage repositories is to your advantage. Were this information stored in a single location, imagine the chaos generated by a downed mainframe! The Web is successful in providing so much information because that information is distributed globally across thousands of Web sites. And the best part about the interconnection is that if one leg of the information route is interrupted, for any reason, an alternate Web link takes over.

Provides Full Bidirectional Communication

An exciting aspect to Web interaction is its provisions for you to "talk back." Take, for example, a radio or television broadcast. This is one-directional output.

The exciting news is that with today's evolution of HTML your document's display instructions are not limited to text only, but now include graphical and auditory elements.

Web Browser Characteristics

While there is only one HTML 4.0 standard, it is not true that there is only one visual interpretation of this standard among all the various browsers. Each Web browser displays HTML elements differently. Matters degrade even more when you find out that not all browsers support all of the HTML 4.0 code standards! Fortunately, any HTML code a browser does *not* understand, it usually just ignores.

The unwarned can spend endless hours, even days or weeks, perfecting and tweaking the visual impression and technical content of their company's Web page, only to find it look like a mosaic on an unfriendly browser. To quote the NCSA General Internet HTML-PrimerAll.html document:

> *Hence these words of advice: code your files using correct HTML. Leave the interpreting to the browsers and hope for the best.*

What Is a URL?

When a Web surfer, or end user, or *client* (the system being used by the Web surfer) makes a request to a server, it uses the HTTP protocol, mentioned earlier, across the network to request the information in the form of a *URL* (Universal Resource Locator—URLs specify the location and name of a World Wide Web resource such as a Web site or an HTML document) from the server.

The server in turn processes the request and, again, using HTTP protocol, transfers the requested information back to the client. It is the server's responsibility to tell the client the type of document being transmitted. This is usually defined as a *MIME* (Multipurpose Internet Mail Extension), an enhancement to Internet e-mail that allows for the inclusion of binary data such as word processing programs, graphics, and sound. The client must then process the information before it splashes on the surfer's screen.

URL

A Universal Resource Locator consists of a protocol name, a colon :, two forward slash characters //, a machine name, and a path to a resource using a single forward slash as a separator. URLs can also specify more than just Web page addresses. For example, you can retrieve a document by preceding the URL with ftp://, or File Transfer Protocol, instead of http://, HyperText Transfer Protocol.

MIME

Designed as a means for embedding complex binary documents within an e-mail message. Browsers take the MIME protocol deciphering the document's type and subtype. At this point the browser decides how it wishes to handle the document type. It may choose to process it internally, or invoke an external program to decipher the information. MIME types consist of a main type and subtype. For example, plain text is "text/plain," but "image/gif" specifies an image stored in GIF format.

Some aspects of the displayed document are fixed, such as titles, paragraphs, lists, and so on, but there are components of the document which are considered live or *dynamic*. These dynamic elements display more current information, for example, the ever-present "hit counter" telling you how many other Web surfers have surfed this page before you.

What Is Scripting?

At this point, now that you have a general overview of HTML and browser capabilities, you might just be asking yourself if there's any more to this whole thing than just displaying formatted text and multimedia images. Well, the answer is yes. Welcome to the world of *scripting*.

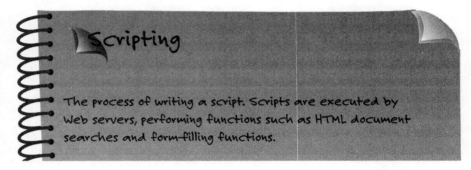

Scripting

The process of writing a script. Scripts are executed by Web servers, performing functions such as HTML document searches and form-filling functions.

CGI

One of the earliest scripting languages was CGI, or Common Gateway Interface. Its most common application is in forms processing. CGI allows you to create pages for users as individual requests come in, and you can customize pages to match that information. The user usually fills out a form and clicks on a submit button. Then the user's browser sends to the server a request that includes the information the user entered into the form. The server then sends this information on to another program for actual processing and responds with the appropriate output at the client or user end. Actually, depending on the kind of server your site resides on, you can write CGI programs in C++, Perl, even AppleScript. If you don't want to go to the trouble of writing complex programs to create pages with server-side interaction, you can purchase products like Microsoft's FrontPage Web site editing program. It incorporates *bots*, which are small programs that attach themselves to the host server. Bots can process forms, provide timestamps, and streamline site-specific search engines.

SCRIPT Tags

HTML page programming takes place via SCRIPT tags which tell script-aware browsers that a script will follow. Within these SCRIPT tags are HTML tags. This approach can be extended to do far more complex things, such as creating *cookies*. Cookies store small amounts of information about a user's preferences on a user's machine and use that information to create customized pages on subsequent visits. You can customize most aspects of Web pages and even the browsers.

Perl

Perl is undoubtedly the most common language used for scripting CGI in UNIX environments with its combination of C syntax and the power of UNIX regular expressions. It is possible to write simple programs in Perl with a minimum of effort.

JavaScript and JScript

Netscape version 2.0 is credited with the introduction of JavaScript. Immediately, Microsoft Internet Explorer 3.0 countered with its own flavors called JScript and VBScript based on the easy-to-learn Visual Basic. The good news is that JavaScript and JScript are evolving toward one another; however various browsers still respond in nonuniform fashion.

These languages provide HTML developers with additional programming horsepower that enables them to make browsers do new and different things. Not everything has to take place on the server end; now the client can take on more of the responsibility of processing.

VBScript

Offering Visual Basic programmers the programming enhancements of a scripting language, VBScript came bundled with Microsoft's

Internet Explorer 3.0. While JavaScript and JScript have a very C- or Java-based flavor, VBScript offers Visual Basic programmers the familiarity of their popular language. VBScript also easily integrates Microsoft's ActiveX controls in a Web environment.

Plug-Ins and ActiveX

Netscape is credited with developing the first plug-ins, Microsoft with developing ActiveX controls. The idea behind both is that the controlling software is loaded onto the user's computer, and then the Web page contains another file that contains the specific instructions or content.

While there are significant structural differences between plug-ins and ActiveX controls, their purpose on the page is basically the same. Like a Java applet, they add additional features and functionality to a Web page without directly affecting the host page. They also create a bidirectional communication between the end user and the plug-in.

The downside to both technologies is they add to the download time of a Web page. In addition to the time it takes to download and install the actual plug-in or control, there's also the extra time to download the content files. In addition, neither technology really provides interaction with other elements on the page. There are some ActiveX controls that provide features like tooltips or pop-up menus, but, like plug-ins, these items are operated directly by the control with no ability to go beyond the feature itself.

What's New in HTML 4.0

Code-named Cougar, the W3C has once again taken on the task of setting the standard that will divide the markup of content from the appearance of a Web page. The Cougar protocol separates the physical style from content markup by more reliance on style sheets (style sheets specify style information whose parameters will govern the formatting of an entire document).

HTML 4.0 is being authored by David Raggett and Arnaud Le Hors, and it continues to recognize frequently used tags from older versions of HTML. If it didn't, we would be looking at all kinds of problems when different browsers accessed pages that exploited its new features. HTML 4.0 isn't really that different from the previous versions of HTML. The key changes can be summed up by the word *dynamic*. HTML 4.0 will now allow the user to manipulate and access the text and image elements directly. The Web page has become dynamically updatable and the properties are easily accessible from code. This might seem like no big deal, since most operating systems have boasted this for years, but in Web pages it's quite a major undertaking.

The updated standard, however, does not simply incorporate a few new tags and attributes. While most of the tags from previous versions remain, it's this new dynamic ability to manipulate and access elements with a scripting language that forms the unique cornerstone of HTML 4.0. For this reason, both Netscape and Microsoft have christened this new HTML version *dynamic HTML*.

Both Netscape Communicator and Internet Explorer 4.0 have changed the structure of just how a Web page is displayed by exposing their browsers to these new dynamic HTML capabilities. For example, with advancement of dynamic or movable images, shoppers can now slide pictures of their purchase items into an image of a shopping cart. While these are new features of dynamic HTML language itself, they do, of course, depend upon the browser to display the results. You can't expect the HTML 4.0–specific parts of a page to do much in Navigator 3 or Internet Explorer 3. As with all other new developments in HTML, the browser must provide support before the page can perform as intended. The following seven features highlight the exciting potential of this latest HTML version:

- Dynamic Fonts–allow you to create your own fonts that others can download, similar to image files. This adds pizzazz to a Web page by making it more eye appealing and unique.
- Absolute Positioning of Elements–allows you to manipulate the x-, y-, and z-coordinates of objects on a page, placing each item where you want it, rather than letting the browser decide.
- Cascading Style Sheets–add even more page format control, are accessible to scripting languages, and allow for a consistent look by applying fonts, colors, and element positioning to multiple pages.

- Canvas Mode–allows the developer to view the HTML-driven page full screen, instead of in the frame of the browser window.
- Dynamic Redraw–allows real-time updating of any element on a page, instead of the time-delayed approach of redrawing the page whenever the user has made a selection.
- New Event-Handling Techniques–event capturing allows events to be passed along from one object to another. It also allows the capturing of events not supported by one object from another.
- Document Object Model–allows the JavaScript language to program the formatting and positioning properties for elements on a page.

HTML—What You Need to Get Started

All you need to create an HTML document is a text editor that is capable of saving files in ASCII format, and a browser such as Netscape's Navigator or Microsoft's Internet Explorer. With a quick click of your mouse and an already established Internet connection, you can download the latest versions of both these browsers to your system via the following addresses:

For Netscape Navigator

http://www.netscape.com

For Internet Explorer 4.0

http://www.microsoft.com

All of the examples and figures for this book were taken using an IBM-compatible PC, running Windows 95, using Windows Notepad text editor for generating the HTML documents. As mentioned earlier however, HTML is a hardware- and platform-independent language. For this reason you can easily create, view, and test, the same HTML documents created throughout the text on a UNIX or Apple Macintosh machine and their associated operating systems.

Should you choose to purchase one of the more popular HTML editors coming onto the market, such as Microsoft's FrontPage, you'll discover a more point-and-click approach to visually creating your Web pages. These programs work much like paint programs only the graphic primitives you place are actually HTML elements and attributes.

While you are graphically designing the page, these products are simultaneously generating the required HTML tags. All of this is fine, as long as the product is designed to do everything you would like from your Web page. However, it is suggested that you stay with a plain text editor for the purposes of this book, since there are some tricks and techniques that even the most powerful HTML editors cannot generate.

Interesting Sites to Visit

www.cern.ch/—The consortium created in 1994 in conjunction with CERN, the European Laboratory for Particle Physics in Switzerland. CERN was the group that gave birth to the Web in 1989.

www.corel.com/products/graphicsandpublishing/—CorelDraw!, a high-end vector program that comes in a bundle by the same name along with Photo-Paint, Dream 3D (a 3D rendering program based on Ray Dream Designer), and Presents (a multimedia presentation program), allows you to export an entire page as HTML.

www.fractal.com/—This site provides excellent painting capabilities such as oil, watercolor, and chalk.

www.cyberdog.apple.com/—This site provides a versatile tool that includes a Web browser, using Apple's OpenDoc technology.

www.hwg.org/—The HTML Writers Guild is an international organization of World Wide Web page authors and Internet publishing professionals. Provides several levels of paid memberships offering benefits such as mentoring programs, educational classes, access to a job board, and software discounts!

www.htmlhelp.com/—This site offers a collection of HTML tips, tricks, and hacks covering both document authoring and Web server management, presented in a question and answer format.

www.browserwatch.iworld.com/—A browser that offers breaking news in the browser and plug-ins industry, plus browser usage statistics and a rich library of plug-ins and *ActiveX* components.

ActiveX

An integration technology developed by Microsoft to add new features to the Internet Explorer Web browser. ActiveX allows programmers to extend Web browser functionality with the programmer's own code. If you consider a Web browser as a miniature operating system, you can see why programmers would love to extend a browser's capabilities.

www.nyu.edu/pages/wsn/susir/lynx/platforms.html/—*Lynx* is a fully featured World Wide Web browser designed for both the UNIX and VMS platforms, using cursor-addressable, character-based terminals or emulators. This is a text-based browser frequently used in universities, libraries, and other environments where affordable access is needed to bring the information of the World Wide Web to as many individuals as possible.

www.developer.netscape.com/index.html/—This Netscape site's DevEdge provides communications, tools, support, and marketing assistance to speed the planning, development, and deployment of Internet and *Intranet* solutions.

Intranet

An internal network that uses Internet technology. Many companies now describe the network they use for intra-company communications as an Intranet.

www.microsoft.com/sitebuilder/—This site provides access to Microsoft's in-depth resources for developing Web sites using Microsoft technology. Their Site Builder network accesses a multilevel library of technical information, products, technologies, services, and ideas and support for using the latest Internet technology, such as the new dynamic HTML 4.0, ActiveX controls, and Java *applets*.

Applet

A program, written in Java, with single or limited function. Many Windows and Win95 special function programs are called applets, and, from that usage, simple Java programs are also called applets. In contrast to an application, which is a program that performs a specific type of work, such as a word processor. Also, applications are standalone products capable of running under an operating system disconnected from the Internet/intranet, while applets are designed to be downloaded by a browser which then executes it.

www.w3.org/pub/www/—Led by Tim Berners-Lee, director of the W3C and creator of the World Wide Web. This platform-independent, vendor-neutral consortium works with the global Internet/intranet community to produce freely available specifications and reference software.

www.w3.org/pub/WWW/TR/REC-CSS/–Accesses the document specifying level 1 of the cascading style sheet mechanism, or CSS1.

www.w3.org/pub/WWW/MarkUp/DOM–A site providing an over-view of materials related to the Document Object Model, or *DOM*.

DOM

A platform-independent, language-neutral interface, allowing programs and scripts to dynamically access and update Web page structure, content, and display style.

WWW.W3.ORG/HYPERTEX/WWW/ADDRESSING/ADDRESSING.HTML
–A site dedicated to defining the various types of URLs available, as well as explaining *URI*s and *URN*s.

URI

A Universal Resource Identifier incorporates not only URLs but also URNs, or Uniform Resource Names, and URCs, or Uniform Resource Citations. URNs and URCs will have wider use in later versions of the HyperText Transfer Protocol.

www.yahoo.com/Computers/WorldWideWeb/–This site links to more than 2,500 pages of HTML documentation. Here you can access multiple sites concerning Internet technology developments such as HTML, CGI, Java, ActiveX, *VBScript*, and *VRML*, in addition to resources for page layout, design, programming, and browser technology updates.

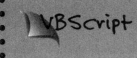

VBScript

Developed by Microsoft and similar to the JavaScript Web page scripting language only it is based on what some consider to be the easiest programming language to learn/use—BASIC.

VRML

Virtual Reality Modeling Language is a language that supports the display of 3D objects in HTML documents.

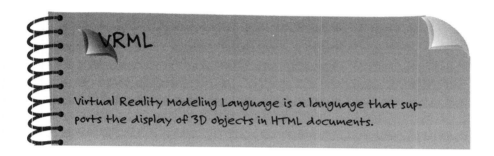

www.ncsa.uiuc.edu/SDg/Software/Mosaic/NCSAMosaic Home.html/—Accesses a Web browser developed by the National Center for Supercomputing Applications (NCSA) at the University of Illinois in Urbana-Champaign.

www.home.netscape.com/trx/comprod/mirror/client-download.html/—Accesses Netscape's Composer, the WYSIWYG editor bundled with the Netscape Communicator suite.

www.microsoft.com/ie/ie40/—Accesses FrontPad, the WYSI-WYG Web page editor used in Microsoft Internet Explorer 4. FrontPad is a streamlined version of Microsoft's *FrontPage*, which you can download for free!

www.adobe.com/prodindex/pagemill/overview.html—Accesses Adobe's PageMill, a powerful WYSIWYG Web page editor. Adobe is the genius behind PageMaker and PDF, or Portable Document Format.

FrontPage

Microsoft's full-fledged total Web site creation and maintenance tool providing HTML editing, site maintenance,
and the FrontPage Web server.

In addition, the following Usenet newsgroups provide a friendly, conversational interchange where you often find a compassionate ear ready to discuss and help solve just about any HTML question you could conceive:

- alt.html
- comp.infosystems.www.authoring.misc
- comp.infosystems.www.browsers.ms-windows
- comp.infosystems.www.browsers.mac
- comp.infosystems.www.browsers.misc

Summary

Since an HTML document is the *host* medium for a JavaScript program and since it is the first visual interface seen by a Web surfer, it is well worth your time to learn or review basic HTML fundamentals. Starting in the next chapter you will see how these standalone HTML features *may* be combined with the programming horsepower missing from the HTML PDL (Page Description Language) and a JavaScript.

CHAPTER 2
SIMPLE HTML AND JAVASCRIPT

- Layout of a Simple HTML Document

- Content versus Controls

- Your First Home Page

All JavaScript statements are included within HTML documents. This chapter explains the fundamental HTML elements or tags necessary to generate a simple Web page and then demonstrates how to modify a straightforward HTML document to host a JavaScript program.

Learning and using HTML is so addicting because each new structure, tag, or attribute you learn about can be edited directly into an existing document. In this chapter you will learn more about the behind-the-scenes proper structure for an HTML document and learn a few tricks to avoid inevitable syntax problems *before* you have them, such as how to put quotation marks within an HTML syntax that uses quotation marks to flag the end of a string.

Layout of a Simple HTML Document

The beauty of HTML is that it does not require a complicated compiler, or endless years of mastering language syntax only to be totally obliterated by some new programming technology that sends us all back to college. The real secret behind HTML is that there is no secret! Everything is right out there in the open just waiting for the right interpretation. HTML documents are just a stream of plain characters waiting to be generated by virtually any text editor capable of generating pure ASCII file output format.

Learning to use HTML requires you to master two fundamentals: the order in which characters occur and the way that they are used to produce the desired results. While it is true that browsers are somewhat forgiving, meaning that you can still see acceptable results even if certain statements have been omitted or misused, the best way to use HTML is to understand and work within its defined boundaries. And rather than concentrate on what makes it easy for *you* to design an HTML document, this book concentrates on teaching you how to design an HTML document that is consistent and easy for the *end user* to access.

In this chapter you will learn about the fundamental components of an HTML document and its overall structure. Along the way, we hope that you begin to appreciate the eloquence, upgradability, and ease of use HTML provides.

Content versus Controls

The first fundamental you need to learn about HTML is that it always separates *content* from the *controls* that act on the content. The content is visually very similar to the text on this page. The controls, sometimes called *markup* or *tags*, are those elements in the HTML document that do not display in your browser's window. These elements appear between pairs of angle-brackets < > and define *how* the content appears on-screen. These tags provide very powerful display possibilities with their header, graphical, hyperlink, and list formats. Before you can read, write, understand, and build a good Web page you not only need to understand the difference between content and controls you also need to use them to their best effect.

Visiphones, Bulletin Boards, and Infomercials

One note of caution before beginning. Remember your target audience. Ask yourself who will be viewing your Web page. And not only who, but how will they view it—on what hardware/software platforms? Are you generating a professional business gateway viewed by corporate-only UNIX sites, or an informal granny-on-line accessed by the grandkids with everything from ancient Commodore computers (basically text-only displays using the text-only *Lynx* browser), university Vax clusters, to your sibling's high-powered Sun workstation? The answers to these questions will decide which HTML components you do or do *not* use to generate navigable display pages.

Your First Home Page

The term *home page* can have several different meanings. If you're reading and browsing the Web, you usually think of the home page as the Web page that loads when you start up your Web browser, or when you choose the browser's Home button. Each browser has its own default home page. Within your browser, you can change the default home page that launches every time you start your daily surf sessions. If you're publishing pages on the Web, however, then the term home page has an entirely different meaning. The home page is the first or topmost page in a hierarchy of pages used to cover all the information on your Web site.

Your home page often resembles a stylized high-level outline enumerating the content of your presentation and consists of list or table of contents or a set of icons. Just remember, you do *not* design your page based on what it looks like on your computer system and on your browser. You *do* design your page so that it works in most browsers by focusing on clear, well-structured content that is easy to read and understand.

\<HTML>, \<HEAD>, and \<BODY> Required

The \<HTML>, \<HEAD>, and \<BODY>, tags, while not at this writing *required* tags, could very easily become standard structure format in the near future. Tools that need these tags may also come along. For this reason, you should not consider creating an HTML document without them, even though most browsers can navigate around their nonexistence. If you get into the habit of including them now, you won't have to worry about updating your files at some later date.

\<HTML> and \</HTML>

The \<HTML> start tag identifies the beginning of the HTML document and its ending tag \</HTML> defines the end of the HTML document, and they encapsulate everything that is supposed to be parsed as HTML. All the text and HTML commands in your HTML document should go within the beginning and ending HTML tags, as in

```
<HTML>
… content and embedded tags here …
</HTML>
```

Theoretically, any content following the \</HTML> end tag is ignored by the browser.

\<HEAD> and \</HEAD>

The \<HEAD> tag marks the beginning of the document header. The header of the document is where global settings are defined and is contained within the \<HEAD>, \</HEAD> tag pair as in

```
<HTML>
<HEAD>
… embedded head tag items here …
</HEAD>
</HTML>
```

This is the document position where you put one or more tags used exclusively within the header portion of an HTML document and it is also an ideal location to include scripting language function definitions. In addition, the \<HEAD> tag pair defines page-level information about the HTML document and can include its title, base URL, index information, next page pointer, and possible links to other HTML documents. Some of the most commonly used tag pairs that can be embedded within the <HEAD> tag pair are <TITLE>, <LINK>, <META>, <SCRIPT>, and <STYLE>. There can be only one <HEAD> tag pair per document. It must follow the opening <HTML> tag and precede the <BODY> tag.

With special HTTP protocol access, headers serve yet another important purpose. Used by search engines, this ability allows them to get some basic information about the page title, file format, last modified date, and any keywords, all without examining the rest of the document's contents.

<TITLE> and </TITLE>

Browsers use a page's title for bookmarks or hotlist programs, while other programs use the title to catalog the Web page. Most browsers display the title within their title bar area. <TITLE> and </TITLE> tags always appear embedded within the page <HEAD> tag pair:

```
<HTML>
<HEAD>
<TITLE>My Specific, Unique, Search-Engine Ready
Title</TITLE>
… embedded head tag items here …
</HEAD>
</HTML>
```

<BODY> and </BODY>

The remainder of your HTML document, including all text and other page elements, such as links and pictures, is encapsulated within the <BODY> tag pair. There can be only one <BODY> and it must follow the <HEAD> tag. Here you add the text you want displayed in the main browser window, add tags and attributes to modify that text, create hyperlinks to other documents, etc. The completed HTML minimal template now looks like

```
<HTML>
<HEAD>
```

```
<TITLE>My Specific, Unique, Search-Engine Ready
Title</TITLE>
… embedded head tag items here …
</HEAD>
<BODY>
Nothing less than the most thought provoking, visu-
ally enticing eye candy,
And memorable quotables you have ever laid eyes on –
goes here!
</BODY>
</HTML>
```

When loaded into Netscape 4, the HTML document just defined looks like Figure 2.1–anything *but* "visually enticing," although somewhat thought provoking. However, there are a few characteristics of this first example worth noting. First, notice that the Netscape browser placed the title "My Specific, Unique, Search-Engine Ready Title" at the top of the window. Examples of good <TITLE>s include

1. *Ford Escort On-line Catalog*
2. *Jim Henson and the Muppets*
3. *Current Movie Reviews*
4. *NYC Opera Ticket Sales Information*
5. *PC Magazine Printer Reviews*

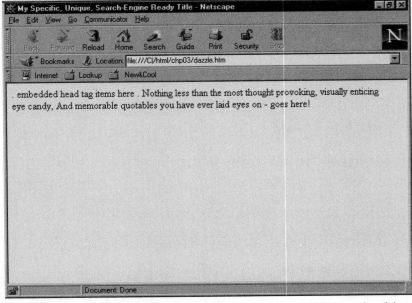

Figure 2.1: *Example HTML document viewed in the Netscape browser.*

Each one of these examples has one, or several, *keywords* which a properly launched search engine can lock onto, while the following selections are found on the one-thousand-three-hundred-and-fifty-third page of your search engine's hit list:

1. *Index of Titles*
2. *The Decade We Live In*
3. *My Personal Home Page*
4. *Musical Instruments*
5. *The Time, Date, and Place of America's Most Important Historical Events*

These <TITLE>s are vague, ambiguous, and general in nature and while they could be found by the most robust end user, most of us wouldn't live that long!

Back to Figure 2.1. Notice also that the displayed line spacing of the <BODY> text does *not* match that of the HTML document. Browsers, by default, simply word wrap text without special formatting tags embedded within the <BODY> of your document.

The good news is that with just a little HTML effort, you can easily improve even this simple document's pupil punch by changing the color of the text, background, etc., of your document. The following list enumerates legal <BODY> attributes:

- TEXT
- BGCOLOR
- BACKGROUND
- LINK
- ALINK
- VLINK

<H1>...<H6> and </H1>...</H6>

Every well-written newspaper article, book review, catalog, or professionally laid out photo album had its origins in a good outline. That outline may have only been in the creator's mind but it was the second most important production step made after deciding the main topic. Clever, unique, and logical level headings help organize and map any media's presentation including Web page design. HTML defines six level headings for this purpose. Headings are a typographical convention designed to aid in the hierarchical organization of text in a document. These six tags, <H1> through <H6>, and their respective end tags of </H1> through </H6>, are shown in Figure 2.2.

Although browsers vary in the size and type style given to the six heading levels, every browser follows the basic rule of giving the biggest and boldest style to <H1>, and the smallest and most insignificant style to <H6>. See Figure 2.3. The six HTML heading styles help to visually detail the level of importance among different parts of your page, much as this book uses different levels of headings to visually organize its contents.

The following HTML document has been loaded into the Microsoft Word and the Netscape and Internet Explorer browsers in order for you to be able to compare their interpretations (see Figures 2.2, 2.3, and 2.4, respectively).

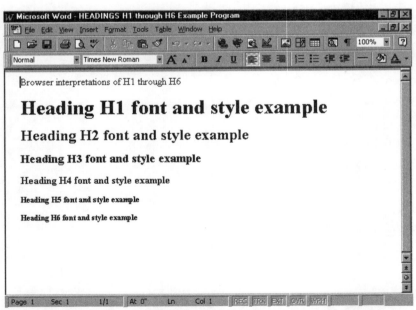

Figure 2.2: Sample HTML document viewed from within Microsoft Word 97.

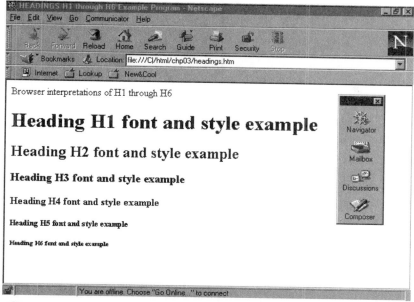

Figure 2.3: *Sample HTML document viewed from within Netscape Navigator.*

```
<HTML>
<HEAD>
<TITLE>HEADINGS H1 through H6 Example Program</TITLE>
</HEAD>
<BODY>
Browser interpretations of H1 through H6
<H1>Heading H1 font and style example</H1>
<H2>Heading H2 font and style example</H2>
<H3>Heading H3 font and style example</H3>
<H4>Heading H4 font and style example</H4>
<H5>Heading H5 font and style example</H5>
<H6>Heading H6 font and style example</H6>
</BODY>
</HTML>
```

Notice that a heading is always placed on its own line, even if it is placed in-line with other material. A new paragraph is started for the heading, and any material following it is placed on the next new line. For this reason, you should *not* use heading tags to create emphasized text within the document. In the next section you will learn HTML tags for this purpose.

In these particular examples you will notice an extreme and atypical similarity in HTML tag interpretations. You would expect both

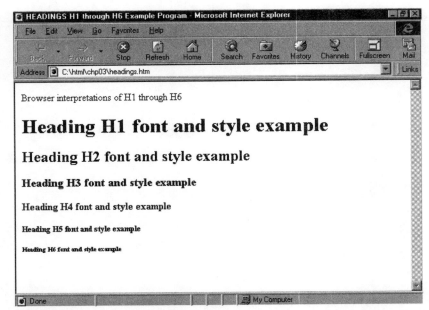

Figure 2.4: *Sample HTML document viewed from within Internet Explorer 4.0.*

Microsoft Word 97 and Internet Explorer to display similar results, but notice too that even here Netscape's browser seems to agree. The point is, depending on which tags you sample, and on which browser software you test, you may conclude you've designed the perfect cross-platform Web page. Examples throughout the remainder of this book will demonstrate otherwise.

<P> and </P>— Paragraphs

Paragraphs are defined with the <P> and </P> tags. Beginning with HTML 32.2 paragraph tags were given an attribute ALIGN, where alignment types include LEFT, CENTER, and RIGHT.

Remember from Chapter 1 that the end tag </P> is optional since every new start tag <P> indirectly flags the end of one paragraph and beginning of the next. The following example HTML document (Figure 2.5) demonstrates how to use these attributes.

```
<HTML>
<HEAD>
```

```
<TITLE>Paragraph Formatting Example</TITLE>
</HEAD>
<BODY>
The following examples demonstrate paragraph format-
ting and alignment.
<P> ALIGN=RIGHT>This way to page two ...</P>
<P> ALIGN=CENTER>--- Separator Bar Section ---</P>
<P> ALIGN=LEFT>Normal default mode positioning</P>
</BODY>
</HTML>
```

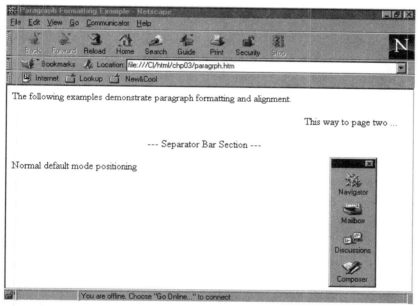

Figure 2.5: <P> ALIGN=RIGHT/CENTER/LEFT> example.

—Line Break

There is actually a subtle difference between line spacing within a paragraph versus line spacing between paragraphs or line breaks. The <BR> tag forces text to begin on a new line but maintains a line spacing point size consistent with intraparagraph formatting. Interparagraph line spacing is a slightly larger point size and proportioned to the font and style chosen for the next paragraph section.

The following HTML document highlights these subtle differences:

```
<HTML>
<HEAD>
<TITLE>Paragraph Formatting Example</TITLE>
</HEAD>
<BODY>
The following examples demonstrate paragraph and
line-break formatting.
Notice that the interparagraph spacing uses a higher
point size.
<P>The following section demonstrates the similarity
in line spacing
within a paragraph whenever the line-break tag is
used.
</P>
<P>Now the section is repeated only this time using
<BR>the line-break tag to separate the sentences.
</P>
</BODY>
</HTML>
```

Notice that the intraparagraph spacing uses a smaller point size than the interparagraph formatting (see Figure 2.6).

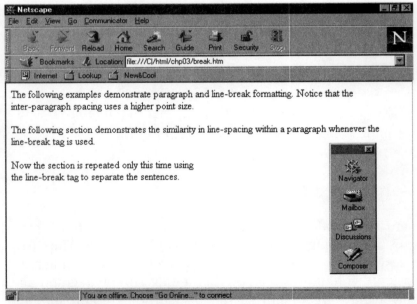

Figure 2.6: *Inter- versus intraparagraph line spacing using <P> and <BR> tags.*

Easy Visual Enhancements

This next section demonstrates a few of the attributes available within the <BODY> tag pair for quickly spicing up your first Web page!

BGCOLOR

You use the BGCOLOR attribute within the <BODY> tag pair to establish the background color of an HTML document. The color can be specified using a color's proper name, a hexadecimal value, or an RGB value.

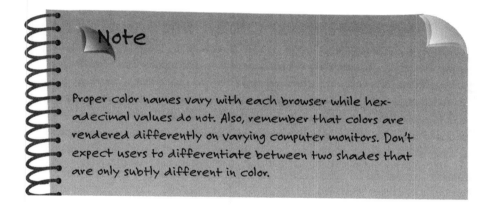

Note

Proper color names vary with each browser while hexadecimal values do not. Also, remember that colors are rendered differently on varying computer monitors. Don't expect users to differentiate between two shades that are only subtly different in color.

For example, White equals #FFFFFF; Red, #FF0000; Green, #00FF00; Blue, #0000FF; Magenta, #FF00FF; and so on. See the TEXT attribute description below for an example HTML document using the BGCOLOR attribute.

TEXT

The <BODY> TEXT attribute allows you to control the color of all the page's body text that isn't a link, including headings, body text, text inside tables, and so on. The following HTML document creates a page with a black background and white text:

```
<HTML>
<HEAD>
<TITLE>Background and Text Color Example</TITLE>
</HEAD>
<BODY BGCOLOR="#000000"TEXT="#FFFFFF>
This page displays white text on a black background.
</BODY>
</HTML>
```

Figure 2.7 uses Microsoft Word 97's ability to preview HTML documents to display the example file.

The following 16 colors are recognized by both Netscape Navigator 4 and Internet Explorer 4.0:

AQUA	GRAY	NAVY	SILVER
BLACK	GREEN	OLIVE	TEAL
BLUE	LIME	PURPLE	WHITE
FUCHSIA	MAROON	RED	YELLOW

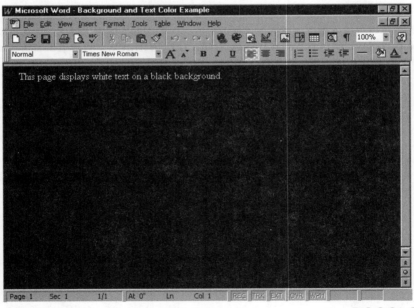

Figure 2.7: *Sample HTML document using the BGCOLOR and TEXT attributes.*

BACKGROUND

You can easily create more visually impressive backdrops by using the <BODY> tag pair's BACKGROUND attribute. BACKGROUND allows you to import an image as a background for your pages rather than simply a solid colored background.

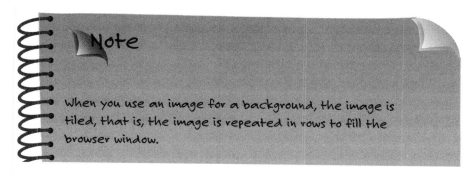

Note

When you use an image for a background, the image is tiled, that is, the image is repeated in rows to fill the browser window.

Creating a tile background involves selecting or making a pattern that flows smoothly from one tile to the next, similar to the challenge experienced when hanging patterned wallpaper! Your goal is to have the edges meet cleanly so that you don't have a seam. The following example borrows this type of image from the Windows 98 selection of wallpapers.

```
<HTML>
<HEAD>
<TITLE>Image Background Example</TITLE>
</HEAD>
<BODY BACKGROUND="RR.gif">
This page displays a Birthday-paced background.
</BODY>
</HTML>
```

Figure 2.8 uses Internet Explorer to render this Birthday background image, repeatedly tiled in a continuous flow:

LINK, ALINK, and VLINK

The three <BODY> attributes, LINK, ALINK, and VLINK, allow you to define the colors used: ALINK sets the color of an active hypertext link. Hypertext links are only active while the mouse is

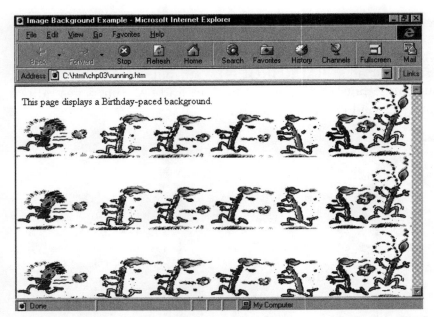

Figure 2.8: *Internet Explorer rendering a visually fun Birthday BACKGROUND.*

clicked on the link. LINK sets the color of the hypertext links that *have not* yet been visited. VLINK sets the color of the hypertext links that *have* been visited.

All three attributes use the same color coding options described for the BGCOLOR and BACKGROUND attributes, meaning you can use color constant names like WHITE, or a hexadecimal RGB value.

Since these attributes are only legal for the <BODY> of your HTML document, their syntax is straightforward:

```
<BODY LINK="BLUE" ALINK="YELLOW" VLINK="RED">
```

Comments

Adding comments to your documents is as good an idea in HTML as it is in C/C++, Fortran, Cobol, etc. Professional programmers use the following definition for a "good comment." A good comment neither insults the intelligence of another programmer, nor assumes too much. The general idea here is this: You should comment any portion of your HTML file that, two months after you've written it, you would come back to look at and say, "Gosh, what *does* that syntax mean?" or "*Why* does that do that that way?" Good comments can give a document a signature indicating who created the file and when any necessary support files needed should the site be shared, and so on.

You start an HTML comment with the following four (no blanks, please) symbols: <!-- and terminate the comment with three consecutive symbols, as in -->. Comments can be single or multiple lines so, for example, the following two styles are both syntactically correct:

```
<!-- Date: Jan 1 98, Created by: J.R.Williams,
Department: Commercial Resources -->
```

or

```
<!--
     Date:        Jan 1 98
     Created by:  J.R.Williams
     Department:  Commercial Resources
-->
```

Last Updated

One of the more meaningful pieces of documentation you can add to any HTML document is a "Last updated:" message. This allows frequent visitors to your site to decide if you have anything new to say or if the Web page contains only previously viewed contents. Although there is no specific HTML tag, attribute, or element specifically for update messages, the following <BODY> <P>aragraph example does the trick:

```
<P ALIGN=RIGHT>Last updated: Jan 1 1998 by
J.R.Williams</P>
```

Formatting Date and TIME

You have several options and variations in the representation of dates and times. The general format looks like

```
YYYY-MM-DDThh:mm:ssTZ
```

Table 2.1 Details each acronym.

Table 2.1: *Explanation of Time Format Acronyms*

YYYY	A four-digit year
MM	A two-digit month (01=January, etc.)
DD	A two-digit day of month (01 through 31)
Hh	A two-digit hour (00 through 23) (am/pm *not* allowed)
Mm	A two-digit minute (00 through 59)
Ss	A two-digit second (00 through 59)
TZ	The time zone designator

The time zone designator is either Z [UTC (Coordinated Universal Time)], +hh:mm (specifies a local time which is hh hours and mm minutes ahead of UTC), or -hh:mm (specifies a local time which is hh hours and mm minutes behind UTC). There can be no variation in the syntax (note that the "T" appears literally in the string, to indicate the beginning of the time element). If a document does not know the time to the second, it may use the value "00" for the seconds (and minutes and hours, if necessary). Both of the following examples correspond to October 5, 1996, 9:20:10 AM, U.S. Eastern Standard Time.

```
1996-10-05T14:20:10Z
1996-10-05T09:20:10-05:00
```

Special Characters

The topic of *special characters* can mean different things to different people. Some individuals will view the German umlaut as a special character, others will have to deal with the UNICODE standard, and still others will just be plagued with how to get greater than symbols, >, into an HTML document without ending some tag!

Many software/hardware combinations will not allow you to enter all UNICODE characters through simple input mechanisms, so

SGML offers character-encoding-independent mechanisms for specifying any character from the document character set.

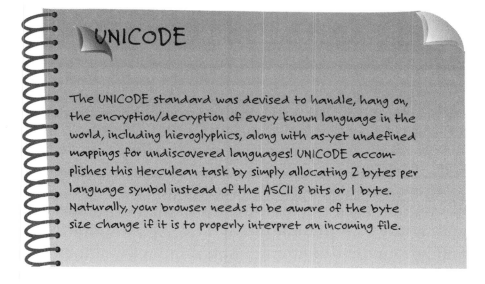

Numeric Character References

Numeric character references specify the integer reference of a UNICODE character. A numeric character reference with the syntax &#D; refers to UNICODE decimal character number D. A numeric character reference with the syntax &#xH; refers to UNICODE hexadecimal character number H. The hexadecimal representation is a new SGML convention and is particularly useful since character standards generally use hexadecimal representations.

Named Character Reference

A more intuitive approach to character set references is the HTML named character reference. Named character references replace integer references with symbolic names. For example, the named entity å refers to the same UNICODE character as å. A full list of named character entities recognized in HTML 4.0 can be found on the W3C Web site.

Four named character entities deserve special mention since they are frequently used to escape special characters. For text appearing as part of the content of an element, you should escape "<" (ASCII decimal 60) as < to avoid possible confusion with the beginning of a tag (start tag open delimiter). The ampersand character "&" (ASCII decimal 38) should be escaped as & to avoid confusion with the beginning of an entity reference (entity reference open delimiter).

You should also escape ampersand within attribute values since entity references are allowed as attribute values. In addition, you should escape ">" (ASCII decimal 62) as > to avoid problems with older user agents that incorrectly perceive this as the end of a tag (tag close delimiter) when coming across this character in quoted attribute values.

Rather than worry about rules for quoting attribute values, it's often easier to encode any occurrence of a quotation mark, ", with &quot, and to only use single quotes, ', for quoting attribute values. The following list enumerates the four most frequently used character references:

> Use " to represent the " mark.
> Use < instead of the less than < sign.
> Use > for the greater than > sign.
> Use & to represent the & sign.

Note, however, that named character references *are* case sensitive. Thus, Å refers to a different character (uppercase A, ring) than å (lowercase a, ring).

<BASE HREF>

The <BASE> tag identifies the base URL, or home reference for the HTML document. Some older browsers do not support the use of <BASE> although others will use it as the URL for an actual bookmark. The <BASE> home reference URL is important in case the document is moved. Moving the HTML document alters the relative links. A *relative link* is an incomplete file reference missing any reference to a server and directory/subdirectory path.

Without a <BASE> reference the browser makes the current HTML document location the base and therefore invalidates any relative links. This is particularly aggravating when a mirror site is the author's fixed drive and the computer is not connected to the Internet at the time the browser starts looking for the original. The syntax for a <BASE> home reference looks like

```
<BASE
HREF=http://myserver.net/mysubdirectory/myfile.html>
```

The HREF attribute is required and must define a fully qualified URL, and the URL must be where the document is located.

<LINK>

The <LINK> tag must be used within a <HEAD> tag and identifies the destination URL named in a hotlink. A <LINK> can identify a point within the same document or the URL of another document. <LINK>s can also identify the current document's relationship with other documents. This document-specific navigation can also define the rendering of specific collections of HTML nodes into the printed documents. The following sections describe the legal attributes for <LINK>.

HREF

Specifies a URL address identifying the hotlinked resource retrieved whenever the user clinks on the link.

ID

The <LINK> ID attribute allows you to specify a URL named file reference or text as a hypertext link to another document or another point in the same document.

MEDIA

Defines the destination medium, for example, print, screen, speech, projection, braille, or all.

REL

The REL attribute defines the hotlinked document's type.

REV

Specifies the reverse <LINK> relationship. <LINK REV="/base/base .htm">. The <LINK REV> tag attribute tells the browser to go to the previous link in the same document.

TARGET

Determines where the resource will be displayed, for example, user-defined name, _top, _blank, _self, or _parent.

TITLE

Specifies a referencing title for the linked resource. Historically, the TITLE attribute defined the title of the document named in the link; however, it can also provide a way to place a browser-invisible string of text in the <LINK>.

TYPE

Defines the Internet content type.

<STYLE>

The <STYLE>, </STYLE> tag pair is one way to use a style sheet in an HTML document. The <STYLE> element has one attribute: TYPE. The LINK element described above imports the style information from a separate style sheet document, while the <STYLE> tag allows you to suggest a presentation form within the document itself.

The advantage of this approach is that there is only one document downloaded, and it also *works* even if the server on which the page resides has not yet been configured to recognize the style sheet MIME type, which would preclude transferring an external style sheet. The syntax for a document-level style sheet is the same as for external style sheets discussed in Chapter 12. (Note: The language used must be given in the TYPE attribute.)

<ISINDEX>

The <ISINDEX> tag dates back to the original days of HTML and addressed the need for searching an HTML document. The <ISIN-DEX> tag caused the browser to present a default prompt symbol where the user would enter keywords that would be sent to the server. The server would execute a search and transmit the results back to the user. If the server did not have a search engine that could handle <ISINDEX>, it simply failed. HTML evolved to include a PROMPT attribute which allowed the author of the HTML document to define a user prompt. Since <ISINDEX> requires a server-side search engine capability, it has fallen into disuse. HTML 4's equivalent use forms and CGI are discussed in later chapters.

Lang

You add the lang attribute to specify the language content of your <BODY>. The syntax for lang is straightforward:

```
lang = language-code
```

Whitespace is not allowed within the language code. All language codes are case insensitive. The default language is "unknown." Language information can be used to control the rendering of a marked-up document in a variety of ways, for example, properly launching a language-specific search engine, selecting the proper typographical glyph for proper font displays, or making sure you use the correct spell checker dictionary and grammar rules.

The lang attribute's value is a language code that identifies a natural language—spoken, written, or otherwise—conveyed by human beings for communication of information to other human beings. Computer languages are explicitly excluded from language codes. These codes consist of a primary code and a possibly empty series of subcodes, as in

```
language-code  = primary-code *( "-" subcode )
```

Here are some sample language codes: "en," English, more specifically "en-US," or the English derivation "en-cockney." Here's another example: "i-cherokee," the Cherokee language spoken by some native Americans. Two-letter primary codes are reserved for language abbreviations. Two-letter codes include fr (French), de (German), it (Italian), nl (Dutch), el (Greek), es (Spanish), pt (Portuguese), ar (Arabic), he (Hebrew), ru (Russian), zh (Chinese), ja (Japanese), hi (Hindi), ur (Urdu), and sa (Sanskrit). Any two-letter subcode is understood to be a country code.

An element inherits language code information according to the following order of precedence (highest to lowest). First, with highest precedent, the lang attribute set for the element itself followed by the closest parent element that has the lang attribute set (i.e., the lang attribute is inherited).

In the following example, the primary language of the document is German ("de"). One paragraph is declared to be in French ("fr"), with an embedded Japanese ("ja") phrase, after which the primary language returns to French.

```
<HTML lang="de">
<BODY>
...German lang here ...
<P lang="fr">...French lang here...
<P>...Interpreted as French again...
<P>...French text interrupted by<EM lang="ja">some
      Japanese</EM>French begins here again...
</BODY>
</HTML>
```

Dir

The dir directive defines which direction, left-to-right, or right-to-left text is processed. The dir element has two attributes: LTR (Left-to-Right) and RTL (Right-to-Left) as in

```
dir = LTR
```

or

```
dir = RTL
```

In addition to specifying the primary language of a document, authors may need to specify the base direction of pieces of text or the text in the entire document. For example, to insert Hebrew text within an HTML document you would enter the following text:

```
<Q lang="he" dir="rtl">...insert Hebrew phrase
here...</Q>
```

The <Q>, </Q> tag pair is designed for short quotations that do not require paragraph breaks and are ideal for simple one-line quotes. In the absence of local overrides, the base direction is inherited from enclosing elements.

<SCRIPT>

The <SCRIPT>, </SCRIPT> tag pair marks that portion of an HTML document containing a script language program, such as VBScript or JavaScript. There must be a start <SCRIPT> tag and an end </SCRIPT> tag, with the script sandwiched between. One of the main advantages of scripts over CGI, both of which allow for considerable interactive Web page content, is that scripts process on the user's computer instead of the CGI-based server counterpart. Even more important is the fact the user-processed scripts provide dynamic Web page content even if the server does not support CGI.

HTML documents may contain more than one <SCRIPT> element, and they can be located in the <BODY> as well as in the <HEAD> tag pairs. Scripts are very powerful and can even allow a document to be modified as it is being parsed, generating, for example, a user-specific index. Great care is needed in designing these types of scripts, as well as testing them to make sure they have consistent and predictable results on the various browsers.

Since scripting languages are not universally understood, some browsers do not recognize any of them. Older browsers will display actual contents of the script if it is not enclosed even further, within a comment block. And should the script contain HTML-specific delimiters like > or −, look out! Some browsers view these symbols as the end of the comment, resulting in the display of whatever follows within the HTML script. To make certain a browser does not misinterpret a nonrecognized <SCRIPT> element, place the script within a comment as in

```
<SCRIPT TYPE="text/javascript">
<!-- beginning of comment block which hides the
script from unfriendly browsers
     …script goes here…
<--
</SCRIPT>
```

The <SCRIPT> tag has three attributes: LANGUAGE, SRC, and TYPE. Changes in the HTML 3.2 to HTML 4.0 standard wean HTML programmers from the older LANGUAGE attribute in place of the newer TYPE specification. Table 2.2 lists the markup tags that can use the <SCRIPT>, </SCRIPT> tags.

Table 2.2: *Markup Tags That Use <SCRIPT></SCRIPT>*

<A>	<ADDRESS>	<B>	<BIG>
<BLOCKQUOTE>	<BODY>	<CAPTION>	<CENTER>
<CITE>	<CODE>	<DD>	<DFN>
<DIV>	<DT>	<EM>	<FIELDSET>
<FONT>	<FORM>	<H*>	<HEAD>
<I>	<KBD>	<LABEL>	<LI>
<OBJECT>	<P>	<PRE>	<S>
<SAMP>	<SMALL>	<SPAN>	<STRONG>

Table 2.2: *Continued*

<SUB>	<SUP>	<TD>	<TEXTFLOW>
<TH>	<TT>	<U>	<VAR>

LANGUAGE

See the <SCRIPT TYPE="type/scriptlang"> attribute which replaces the older style <SCRIPT LANGUAGE="scriptlang"> attribute.

SRC

In the form <SCRIPT SRC=" URL"> where the URL routes the server to the specified plain text script code file. An example statement would look like

```
<SCRIPT SRC="./Jscripts/AJScript.js"
TYPE="text/javascript"> </SCRIPT>
```

TYPE

Beginning with HTML 4, <SCRIPT> tags use the TYPE attribute instead of the LANGUAGE attribute to define the type of file and its associated language. The syntax for TYPE is

```
<SCRIPT TYPE="typefile/scriptlang"> </SCRIPT>
```

See the SRC attribute for an example of a complete <SCRIPT> element definition. For reference purposes only, the older LANGUAGE attribute was used in the following syntax:

```
<SCRIPT LANGUAGE="VBScript"> </SCRIPT>
```

ONLOAD

The ONLOAD event attribute may be used with <BODY> and <FRAMESET> elements and is triggered whenever the user finishes loading a window or all frames within a <FRAMESET>:

```
onload = script
```

ONUNLOAD

The ONUNLOAD event attribute may be used with <BODY> and <FRAMESET> elements and is triggered whenever the user removes a document from a window or frame:

```
onunload = script
```

<NOSCRIPT>

The <NOSCRIPT>, </NOSCRIPT> tag pair marks the alternate route for browsers incapable of interpreting <SCRIPT> language documents. Authors should never use the <SCRIPT> element as the sole element of a page without also using <NOSCRIPT> to provide content to users of browsers that do not support scripts or that have script support turned off for security purposes.

<META>

The <META> tag is used to indicate special instructions for the client browser or a server performing a parsing operation. Other text can be included to define the date of creation, and so on. Search engines may post information specified by the <META> tag. The following sections describe the two <META> attributes HTTP-EQUIV and NAME.

HTTP-EQUIV

The <META> tag itself is placed within the <HEAD> in an HTML document and must include the CONTENT attribute. It should also contain either the NAME or HTTP-EQUIV attribute as in

```
<META HTTP-EQUIV="REFRESH" CONTENT="3;
URL=HTTP://www.server.net/index.html>
```

You use the NAME attribute whenever HTML document is to be interpreted by the browser and the HTTP-EQUIV attribute when interpretation is done on the server end. HTTP-EQUIV directs the browser to make requests of the server in order to execute various HTTP functions within the capabilities of the client. REFRESH is just one value that directs the client to repost the URL named or the current document if no URL is present, in the example above, after *three* seconds.

This next example uses the HTTP-EQUIV attribute to ensure that when a page is reloaded after the specified expiration date, it is reloaded from the server instead of a cached copy guaranteeing the latest edition:

```
<META HTTP-EQUIV="Expires" CONTENT="Mon, 12 Dec 1997
16:23:00 GMT">
```

<META> information can make your information more accessible to spiders and robots for automatic indexing, and more accessible to other programs that you might use to help you manage an HTML document collection.

NAME

Some search engines will describe your site from the first few sentences on the index page. A search engine that is indexing a page with

```
<META NAME="keywords" CONTENT="SCUBA, Diving, Bahamas">
```

would use the words contained within the content to index the page. This is more precise and guarantees more direct hits to your site.

If you prefer, you can use the CONTENT attribute to specify the description instead as in

```
<META NAME="description" CONTENT="This site is dedi-
cated to all those dry SCUBA Divers who wish they were
wet in the Bahamas right now!">
```

UNIVERSAL ATTRIBUTES

Any text block, for example the text between <H1> and </H1> tags, is a candidate for dynamically changing text styles. This is possible by simply including the ID, CLASS, and an event name attribute. These are described next.

ID

```
ID = AnElementName
```

The ID attribute assigns a documentwide name to a specific instance of an element. Values for ID must be unique within a document. Furthermore, this attribute shares the same name space as the name attribute.

CLASS

```
CLASS = ElementInstance
```

This attribute assigns a CLASS or set of CLASSes to a specific instance of an element. Any number of elements may be assigned the same CLASS name. All CLASS names must be separated by at least one blank. *AnElementName* specified by ID must be unique within a document. An *ElementInstance* specified by CLASS may be shared by several element instances.

Class values should be chosen to distinguish the role of the element with which the class is associated, for example, comment, sample, or error. These attributes can be used in the following ways. The ID attribute may be used as a destination for hypertext. Scripts can use the ID attribute to reference a particular element. Style sheets can use the ID attribute to apply a style to a particular element. The ID attribute is used to identify OBJECT element declarations.

Style sheets can use the CLASS attribute to apply a style to a set of elements associated with this CLASS, or to elements that occur as the children of such elements. Both ID and CLASS can be used for further processing purposes, for example, for identifying fields when extracting data from HTML pages into a database, translating HTML documents into other formats, etc.

Almost every HTML element may be assigned ID and CLASS information. Suppose, for example, that we are writing a document about Web page design. The document is to include a number of pre-formatted code samples. We use the FRMT element to format the code samples. We also assign a background color (blue) to all instances of the FRMT element belonging to the class "codesamp."

```
<HEAD>
<STYLE
FRMT.codesamp { background : blue }
</STYLE
</HEAD>
<BODY>
<FRMT CLASS="codesamp" ID="First Section">
...formatted code section goes here...
</FRMT>
</BODY>
```

By setting the ID attribute for this example, we can (1) create a hyperlink to it and (2) override CLASS style information with instance style information. Chapter 12 is dedicated exclusively to understanding HTML styles.

EMBEDDING JavaScript IN HTML

The syntax for embedding a JavaScript looks like

```
<SCRIPT language="JavaScript">
  … insert your JavaScript code here …
</SCRIPT>
```

However, browsers that do not support JavaScript will happily attempt to display or parse the content of a JavaScript. Beginning with Netscape 3, Netscape introduced the <NOSCRIPT> tag described above as a way for alternative text to be specified for non-JavaScript browsers. Any text between <NOSCRIPT> and </NOSCRIPT> tags is ignored. A modification of the previous syntax incorporating this necessary option would look like

```
<SCRIPT LANGUAGE="JavaScript">
  … insert your JavaScript code here …
</SCRIPT>

<NOSCRIPT>
  This Web page is unable to run the JavaScript com-
ponent.
</NOSCRIPT>
```

The following example brings together all of the necessary HTML and JavaScript fundamentals necessary for a simple JavaScript-enabled Web Page:

```
<HTML>

<HEAD>
<TITLE>Your First JavaScript Hosted Web Page</TITLE>
</HEAD>

<BODY>
  HELLO Universe!

<SCRIPT LANGUAGE="JavaScript">
document.writeln("We ARE here!");
</SCRIPT>
</BODY>
</HTML>
```

Summary

In this chapter you learned the fundamental HTML elements or tags necessary to generate a *simple* Web page and how to modify a straightforward HTML document to host a JavaScript program. You also learned more about the behind-the-scenes proper structure for an HTML document and a few tricks to avoid inevitable syntax problems *before* you have them, such as how to put quotation marks within an HTML syntax that uses quotation marks to flag the end of a string. In the next chapter you will learn the basic fundamentals of organizing and formatting text output.

PART TWO

HTML 4.0 Fundamentals

Part Two provides a quick review of HTML fundamentals and at the same time introduces you to many of the new HTML 4.0 concepts. If you are familiar with HTML, you'll find this section a snap to master. You'll quickly grasp concepts, such as image maps, forms, style sheets, and scripting. If you have been working with earlier versions of HTML, you'll find the material in this section to be new and exciting.

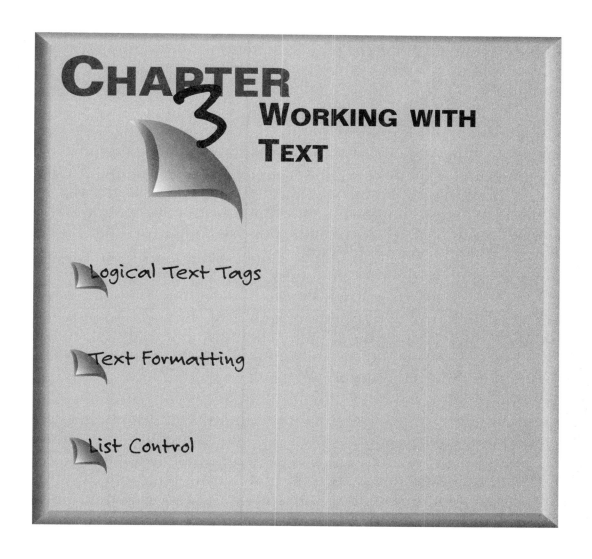

CHAPTER 3
WORKING WITH TEXT

- Logical Text Tags

- Text Formatting

- List Control

Since all JavaScripts are hosted by HTML documents, you need to understand how to create an interesting Web page with standard HTML elements that can interact with your JavaScript. The idea behind any well-designed Web page is to *convey information!* One of the ways to create drama, interest, and focus a reader's attention is to change the rendered text's font face, font size, and position and use **bold**, <u>underline</u>, and *italics*. And since most Web sites are logically related collections of Web pages, lists provide one of the most efficient means of conveying this relationship. The examples in this chapter illustrate the rendering of some of the textual markup elements and list features. You'll see how these tags are used with the various attribute options available to the developer.

Logical Text Tags

Previous chapters demonstrated several basic page elements and links. With this background, you are now ready to learn more about what HTML can do in terms of text formatting and layout. Table 3.1 describes most of the remaining tags in HTML that you'll need to know to construct your Web page.

Table 3.1: Text Formatting Tags

HTML Tag	Description
<ABBREV>	Logically flags an abbreviation.
<ACRONYM>	Logically flags an acronym.
<ADDRESS>	Used for addresses (frequently rendered in italics). Addresses are often rendered, indented, on their own lines.
<BIG>	Outputs text one size larger.
<CITE>	Used for quotations (frequently rendered in italics).
<CODE>	Used for rendering code listings (frequently rendered as Courier).
<EM>	Used for emphasis (frequently rendered in italics).
<Hn>	Headings.
<KBD>	Used to represent user keyboard-entry key sequences (frequently rendered as Courier).
<PERSON>	Marks a name for indexing purposes.
<Q>	Used for in-line quotations.
<SAMP>	Used for rendering sample text (frequently rendered as Courier).
<SMALL>	Outputs text one size smaller.
<STRONG>	Strong (frequently rendered in bold).

Table 3.1 *Continued*

69

Working with Text

3

HTML Tag	Description
<SUB>	Used for subscripting.
<SUP>	Used for superscripting.
<VAR>	Defines a variable name (frequently rendered in italics).

Most of the text formatting tags are self-evident; however <ACRONYM> needs a little clarification. <ACRONYM> allows authors to clearly indicate a sequence of characters that compose an acronym, for example, "WWW," "NASA," "IRS," and so on. <ACRONYM>s are useful to spell checkers, speech synthesizers, and other browser tools. The content of the <ACRONYM> element defines the acronym itself and is frequently used in conjunction with a TITLE attribute to provide the text to which the acronym expands. Here is a sample acronym definition:

```
<ACRONYM TITLE="World Wide Web">WWW</ACRONYM>
```

The following HTML document uses all of the tags listed in Table 3.1. Figure 3.1 highlights the first few lines of the complete listing below. Figure 3.2 completes the browser output display view.

```
<HTML><HEAD>
<TITLE>Example demonstrating Structured Text.</TITLE>
</HEAD>
<BODY>
<P><H1>Program Demonstrates Structured Text
Options</H1></P>
<P>The EM tag <EM>italicizes</EM> text.</P>
<P>The STRONG tag <STRONG>BOLDS</STRONG> text.</P>
<P>The ADDRESS tag formats <ADDRESS>1 Main
Street</ADDRESS>.</P>
<P>Putting a <CITE>citation</CITE> within a sen-
tence.</P>
<P>Inserting <CODE>code</CODE> fonts.</P>
<P><SAMPLE>Sample</SAMPLE> looks similar.</P>
<P>Press <KBD>Enter</KBD> to continue.</P>
<P>Making text <BIG>BIGGER</BIG>.</P>
<P>Making text <SMALL>small</SMALL>.</P>
<P>Lifting things<SUP>up</SUP> a bit.</P>
<P>Dropping them <SUB>down</SUB> a little.</P>
<P>World Wide Web = <ABBREV>WWW</ABBREV>.</P>
<P><ACRONYM>Acronym</ACRONYM>.</P>
```

```
<P><PERSON>Smith,John</PERSON> name indexing.</P>
<P>Please <Q>quote me</Q>.</P>
<P>This is a <VAR>variable</VAR> name.</P>
</BODY>
</HTML>
```

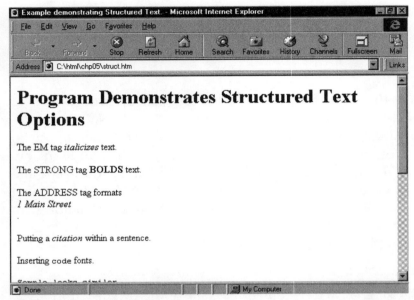

Figure 3.1: First part of rendered text formatting attributes.

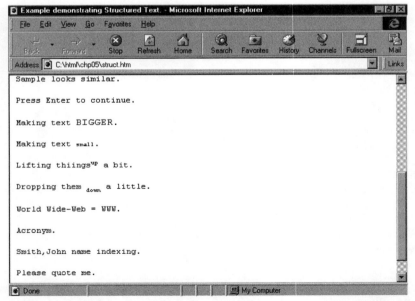

Figure 3.2: Remainder of rendered text formatting attributes.

Whitespace

Since the big brother to HTML, SGML, has a rather unique parsing convention when it comes to the topic of whitespace, its worth the time to take a closer look. SGML discriminates between statement start characters, or line feeds, and statement end characters, or carriage returns. Some architectures use just carriage returns, some use just line feeds, and others carriage return/line feed pairs for line breaks. You should consider single carriage returns, single line feeds, and carriage return/line feed pairs to be a single line break.

HTML always ignores a line break occurring immediately following a start tag, and any line break occurring immediately before an end tag. This applies to all HTML elements. With the exception of the PRE element, all leading whitespace characters (multiple spaces, horizontal tabs, form feeds, and line breaks) following the start tag are always ignored. Multiples of whitespace characters are always replaced by a single space. Using this rendering syntax, the following four examples are rendered identically:

```
<P>
Example highlighting whitespace and line break pars-
ing.
</P>
```

or

```
<P>
   Example highlighting whitespace and line break
parsing.
</P>
```

or

```
<P>Example highlighting whitespace and line break pars-
ing.</P>
```

or

```
<P>Example      highlighting whitespace and line break
parsing.</P>
```

Care should be taken when considering the topic of whitespace since the notion of what whitespace is varies from one language to another. The rule is to collapse whitespace in script-sensitive ways. For example, in Latin scripts, a single whitespace is just a space, ASCII decimal 32, while in Thai it is a zero-width word separator, and in Chinese, a whitespace is ignored entirely.

However, when used constructively, these rules allow you to use whitespace to your advantage, for example to clarify your HTML source with additional whitespace that will not be rendered by the browser, as in the following HTML document:

```
<P>
This example shows left justification of a paragraph
and a list, with no extra line-spacing for clarity to
the human reader.
</P>
<UL>

<LI>
This is <EM>ITEM 1</EM> .
</LI>
<LI>
This is <EM>ITEM 2second</EM> .
</LI>
</UL>
```

This next example omits end tags and uses less whitespace, making the code easier for a human to understand:

```
<P>This example shows a more meaningful HTML document
format for a paragraph and a list.
<UL>
   <LI>This is <EM>ITEM 1</EM> .
   <LI>This is <EM>ITEM 2</EM> .
</UL>
```

while being rendered identically by the browser.

Physical Text Tags

HTML defines an additional set of tags, some of which overlap the logical tags previously defined for detailing how text is rendered. Table 3.2 lists the physical tag styles available in most popular browsers.

(Note: <BLINK> is currently available to Netscape browsers only.)

Table 3.2: *Physical Tags*

HTML Tag	Description
\<B\>	Bold
\<I\>	Italics
\<U\>	Underline
\<TT\>	Tele-Typewriter
\<S\>	Strikeout
\<DFN\>	Definition
\<BLINK\>	Netscape (simply ignored by other browsers)

The following HTML document demonstrates how to use physical tags and is rendered in Figure 3.3.

```
<HTML><HEAD>
<TITLE>Physical Tags Example</TITLE>
</HEAD>
<BODY>
<P>This is a <B>BOLD</B> word.</P>
<P>This statement uses italics for
<I>emphasis.</I></P>
<P><U>This line is completely underlined.</U></P>
<P><TT>Now, U.S. News and World Report,
reports...</TT></P>
<P>Parts of this line are <S>struck-out.</S></P>
<P>This line contains a <DFN>Definition.</DFN></P>
<P>This is a Netscape <BLINK>blinker</BLINK>!</P>
<P></P>
</BODY>
</HTML>
```

Text Formatting

Remember the day when source code was entered in all CAPITAL LETTERS? Well those days are long gone. Nowadays, *everybody* needs to be a typesetter! Even MiXeD CaSe, **BOLD**, *italics*, and <u>underline</u> are no longer visually interesting enough to hold a reader's

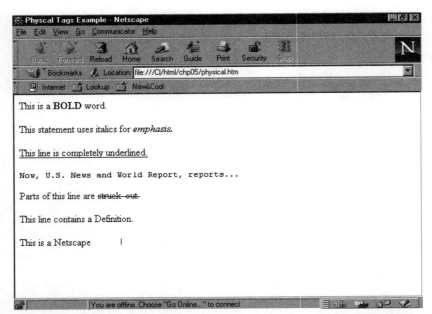

Figure 3.3: *Netscape rendering of physical tag BLINK. (Hint: It's flashing!)*

eye. HTML defines tags that allow you to select a text's font face, color, size, and alignment. This section describes Web page type setting fundamentals.

Alignment

There are three types of alignment associated with the ALIGN tag: LEFT, CENTER, and RIGHT. The following example HTML document details these options (see Figure 3.4).

```
<HTML>
<HEAD>
<TITLE>Paragraph Alignment: LEFT, CENTER, and
RIGHT</TITLE>
</HEAD>
<BODY>
<P ALIGN=LEFT>
LEFT alignment
</P>
<P ALIGN=CENTER>
CENTER alignment.
</P>
```

```
<P ALIGN=RIGHT>
RIGHT alignment.
</P>
</BODY>
</HTML>
```

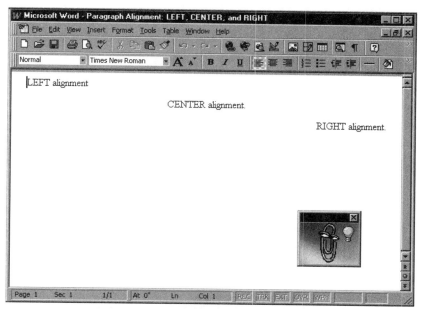

Figure 3.4: LEFT, CENTER, and RIGHT alignment.

Additional Line Breaks

To add additional line spacing between paragraphs you use the <BR> tag. You should *not* use multiple <P>, </P> tag pairs, since by definition, a paragraph cannot be empty. Browsers treat multiple paragraph tags in different ways: They may either ignore all but the first tag, insert the extra spaces, or flag the use as an invalid HTML tag. Adding multiple breaks is as simple as adding the following statements within the <BODY> of your HTML document:

```
<BR>  <BR>  <BR>  <BR>
```

CLEAR

The CLEAR attribute is associated with the <BR> tag and allows you to define the text wrapping options around an image. CLEAR forces the browser to render text below the image to the LEFT, CENTER, or first clear RIGHT margin. The syntax for CLEAR is

```
<BR CLEAR=LEFT | CENTER | RIGHT>
```

<FONT>

The <FONT>, </FONT> tag pair allows you to use specific fonts and colors in your pages, just as you can in a printed document. This is accomplished using the <FONT> tag and one of its two attributes, SIZE and COLOR. Some browsers also support a FACE attribute, which is used to specify one or more typefaces to use for the selection. Most browsers allow users to override these settings, so don't count on them to convey content.

SIZE

The SIZE attribute defines the size of the contents of the tag to a specific or relative size. The value supplies the desired size expressed as an integer from 1 to 7 (the default is 3), or as a relative value from –6 to +6. If a relative value is used, it is added to the current setting for <BASEFONT> (see below). The specific values 1 to 7 render inversely to <H1> through <H6>. Where <H1> is the largest font size, the specific value 1 is the smallest font size. The syntax is

```
<FONT SIZE=value>… text goes here …</FONT>
```

The following program uses specific values (see Figure 3.5):

```
<HTML><HEAD><TITLE>Example of FONT SIZE
attributes</TITLE>
</HEAD>
<BODY>
<P> <FONT SIZE=1>
Example SIZE = 1
</FONT></P>
<P> <FONT SIZE=2>
Example SIZE = 2
</FONT></P>
```

```
<P> <FONT SIZE=3>
Example SIZE = 3
</FONT></P>
<P> <FONT SIZE=4>
Example SIZE = 4
</FONT></P>
<P> <FONT SIZE=5>
Example SIZE = 5
</FONT></P>
<P> <FONT SIZE=6>
Example SIZE = 6
</FONT></P>
<P> <FONT SIZE=7>
Example SIZE = 7
</FONT></P>
</BODY>
</HTML>
```

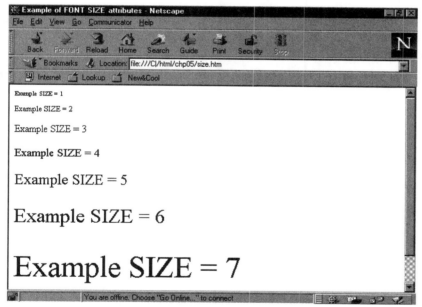

Figure 3.5: *Setting a font's SIZE attribute.*

COLOR

The COLOR attribute defines the color of the text being rendered. There are three forms of color description: a color's name, its hexadecimal value, or an RGB value. The syntax looks like

```
<FONT COLOR="BLUE"...text goes here...</FONT>
```

The FACE attribute is an extension to HTML 3.2 also and is supported by most popular browsers. FACE allows you to specify a list of fonts. Whenever the first font specified isn't found, the second one is tried, and so on. If none of the selected fonts exists on the user's system, the default font is used. A sample looks like (see Figure 3.6):

```
<HTML>
<HEAD>
<TITLE>Example of FONT FACES</TITLE>
</HEAD>
<BODY>
```

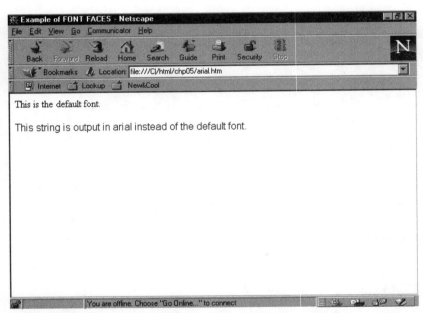

Figure 3.6: Changing the font's FACE attribute.

<BASEFONT>

You use the <BASEFONT> without an end tag to set the default font size for all text that follows in a document. The default <BASEFONT> size is 3. If a <FONT>, </FONT> tag pair is found after the <BASEFONT> setting, the newer <FONT> value is in effect until the closing tag, as seen in the following example (see Figure 3.7):

```
<HTML><HEAD><TITLE>Example of FONT and
BASEFONT</TITLE></HEAD><BODY>
<FONT BASEFONT=0
<P>This is the BASEFONT of 0.</P><P> <FONT
SIZE=7>This string is output in FONT SIZE
7.</FONT></P>
<P>This text once again defaults to the BASEFONT of
0.</P></BODY></HTML>
```

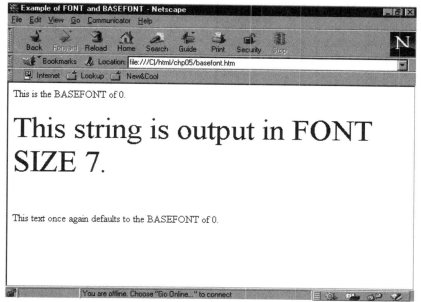

Figure 3.7: *Setting the BASEFONT attribute.*

When using <BASEFONT> you can use the "relative" version of <FONT SIZE=n> where you use positive or negative integer values to proportion rendering to the base font, as in

```
<BASEFONT SIZE=5>
<P>…text goes here…</P>
<P><FONT SIZE=-2>…two sizes smaller than base
font…</P>
<P><FONT SIZE=+1>…one size larger than base font…</P>
```

Visual Bar Separators

One easy way to apply visual demarcation is known as a horizontal rule, or visual separator bar. The following section describes horizontal rule attributes and is followed by an example HTML document using the various options.

Alignment

Horizontal rules have three alignment options: LEFT, CENTER, and RIGHT.

\<HR ALIGN=LEFT>Size

You use the SIZE attribute to set the height of the separator, as in

```
<HR SIZE=5>
```

Width

The WIDTH attribute defines the width of the rule in numbers of pixels. This can become quite difficult to calculate ahead of time for all output display formats. A simple approach is to use the percent modifier, as in

```
<HR WIDTH=75%>
```

Color

Though not an actual formal part of the HTML definition, most popular browsers accept a color attribute in an RGB format, as in

```
<HR COLOR="#RRGGBB">
```

Shading

Normally horizontal rules render with a three-dimensional image. Depending on background colors, this rule style is difficult to see. For this reason there is a NOSHADE attribute (see Figure 3.8). The syntax looks like

```
<HR NOSHADE>

<HTML><HEAD>
<TITLE>Example demonstrating horizontal rule
options.</TITLE>
</HEAD>
<BODY>
<P>This is a fifty-percent rule.</P>
<P><HR WIDTH=50%></P>
<P>This is a fifty-percent rule, RIGHT aligned.</P>
<P><HR WIDTH=50% ALIGN=RIGHT></P>
<P>This is a 10 pixel rule, default width.</P>
<P><HR SIZE=10></P>
<P>This rule is the same except for the NOSHADE.</P>
<P><HR SIZE=10 NOSHADE></P>
</BODY>
</HTML>
```

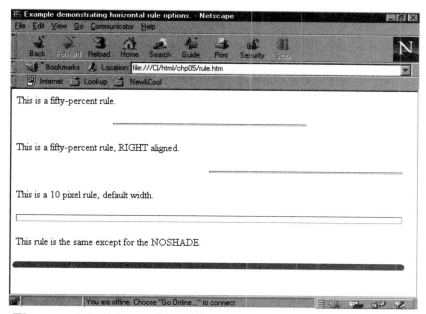

Figure 3.8: Using the <HR> horizontal rule element.

List Control

List structures are an invaluable tool to quickly hit the high points of a subject, whether that be the hierarchy of information presented on a Web site's hotlinked pages, or describing your personal interests. There are three types of lists: unordered or bulleted, ordered, and a special category for generating a list of defining terms.

Unordered

You use the <UL>, </UL> tag pair to delimit an unordered bulleted list. You use the <LI> and optional </LI> tags to define list items. When using the <UL>, </UL> tags for unordered or bulleted lists, you can select the type of bullet by using one of the following three attributes, CIRCLE, DISC, SQUARE, rendered in Figure 3.9.

```
<HTML><HEAD>
<TITLE>Unordered List Bullet Options Example</TITLE>
</HEAD>
<BODY>
```

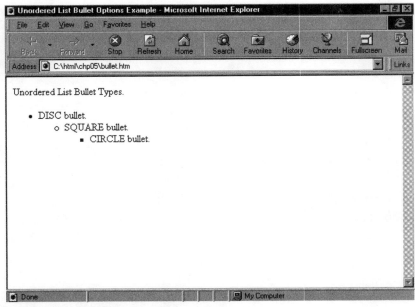

Figure 3.9: *Bulleted list options.*

```
<LH>Unordered List Bullet Types.</LH>
<UL TYPE=DISC>
<LI>DISC bullet.</LI>
<UL TYPE=SQUARE>
<LI>SQUARE bullet.</LI>
<UL TYPE=CIRCLE>
<LI>CIRCLE bullet.</LI>
</UL>
</BODY>
</HTML>
```

Ordered

You use the <OL>, </OL> tag pair to delimit a numbered ordered list, along with <LI> and </LI>, with the addition of the attributes listed in Table 3.3.

Table 3.3: Ordered List Attributes

Attribute	Description
1	Arabic numerals–this is the default mode.
A	All capital letters.
a	All small letters.
I	Uses large Roman numerals.
i	Uses small Roman numerals.

The following example demonstrates how you could use these options to generate a meaningful outline format. See Figure 3.10 for the rendered results.

```
<HTML><HEAD>
<TITLE>Ordered List Example</TITLE>
</HEAD>
<BODY>
<LH>Generating an Outline Format</LH>
<OL TYPE=I>
<LI>Large Roman Numeral Item</LI>
<OL TYPE=A>
<LI>Capital Letter Item</LI>
<OL TYPE=1>
<LI>Arabic Item</LI>
```

```
<OL TYPE=a>
<LI>Small Letter Item</LI>
<OL TYPE=i>
<LI>Small Roman Numeral Item</LI>
</OL>
</BODY>
</HTML>
```

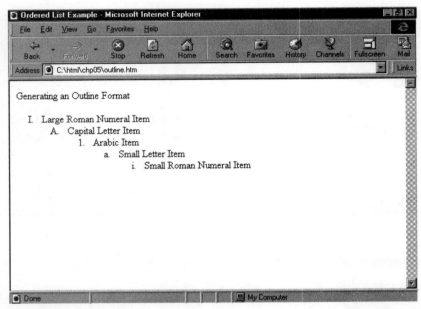

Figure 3.10: Ordered list used to create an outline format.

Dictionary Tables

When you want to add a definition list with associated descriptions for each list item, use the <DL>, </DL> definition list tag pair (see Figure 3.11). Associated with the <DL>, </DL> pair are <DT>, used for the defining term, and <DD>, used for the defining description. These last two tags do *not* have end tag counterparts.

```
<HTML><HEAD>
<TITLE>Definition List Example</TITLE>
</HEAD>
<BODY>
<DL>
<DT>TERM 1
<DD>TERM 1 definition here.
<DT>TERM 2
```

```
<DD>TERM 2 definition here.
<DT>TERM 3
<DD>TERM 3 definition here.
</BODY>
</HTML>
```

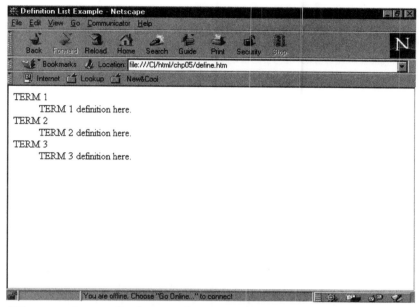

Figure 3.11: *Definition list example.*

Nested Lists

Lists can easily contain items that are in themselves, lists, as in the following example:

```
<HTML><HEAD>
<TITLE>Nesting Lists Example</TITLE>
</HEAD>
<BODY>
<LH>Nested Lists Example.</LH>
<UL TYPE=DISC>
<LI>LEVEL 1 ITEM.
<UL TYPE=SQUARE>
<LI>Level 2 item.
<LI>Level 2 item.
<LI>Level 2 item.
</UL>
<LI>LEVEL 1 ITEM.
```

```
<LI>LEVEL 1 ITEM.
</UL>
</BODY>
</HTML>
```

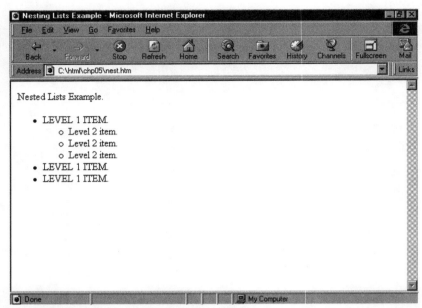

Figure 3.12: *Nested list example.*

JavaScript write()

Of course JavaScript has its own methods for outputting text to the document object. JavaScript defines the function write(). The syntax for write() looks like

```
write(expression1[,expression2…..expressionn])
```

The function write() outputs the values of the expressions to the document. Javascript supports the standard C/C++ output format controls: /n (new line), /r (carriage return), /f (form feed), /t (horizontal tab), and /b (backspace).

More similar to Assembly Language programming than C/C++, JavaScript allows you to delimit any string with either a matching pair of double quotes, as in "JavaScript double-quoted string," *or* a matching pair of single quotes, as in 'JavaScript single-quoted string.' However, as with C/C++, whenever you need to include a quoted statement within an output string, you simply precede the nested quote symbol with a backslash, as in, "He said, \"In the beginning…\" and then was interrupted." Similarly, adding apostrophes is just as easy, as in. "That\'s not true!"

Also, just to add a little variety to your programming technique, JavaScript output string formatting can also use standard HTML tags *or* their JavaScript counterpart. The following HTML document demonstrates many of these concepts.

```
<HTML>
<HEAD>
<TITLE>Using JavaScript and HTML tags to output
strings</TITLE>
</HEAD>
<BODY>
<SCRIPT LANGUAGE="JavaScript">
<!-- Hide from older browsers
document.write("String output using the BR HTML car-
riage return.<BR>")
document.write("String using C/C++ carriage return
syntax.")
// End hide from older browsers -->
</SCRIPT>
</BODY>
</HTML>
```

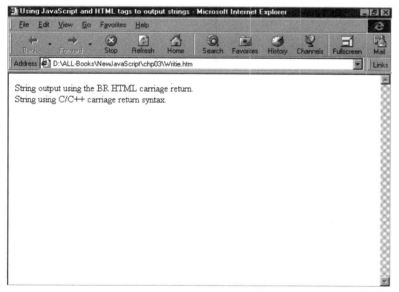

Figure 3.13: *Figure showing the similarity between <BR> and \n with write().*

Figure 3.13 illustrates the results of the output syntax. This frequently used JavaScript output method is used in all its various forms beginning with Chapter 10 and following through the remaining chapters.

Summary

In this chapter you have seen how HTML documents can create interesting Web page formatting with standard HTML elements that can interact with your JavaScript. Remember, the *idea* behind any well-designed Web page is *to convey information!* One of the ways to create drama, interest, and focus a reader's attention is to change the rendered text's font face, font size, and position and use **bold**, underline, and *italics*. And since most Web sites are logically related collections of Web pages, lists provide one of the most efficient means of conveying this relationship. In the next chapter you will learn about HTML and JavaScript's image and multimedia symbiosis.

CHAPTER 4

WORKING WITH IMAGES AND MULTIMEDIA

- Images
- <IMG> Tag
- Attributes
- Sounds
- Video

This chapter will introduce you to many of the common HTML techniques for adding image, sound, and multimedia capabilities to your documents. You'll see many of these concepts used in later chapters. For example, much of the work done with images will be reintroduced when you work with image maps in Chapter 6.

Images, sound, and multimedia tools add a professional touch to your HTML documents. JavaScript can also be included for manipulating images as you'll see in the next section.

Images

There are several techniques used by HTML for rendering images on a Web page. Traditionally, this has been the job of the <IMG> element but with the release of HTML 4.0 images can also be rendered with the use of the <OBJECT> container. In this chapter we'll concentrate on using the <IMG> element. In Chapter 18 you will learn how many of these same feats can be accomplished with the <OBJECT> container.

The <IMG> element has one major advantage over the use of the new <OBJECT> container—all popular browsers supported its use.

You'll find that it is relatively easy to add images to a user's Web page. Adding images tastefully is quite another feat. There are always additional considerations that accompany the use of images. These include download time, navigation considerations, readability, usability, and so on.

Have you ever entered a Web site and become frustrated when waiting for a large collection of graphic images to appear? If you are like many of us, you have probably selected the alternate text option to navigate to the proper location. In this case, the multiple graphic images only tend to slow up the navigation process in the Web page.

A well-designed Web page layout is essential for efficient navigation of the site. Have you ever entered a site to update file software and then had to read just about every paragraph of information to determine where to go to get the software? Poor Web page design is both time consuming and frustrating to the user.

In the following section, we'll look at examples that will help you load, size, place, and use graphic images effectively. You'll also learn the syntax and parameters associated with the <IMG> element and investigate how it relates to the manipulation of images destined for Web pages.

Using the <IMG> Tag

The <IMG> tag is perhaps the most popular method available under HTML for adding images to a Web page. The <IMG> element uses a large number of attributes that are listed and described in Table 4.1.

Table 4.1: *<IMG> Element Attributes*

Attribute	Description
align	Gives the image's location in the viewing area. Use bottom to align the bottom of the element with the current baseline. Bottom is the default. Use middle to vertically align the center of the object with the current baseline. Use top to vertically align the object with the top of the current text line. Use left or right to align the image with the current left or right margin, respectively.
alt	Gives text to be rendered when the image cannot be displayed.
border	Gives the border width placed around the image in pixels. When the image serves as a hyperlink, the border is drawn in the hyperlink color. Use a value of 0 for no border.
height	Gives the height of an image in pixels. Specifying a value often speeds up image loading by relieving the browser from determining layout size.
hspace	Gives the amount of space to the left and right of an image. The amount of space is specified in pixels. No default is specified.
ID	Gives the image for the viewing area. It can also be used to locate other images or hyperlinks.
ismap	Gives that an image map is a server-side image map.
lang	Gives language information.
longdesc	Gives a link to a long description
onclick	Gives an action relating to a mouse click (push/release).
ondblclick	Gives an action relating to a mouse double-click (push/release).
onkeydown	Gives an action relating to a key down event.
onkeypress	Gives an action relating to a key press (down/release) event.

Table 4.1: *<IMG> Element Attributes (Continued)*

Attribute	Description
onkeyup	Gives an action relating to a key release event.
onmousedown	Gives an action relating to a mouse button push.
onmousemove	Gives an action relating to the movement of the mouse.
onmouseout	Gives an action related to moving the mouse out of the area.
onmouseover	Gives an action related to moving the mouse into the area.
onmouseup	Gives an action relating to a mouse button release.
src	Gives the source of the image. This can be a file location or a full URL.
style	Gives in-line style information.
title	Gives element titles.
usemap	Gives a URL used with a client-side image map.
vspace	Gives the amount of space above and below an image. The amount of space is specified in pixels. No default is specified.
width	Gives the width of an image in pixels. Specifying a value often speeds up image loading by relieving the browser from determining layout size.

Image types are rendered by built-in mechanisms provided by the browser for all common image formats. These image types may include, but are not limited to, gif, jpeg, and png. When the data type isn't supported, the browser can use the alt attribute to specify a text alternative to the image. This attribute is useful in cases where images are not supported, a particular image format is not supported, or they cannot display images for a particular reason.

Browsers interpret an <IMG> element in-line and attempt to render the image at the current element's definition. Here is a simple example that will load a jpeg image to the viewing area from a Web site.

```
<HTML>
```

```
<HEAD>
<TITLE>Viewing Flowers from Barbados</TITLE>
</HEAD>
<BODY>

<IMG src= "http://barbadosphotogallery.com/jpgees/
        plants/flower13.jpg"

</BODY>
</HTML>
```

Figure 4.1 shows how this image is rendered in the viewing area.

Figure 4.1: *The image of a flower is rendered in the viewing area.*

The same image, if used frequently, could be saved and loaded from the hard disk. Here is the required modification to the previous example:

```
<IMG src="flower13.jpg">
```

When images are saved to a hard disk you will find that they will reload more quickly than downloading from a Web site. If you are working with multiple images or large image files, this might save you time under certain circumstances.

In the following sections, we'll investigate the use of several of the attributes listed in Table 4.1 to give you an idea of how they can be used.

Using the alt Attribute

The alt attribute allows alternative text to be specified that will be rendered if the image cannot. Here is a simple example that will not load the image because it doesn't exist.

```
<HTML>
<HEAD>
<TITLE>Viewing Flowers from Barbados</TITLE>
</HEAD>
<BODY>

<IMG src="http://barbadosphotogallery.com/jpgees/
        plants/flower300.jpg"

    alt="Attempted to load a Barbados flower">

</BODY>
</HTML>
```

Figure 4.2 shows the resulting screen message.

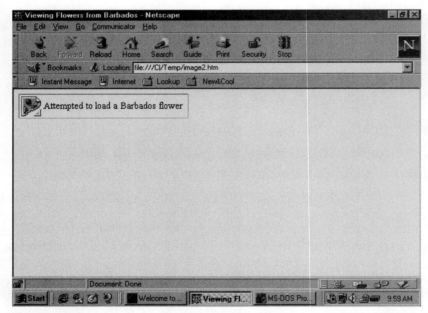

Figure 4.2: Use the alt attribute when an image might not be rendered.

The alt attribute is useful when a browser cannot display images or cannot display a particular image format.

Using the Align Attribute

The align attribute is used for placing images in the viewing area. This attribute aligns images relative to text placed in the viewing area or against the left or right borders.

The example aligns the image relative to the top of the line of text.

```
<HTML>
<HEAD>
<TITLE>Viewing Flowers from Barbados</TITLE>
</HEAD>
<BODY>

A flower from Barbados.
<IMG src="http://barbadosphotogallery.com/jpgees/
         plants/flower19.jpg"
    align="top">

</BODY>
</HTML>
```

Examine Figure 4.3 and notice where the text and image are placed.

Figure 4.3: *Aligning images with the align attribute set to "top."*

To align the same image with the align attribute set to "middle," use this variation of the previous example:

```
A flower from Barbados.
<IMG src="http://barbadosphotogallery.com/jpgees/
          plants/flower19.jpg"
    align="middle">
```

The align attribute can be used to align the image relative to the left edge of the viewing area by setting it to "left." Here is a portion of code to achieve this result:

```
A flower from Barbados.
<IMG src="http://barbadosphotogallery.com/jpgees/
          plants/flower19.jpg"
    align="left">
```

The align attribute is used to place the image in a relative position. Other attributes can determine the size of the image, as you'll see in the next section.

Using the Width and Height Attributes

The width and height attributes can be used to stretch or shrink the image. The value used is measured in pixels. In the following example the width of the image is forced to 400 pixels.

```
<HTML>
<HEAD>
<TITLE>Viewing Flowers from Barbados</TITLE>
</HEAD>
<BODY>

A flower from Barbados.
<IMG src="http://barbadosphotogallery.com/jpgees/
          plants/flower15.jpg"
    width=400>

</BODY>
</HTML>
```

Figure 4.4 shows the results of setting the image's width to 400 pixels.

Figure 4.4: *Use the width attribute to set the width of the image in pixels.*

The height attribute can be used to alter just the height of an image. In the following code the height of an image is forced to 100 pixels.

```
A flower from Barbados.
<IMG src="http://barbadosphotogallery.com/jpgees/
        plants/flower15.jpg"
    height=100>
```

If only one attribute is set, such as height or width, the unspecified attribute will remain at the default value. Both the height and width of an image can be altered simultaneously.

```
A flower from Barbados.
<IMG src="http://barbadosphotogallery.com/jpgees/
        plants/flower15.jpg"
    width=400 height=200>
```

By using both the height and width attributes, an image can be expanded or collapsed to fit any viewing area.

Using the Border Attribute

The border attribute can be used to render a border around the image. The width of the border is specified in pixels. A default border is 1 pixel wide.

In the following example a border 10 pixels thick is drawn around an image whose width and height have been set to 200 pixels.

```
<HTML>
<HEAD>
<TITLE>Viewing Flowers from Barbados</TITLE>
</HEAD>
<BODY>

A flower from Barbados.
<IMG src="http://barbadosphotogallery.com/jpgees/
         plants/flower22.jpg"
   border=10 width=200 height=200>

</BODY>
</HTML>
```

Figure 4.5 shows a bold border drawn around the image.

Figure 4.5: *Borders help emphasize images.*

The border value can be set to zero to make the border invisible.

Using the hspace and vspace Attributes

The hspace and vspace attributes are used to set the whitespace that surrounds the image. In the following example the hspace and vspace attributes are set to 50 pixels each.

```
<HTML>
<HEAD>
<TITLE>Viewing Flowers from Barbados</TITLE>
</HEAD>
<BODY>

A flower from Barbados.
<IMG src="http://barbadosphotogallery.com/jpgees/
          plants/flower24.jpg"
 hspace=50 vspace=50 border=2 width=300 height=200>

</BODY>
</HTML>
```

Examine Figure 4.6 and observe the whitespace surrounding the figure.

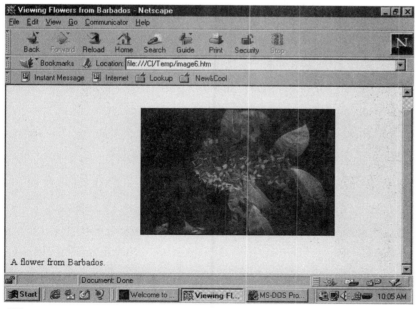

Figure 4.6: *The hspace and vspace attributes add whitespace to the area surrounding an image.*

Notice, too, that this image is fixed at 300 x 200 pixels. Look closely and you will see that it is surrounded by a 2-pixel width border, too.

JavaScript and Images

Images can also be manipulated with simple JavaScript code. The following listing shows how the JavaScript Image() constructor can be used to preload images for later use. Any JPEG images can be used for the example; we just decided to use a few beach scenes from Barbados.

```
<HTML>
<HEAD>
<TITLE>Barbados Beaches</TITLE>

<SCRIPT LANGUAGE = "JavaScript">
var testimage = new Array(2)

testimage[0] = new Image(400,200)
testimage[0].src = "beach1.jpg"
testimage[1] = new Image(400,200)
testimage[1].src = "beach2.jpg"

function getit() {
 document.images[0].src = testimage[1].src
}

</SCRIPT>
</HEAD>
<BODY>

<IMG SRC="beach1.jpg" width = 400 height = 200>

<FORM>
<INPUT type = "button" name = "new"
    value = "get new image" onClick="getit()">
</FORM>
</BODY>

</HTML>
```

Figure 4.7 shows the screen once the button has been activated.

The advantage of using the Image() constructor is that large images can be downloaded in advance of their use. The application downloads both beach1 and beach2 from the hard disk in this example. If you download images from a Web site, you know how time consuming it can be. If you use this technique, you'll find your application is much faster. In this example, the beach1.jpg image is initially displayed. The beach2.jpg image is displayed when the user selects the "get new image" button. Since it has been preloaded, it will appear almost instantly.

Figure 4.7: *Push the button for a new beach scene.*

Multimedia

Multimedia-enhanced Web pages are as enticing to the senses as television is over a magazine. In this section you will learn how to add sound and animation (via AVI and MOV files) to your design. But first a note of caution. With today's average Web surfer riding no faster than 56K, a Web site flooded with too much multimedia content leaves them stranded in the middle of the ocean, never quite making it to shore. Needless to say, the surfer never returns to your crowded beach!

Story Boards

The simplest way to guarantee a successful, multimedia-enabled Web page is to make your site's content as clear, straightforward, and interesting as possible, *without any multimedia*. Once you have succeeded in this, adding multimedia is the icing on the cake.

Take a moment to do what the most successful entertainment giants have done to make certain a presentation's contents *flow*—create a story board. A *story board* is a sequence of sketched images, laid out in a logical progression, hitting the highlights of a production's story sequence. So, too, your Web page should be a logical and hopefully interesting narrative, either about you, your club, or your company. Skipping this preproduction development phase is like not doing a structured design for a program—the end result is confusing, missing necessary details, and a patch over a patch—impossible to port, maintain, or upgrade.

Internal and External Multimedia Content

There are actually two distinct sources for multimedia files, internal and external. Internal or in-line images appear directly on a Web page, whereas external images are stored externally and are only loaded when a user chooses the appropriate hotlink on a Web page. In general, external media is defined as any file that cannot be automatically loaded, played, or displayed by a Web browser on a Web page.

Internal or in-line multimedia file use is limited to the types of files supported by most browsers. This usually means you can only use GIF and JPEG images. External files can include just about any kind of file you can create. These include PostScript, zipped, MPEG video, and nonin-line GIF files. In other words, external file formats can be just about any type of file you can store on a disk.

Internal file formats are supported directly by most browsers so let's look instead at what happens when you use external file formats. Browsers handle external files by first downloading the file and then passing it to some other application on your system that is designed to read and handle the specific file format. Technically, the decision as to what application handles the file is settled by one of two factors: the extension to the filename or the content type of the file.

When a file is accessed from the server, the Web server does not actually send the filename. In some cases, the data it sends back may be automatically generated and not have a filename at all. What the server does send back is a special code called the content type, which tells the browser what kind of file it is sending. Content types look similar to text/html, image/gif, video/mpeg, video/avi, and so on.

The browser and the Web server maintain lists in their configuration or preference files so they can easily map file extensions to content type. The server uses its list to decide which content-type to send to the browser with a given file extension. The browser uses its list to map these content types to the appropriate plug-in on the user's system.

URLs and Multimedia Files

When a URL references a multimedia file on an external, remote location, it means that each time the user's browsers loads the file, that browser actually links to the remote location. This increases the time needed for the browser to load the file. If the remote location is not online, the browser can't load the image. For this reason, having your graphic files on your own WWW server usually works better.

An exception to this takes place when you want to include an image from another location that changes over time, such as a digital clock or weather map, or a very large image. In the first case, the other site maintains the changing image and you see it directly from their site, but included in your Web page. In the second case, you save your server's disk space by pointing to the remote location for the multimedia image. And, reusing the same graphic on a single Web page doesn't add significant time or disk storage requirements when the user's browser activates caching (or the retrieval of previously accessed files).

Adding Sound

There are several ways you can add audio to your HTML document, including

- The Anchor tag <A> and HREF attribute.
- Plug-ins like RealAudio.
- Browser-specific tags, such as Microsoft's Internet Explorer <BGSOUND> tag.
- Intel processor-specific TrueSpeech.

Is Anyone Listening?

Before discussing *how* to add sound to an HTML document, a few notes of caution. First, remember that an end user may not even own a sound card and therefore won't hear any sounds, and that even more end users turn their sound off even if they *do* own a sound card!

Using the <A> Anchor Tag

The <A> anchor tag is undoubtedly the simplest method to add sound to your HTML document. You simply use the <A>, </A> tag pair to encapsulate the sound file's name, as in

```
<A HREF="MyWelcome.au">Allow me to introduce
myself."</A>
```

The anchor tag is used to insert hyperlinks into an HTML document. To include a link to an external sound on your Web page, you must have the sound file in the right format, just as you would for an image file. Presently, the only fully cross-platform sound file format for the Web is Sun Microsystem's AU file format.

The AU audio format provides different types of sound sampling encryption. The most popular one is the 8-bit format. However, AU files are not the best audio quality. Other, better-quality sound formats include the Macintosh AIFF, the Windows WAV, or the more cross-platform MPEG audio.

There are also plug-ins, such as RealAudio, with their associated proprietary file formats, developed specifically for playing audio files on the Internet and the World Wide Web. Unlike most other audio files where you wait for the entire file to download before you can hear it, RealAudio uses a technique called streaming. *Streaming* allows a sound file to begin playing at the same time it is being downloaded–there is only one slight initial pause, as the file first arrives at your machine.

Unfortunately, like all other plug-ins, there is the need to set up a special server to deliver real audio files, and linking to them involves a slightly different process than linking to regular audio files. For both reasons, this subject's discussion is delayed to later on in the chapter.

Common sound file formats and their extensions recognized by today's browsers are listed in Table 4.2.

Table 4.2: *Sound File Formats and their File Extensions*

Sound File Format	Sound File Extension
AIFF/AIFC	.aiff, or .aif (for 8.3 file formats)
AU	.au
MIDI	.mid
MPEG	.mp2 (video and sound)
Wave	.wav

USING MICROSOFT'S <BGSOUND> TAG

The background sound tag, <BGSOUND>, provides an elevator-background-like way to audibly enhance the viewing of a Web page. <BGSOUND> allows you to link to any WAV file using the SRC attribute and set a repeat play count, as in the following example:

```
<BGSOUND SRC=http://www.mysite.com/elevatormusic.wav
LOOP=INFINITE>
```

The LOOP attribute repeats indefinitely if set to a value of -1 or INFINITE; otherwise the integral value limits the repeat play to the value specified, for example, four iterations. Note, the sound will start to play as soon as it has finished downloading and does *not* require the user to click on any hotlink. Be careful when using sound in your documents. A constantly repeating sound can be even more annoying than overusing blinking text. It is better to have one short sound that grabs your reader's attention than a 30-minute long WAV file that irritates. In general, the only reason for using sound is for a *special* effect and therefore it should be brief.

Image File Size

Before launching off into the world of visual imagery, you need to know a little about controlling image file size. One way to control a file's size is to limit the number of bits stored per pixel. Although reducing the bits per pixel reduces the resolution of the image as rendered by the browser, try storing your image with 7 or 5 bits per pixel if you really need to show a large image as quickly as possible. Another approach is to reduce the number of colors in the picture to lower its overall image size.

Various graphics programs allow you to import an image in one resolution and change its parameters and save a streamlined rendition. Standard GIF images require an 8-bit-per-pixel format providing 256 colors. Changing the bits-per-pixel ratio down to 7 bits limits reproductions to 128 colors, while a 5-bit version contains only 32 color variations.

Applications like Corel7 even allow you to set the number of colors, for example 43, with the software selecting the appropriate number of pixels, in this example, 7 bits-per-pixel. There is an advantage to this approach, since the 85 unused color definitions are set to all zeros, resulting in a smaller image, with faster rendering, than one set explicitly to a 7-bits-per-pixel standard format.

Adding Animated GIFs

Many developers are surprised to discover that a GIF file format is not just for single-frame images, but also multiple images, stored in a single file, which can be rendered into an animation sequence. Incorporating animated images into your Web page is straightforward when using the <IMG> image tag and its associated SRC tag, as in

```
<IMG SRC = "http://www.mysite.com/animate.gif">
```

The following HTML document launches the Norton Utilities tutorial genie-animated GIF file:

```
<HTML>
<HEAD>
<TITLE>Adding Animated GIFs to a Web Page</TITLE>
</HEAD>
<BODY>
<P>An Animated Nortun Utilities Genie!"</P>
<IMG src="c:/UT/Norton/HTML/nsgmain.gif">

</BODY>
</HTML>
```

Figure 4.8 displays the magical guide. The good news is that an animated GIF is treated the same way as any other image file on your Web page.

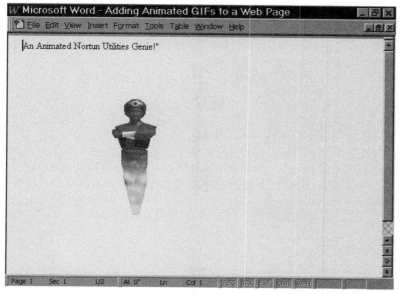

Figure 4.8: *Adding an animated GIF to a Web page.*

ADDING DIFFERENT TYPES OF MEDIA WITH < E M B E D >

The <EMBED> tag, originally introduced by Netscape, allows you to add different types of multimedia to your HTML document. File formats currently supported include

- LiveVideo AVI (Audio Video Interleave) file format.
- LiveAudio MIDI, AIFF, AU, and WAV file formats.
- QuickTime multimedia movies in MOV file format.

The <EMBED> tag has three attributes: SRC, HEIGHT, and WIDTH. The <EMBED> tag also works with special downloaded plug-ins and may contain additional plug-in-specific attributes such as Netscape's PLAY_LOOP repetition parameter, or Microsoft's PALETTE selector. (Note: Netscape's PARAMETER_NAME attribute is equivalent in function to Microsoft's OPTIONAL_PARAMETER.)

SRC Attribute

The SRC attribute allows you to define the URL multimedia file source.

HEIGHT and WIDTH Attributes

Defined in number of pixels, the HEIGHT and WIDTH attributes give the height and width of the embedded multimedia file.

Adding an AVI File

The following HTML document shows how to add an insert disk animated AVI file to your Web page:

```
<HTML>
<HEAD>
<TITLE>Adding AVI Files to a Web Page</TITLE>
</HEAD>
<BODY>
<P>Adding a Simple Downloading AVI File Image.</P>
<EMBED SRC="D:/BK/JAVASCRIPT/CHP04/setup.avi"WIDTH=40
HEIGHT=30
PLAY_LOOP=3>

</BODY>
</HTML>
```

Figure 4.9 shows the resulting image and the AVI player frame including the play, stop-play, and file image slider-selector controls.

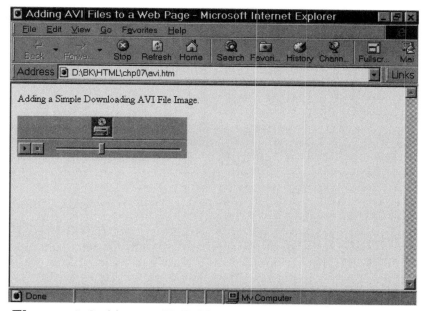

Figure 4.9: *Using <EMBED> with Microsoft's Internet Explorer and an AVI file.*

A properly designed Web page using the <EMBED> tag should always include a <NOEMBED> counterpart for those Web surfers.

<NOEMBED> for Nonmultimedia-Aware Browsers

A good habit to get into is always including a <NOEMBED> for every <EMBED> tag you use in an HTML document. This practice politely prompts the end user with a message informing them of an unrecognized multimedia file format.

<NOEMBED> is used in conjunction with the EMBED element to indicate content/HTML markup that will only appear if the browser does not support the EMBED syntax. Browsers that *do* support the EMBED element will ignore the contents of the NOEMBED element.

An example of <NOEMBED> for the previous HTML document would look like

```
<HTML>
<HEAD>
<TITLE>Adding AVI Files to a Web Page</TITLE>
</HEAD>
<BODY>
<P>Adding a Simple Downloading AVI File Image.</P>
<EMBED SRC="D:/BK/JAVASCRIPT/CHP04/setup.avi"WIDTH=40
HEIGHT=30
PLAY_LOOP=3>
<NOEMBED>
Unfortunately, your browser does not support AVI file
Playback - you will not see the animated download file
Image.
</NOEMBED>

</BODY>
</HTML>
```

Adding Video Using Internet Explorer's DYNSRC Attribute

Since the introduction of Microsoft's Internet Explorer 2.0 browser, HTML programmers have been able to use the <IMG> proprietary attribute DYNSRC, which stands for Dynamic Source. This attribute must be used as part of the standard <IMG> HTML tag. It is designed to allow you to embed in-line video clips in an AVI file format. DYNSRC is also extended to allow you to embed VRML elements! The syntax for an image looks like

```
<IMG SRC = "http://www.mysite.com/staticlogo.jpg" DYN-
SRC="animlogo.avi">
```

If the browser does not support the DYNSRC attribute it is simply ignored and instead uses the alternate image specified by the SRG attribute.

Microsoft added several parameters to the DYNSRC attribute that allow you to control the playback:

- CONTROLS–The CONTROLS parameter allows you to add VCR-type buttons below the video frame providing play and stop capabilities.
- LOOP–Similar to the standard HTML LOOP attribute, LOOP defines the number of video playback repetitions. The value can be set explicitly, as in LOOP=4, or a value of –1 or INFINITE, generate nonstop playback-rewind-playback cycles. LOOPDELAY, specified in milliseconds, states how long a video clip will wait between play loops. Also, because the DYNSRC is an attribute of the <IMG> element, other attributes of the IMG element, such as HEIGHT, WIDTH, HSPACE, VSPACE, BORDER, etc., are also acceptable and, if specified, will format the display window for the video clip.
- START–The START parameter selects one of two start-play modes. The first is FILEOPEN, which automatically plays the AVI file video as soon as the entire HTML page and AVI file are downloaded. The alternate START mode is called MOUSEOVER. MOUSEOVER prevents the video from starting until the user passes the mouse over the top of the video frame. Both values can be set, but they must be separated with a comma. You would use both values together if you wanted the video to play as soon as the Web page opens, and then again whenever the user moved the mouse over it.

A complete example using DYNSRC would take on this form:

```
<IMG DYNSRC="myvideo.avi" SRC="staticvideo.jpg" WIDTH=160
HEIGHT=120 START="FILEOPEN,MOUSEOVER" CONTROLS>
```

Notice that DYNSRC also supports the WIDTH and HEIGHT attributes. Also, when selecting MOUSEOVER, it does not make any sense to implement the LOOP=INFINITE attribute. This is because MOUSEOVER will be ignored, because you have set the video to loop indefinitely.

Using ActiveX Controls

ActiveX is yet another option by which Web page designers can deliver specialized content to the user. ActiveX controls are objects that can be inserted into Web pages or other applications. This standard, developed by Microsoft, is a bit of a cross between Java and plug-ins. Like Java, it is loaded automatically when it encounters the browser. Like a plug-in, after it is downloaded onto the user's system, it remains there for the future and doesn't have to be reloaded. If you are a Visual Basic developer, you will be very familiar with ActiveX controls, since they were formerly known as OLE controls or OCXs.

ActiveX controls also offer a wide variety of content options, including Windows-type controls, spreadsheets, and Shockwave. There are even several ActiveX controls that are included with Internet Explorer which give you the ability to make your own Web page come alive by providing special formatting features, animation, video, and much more.

ActiveX controls can range from simply controlling the label displayed inside a standard control, to an ActiveX control that gives you the ability to see another desktop across the Internet. If you can think of a particular control that you need for some specialized purpose, chances are that someone has probably already created it.

To include an ActiveX control, you simply use the <OBJECT> tag as in

```
<OBJECT CLASSID="classID" DATA="data.fil" HEIGHT=140
WIDTH=120> </OBJECT>
```

The classIDs are supplied by the software vendor that developed the ActiveX control and the data.fil identifies the file containing the ActiveX content, for example, a DCR file for a Shockwave Director movie. The following additional attributes are available:

- ALIGN—Similar in use to the <IMG> tag ALIGN attribute, ALIGN sets the alignment of an ActiveX control's spacing in relation to surrounding text. Options include BOTTOM (the default), MIDDLE, TOP, LEFT, or RIGHT.
- CODEBASE—CODEBASE is a URL specifying the source for the ActiveX control. Windows maintains an internal registry contain-

ing virtually every bit of information about a particular machine's hardware and software configuration. When your browser loads the ActiveX's classID, it automatically scans the Windows registry for a match. If a match is found, the local version is used; if not, the browser automatically uses the CODEBASE URL to find the missing ActiveX control and downloads it.

- CODETYPE–The <OBJECT> tag supports the CODETYPE attribute allowing you an alternate approach to letting your browser decide whether or not it can handle the specified ActiveX object. ActiveX controls have a CODETYPE of *application/x-oleobject*.

- PARAM and VALUE–These ActiveX control-specific attributes allow you to uniquely communicate with a third-party vendor's ActiveX control. As each custom control needs to communicate with your Web page, the vendor supplies the list of parameters used for the interface. You pass parameters to the control using the PARAM and VALUE attributes. To do this you simply use the <PARAM> tag between the <OBJECT>, </OBJECT> tag pair (consult the documentation supplied by the vendor for specific details on the use of PARAM and VALUE).

A generic example would have the following form:

```
<PARAM name="param" VALUE="value">
```

Summary

You learned that sound and images can be used to enhance any Web site. A good rule of thumb, however, is to use them only when necessary and to keep their sizes as small as possible. You also learned just how easy it is to add multimedia content to an HTML document.

Don't forget as you design your applications that some end users do not have sound capabilities, or their sound may be turned off. Other users may resent the increased download time generated by too much or too high a resolution image and never return to your site. Finally, don't forget that multimedia splash is never a substitute for quality content.

CHAPTER 5

WORKING WITH LISTS, DOCUMENTS, AND IMAGES

- Tables
- Attributes
- Links

Many of the elements discussed in this chapter enable you to visually clarify and enhance the display of JavaScript screen output. This chapter provides a discussion of several important HTML concepts: tables or lists of information, links used for document navigation, and anchors used in image placement. While each topic is independent of the others, you will find that a complete understanding of HTML capabilities requires a through knowledge of these three topics.

Tables

The HTML table model allows you to arrange all types of data into rows and columns of cells. These cells may include text, preformatted text, images, links, forms, form fields, other tables, etc. Table cells may either contain header information using the <TH> tag or data using the <TD> tag. Cells may span multiple rows and columns.

You can use tables for many different purposes. The obvious use is for structuring information, for example, international exchange rates, technical data, and so on. Tables can also be used to improve the layout of your HTML document by allowing you to place text in columns like a newspaper, or even to align images.

In the following sections of this chapter we'll investigate the versatility of table elements for rendering text in columnar formats. To create tables in HTML, you define the parts of your table and which bits of HTML go where, and then you add HTML table code around those parts. Then you refine the table's appearance with alignments, borders, and colored cells.

However, before launching off into your first table example, a word of caution. Creating tables by hand in HTML is no fun. The code for tables was designed to be easy to generate by programs, not to be written by hand. As such it can be a bit confusing. Initially, you will do a lot of experimenting, testing, and going back and forth between your browser and your code to get a table to look and work the way you would like.

<TABLE> Creation

To create a table in HTML, you use the <TABLE>, </TABLE> tags surrounding the text for the table's caption and then the contents of the table itself, as in

```
<TABLE>
...Caption and table contents go here...
<TABLE>
```

Defining Rows and Columns with \<TR> and \<TD>

You define a table's contents, row by row, by nesting the associated text between a \<TR>, \</TR> tag pair. Each table row has, in turn, a number of columns or table cells, which are surrounded with the \<TH>, \</TH> tag pair for column headings, or \<TD>, \</TD> tags for cellular data items, as in

```
<HTML>
<HEAD>
<TITLE>Table Row and Column Elements</TITLE>
</HEAD>
<BODY>
<TABLE>
<TR>
     <TH>Column I</TH> <TH>Column II</TH> <TH>Column
III</TH>
</TR>
<TR>
     <TD>Data 1-1</TD> <TD>Data 1-2</TD> <TD>Data 1-
3</TD>
</TR>
<TR>
     <TD>Data 2-1</TD> <TD>Data 2-2</TD> <TD>Data 2-
3</TD>
</TR>
</TABLE>
</BODY>
</HTML>
```

Figure 5.1 displays the resulting page. Compare this with Figure 5.2 which adds the BORDER = 5 attribute.

Other Ways to Define Columns

There are actually multiple methods for defining the number of columns. The first approach is to specify the number of columns with the COL and COLGROUP tags. (Note: These tags can only occur at the start of the table, immediately after the optional CAPTION attribute.)

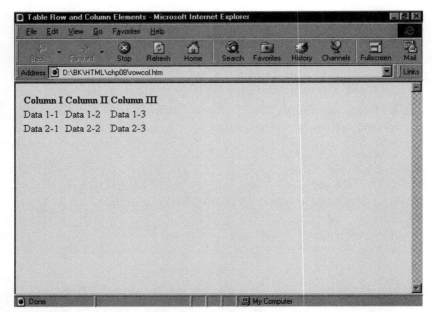

Figure 5–1: Using the <TABLE>, <TH>, and <TD> elements.

The second method for defining columns is to scan each row in turn to compute the number of columns needed for each row, taking into account cells that span multiple rows and/or columns. Set the number of columns for the table to be the maximum number of columns from each row. For any row that has less than this number of columns, the end of that row should be padded with empty cells. The "end" of a row depends on the directionality of the table (see the description of the DIR attribute later in this chapter).

The third means of defining numbers of columns is to use the use the COLS attribute in the <TABLE>, </TABLE> tag pair. This is the weakest method since it doesn't provide any additional information about column widths. This may not matter, however, if the author uses style sheets to specify widths.

The following examples demonstrate the various options for defining table columns. Each example renders a table with three columns.

```
<TABLE>
  <COL><COL><COL>
…Table contents go here…
</TABLE>
or
<TABLE>
  <COL span="3">
```

```
…Table contents go here…
</TABLE>
or
<TABLE>
<TR>
  <TD><TD><TD>
</TR>
</TABLE>
or
<TABLE cols="3">
…Table contents go here…
</TABLE>
```

Setting up Column Groups with COLGROUP

You use the <COLGROUP> tag to create an explicit column group. Each column group defined by <COLGROUP> may contain zero or more <COL> elements. The width attribute of the <COLGROUP> defines a default width for each column in a column group. The special value "0*" tells the browser to set every column in a group to its minimum width. This behavior may be overridden by the presence of a <COL> element. The table in the following example contains two column groups. The first column group contains seven columns and the second contains five columns. The default width for each column in the first column group is 40 pixels. The width of each column in the second column group will be the minimum for the column.

```
<TABLE>
<COLGROUP span="7" width="40">
<COLGROUP span="5" width="0*">
<THEAD>
<TR> ...
</TABLE>
```

In this next example the table is defined to have two column groups. The first group contains four columns, the second contains two columns. The available horizontal space will be allotted as follows: First the browser will render 40 pixels to the first column, with the second group allotted 20 pixels. Then, the minimal space required for the second column will be allotted to it. The remaining horizontal space will be divided into six equal portions. Column three will receive two of these portions, column four will receive one, and column five will receive three.

```
<TABLE>
<COLGROUP>
   <COL width="40">
   <COL width="30">
   <COL width="0*">
   <COL width="2*">
<COLGROUP align="right">
   <COL width="1*">
   <COL width="3*" align="char" char=".">
<THEAD>
<TR> ...
</TABLE>
```

We have set the value of the **ALIGN** attribute in the second column group to right. All cells in every column in this group will inherit this value but may override it. In fact, the final <COL> does just that, by specifying that every cell in the column it governs will be aligned along the period, ., symbol.

COLSPAN, ROWSPAN, NOWRAP

You may also use the <TD> COLSPAN attribute to define the number of table columns that a cell spans. COLSPAN allows you to combine cells, just as you can do in a spreadsheet application. If you need to include the same data in more than one adjacent cell in a row, use COLSPAN. The syntax is straightforward:

```
<TD COLSPAN=number_of_adjacent cells>
```

ROWSPAN is similar in that it defines the number of table rows that a cell spans. ROWSPAN also allows you to join adjacent cells so that you can render one set of data across multiple rows. The syntax looks like

```
<TD ROWSPAN=number_of_adjacent_rows>
```

Finally, NOWRAP prevents cell contents from wrapping within a cell. You use this attribute when you are formatting data. A note of caution though. Using this attribute can generate extremely wide cell dimensions. The syntax for NOWRAP looks like

```
<TD NOWRAP>
```

Adding a \<BORDER>

One of the first options you can add to the table's visual appearance is a border. The BORDER element is defined in numbers of pixels. BORDER has a default value of 1 pixel when left undefined.

```
<HTML>
<HEAD>
<TITLE>Table Row and Column Elements with
Border</TITLE>
</HEAD>
<BODY>
<TABLE BORDER="5">
<TR>
    <TH>Column I</TH> <TH>Column II</TH> <TH>Column
III</TH>
</TR>
<TR>
    <TD>Data 1-1</TD> <TD>Data 1-2</TD> <TD>Data 1-
3</TD>
</TR>
<TR>
    <TD>Data 2-1</TD> <TD>Data 2-2</TD> <TD>Data 2-
3</TD>
</TR>
</TABLE>
</BODY>
</HTML>
```

Figure 5.2 is the screen from this HTML document. Compare it with the results shown earlier in Figure 5.1.

Adding Table \<CAPTION>s

To add a brief table description for your table you immediately follow the \<TABLE> tag with a \<CAPTION>, \</CAPTION> tag pair. You can think of the \<CAPTION> tag for tables as being equivalent to the \<HEAD> tag for the \<BODY> of your HTML document. \<CAPTION> has a placement option of TOP or BOTTOM. The following example places the caption in the more common BOTTOM position:

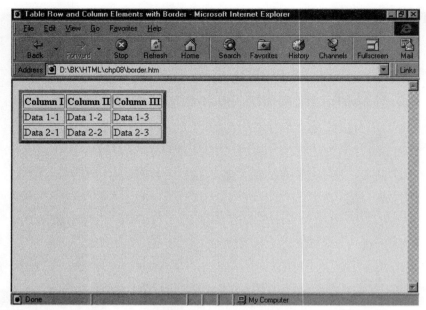

Figure 5–2: *Original table redefined with a rendered border attribute.*

```
<HTML>
<HEAD>
<TITLE>Table Row and Column Elements with Border and
Caption</TITLE>
</HEAD>
<BODY>
<TABLE BORDER="5">
<CAPTION ALIGN=BOTTOM>Completed Example Table with
caption.</CAPTION>
<TR>
    <TH>Column I</TH> <TH>Column II</TH> <TH>Column
III</TH>
</TR>
<TR>
    <TD>Data 1-1</TD> <TD>Data 1-2</TD> <TD>Data 1-
3</TD>
</TR>
<TR>
    <TD>Data 2-1</TD> <TD>Data 2-2</TD> <TD>Data 2-
3</TD>
</TR>
</TABLE>
</BODY>
</HTML>
```

Figure 5.3 now renders the table with a bottom-aligned caption.

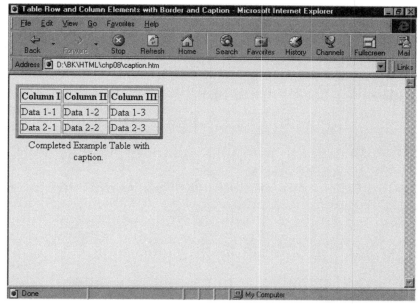

Figure 5–3: *Original table rendered with a CAPTION.*

Selecting Table Position with ALIGN

Depending on your table's contents, you may generate a more easily viewed rendering by instructing the browser to align the table either to the LEFT (the default mode), CENTER, or RIGHT on your Web page. The following HTML document adds CENTER table alignment to the previous example.

```
<HTML>
<HEAD>
<TITLE>Table Rendered with CENTER Alignment</TITLE>
</HEAD>
<BODY>
<TABLE ALIGN=CENTER BORDER>
<TR>
     <TH>Column I</TH> <TH>Column II</TH> <TH>Column
III</TH>
</TR>
<TR>
     <TD>Data 1-1</TD> <TD>Data 1-2</TD> <TD>Data 1-
3</TD>
</TR>
<TR>
     <TD>Data 2-1</TD> <TD>Data 2-2</TD> <TD>Data 2-
3</TD>
```

```
</TR>
</TABLE>
</BODY>
</HTML>
```

Figure 5.4 displays the modified table alignment.

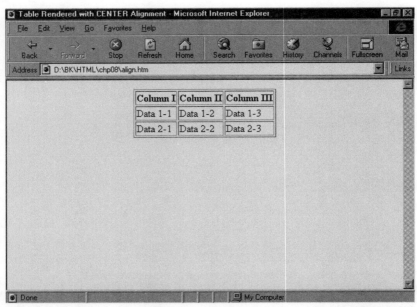

Figure 5-4: *Table centering using ALIGN=CENTER attribute.*

This next example demonstrates how to align cell contents. Once again, data elements have LEFT, CENTER, and RIGHT alignment options only.

```
<HTML>
<HEAD>
<TITLE>Table Rendered with Varying Cell Content
Alignment</TITLE>
</HEAD>
<BODY>
<TABLE ALIGN=CENTER BORDER>
<TR>
    <TH>Column I</TH> <TH>Column II</TH> <TH>Column
III</TH>
</TR>
<TR ALIGN=CENTER>
```

```
    <TD>Center 1-1</TD> <TD>Center 1-2</TD>
<TD>Center 1-3</TD>
</TR>
<TR ALIGN=RIGHT>
    <TD>Right 2-1</TD> <TD>Right 2-2</TD> <TD>Right
2-3</TD>
</TR>
</TABLE>
</BODY>
</HTML>
```

Figure 5.5 renders the modified cell contents. Row one aligns each cell using the CENTER attribute and row two uses RIGHT alignment. The default is LEFT.

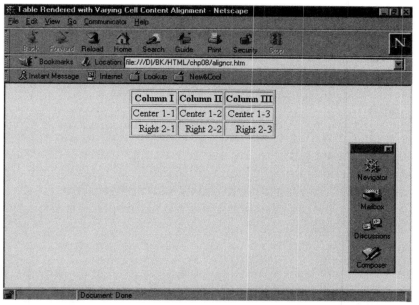

Figure 5–5: *Modifying cell ALIGNment with CENTER and RIGHT.*

VALIGN, CHAR, AND CHAROFF

The VALIGN attribute is similar to ALIGN only it defines the vertical alignment of text in the cells in the row. The syntax is

```
<TR VALIGN="TYPE">
```

where TYPE is either TOP, MIDDLE, BOTTOM, or BASELINE. Table 5.1 describes each option.

Table 5–1: *VALIGN Types and Descriptions*

Type	Description
TOP	Cell contents are aligned with the top of each cell space.
MIDDLE	Cell contents are aligned with the middle of each cell space.
BOTTOM	Cell contents are aligned with the bottom of each cell space.
BASELINE	Cell contents are aligned along a common baseline.

The <TR> CHAR attribute allows you to align cell contents with a specific character. The default character is the decimal point. The syntax looks like

```
<TR CHAR="single_character">
```

CHAR and CHAROFF attributes usually appear in pairs. CHAROFF defines the offset to the first alignment character. The offset is usually from the left margin for Latin-based cell text contents. If a line doesn't include the alignment character, browsers usually shift the cell contents so that they end at the alignment poisiton. The syntax for CHAROFF looks like

```
<TR CHAROFF="25%">
```

Setting Internal Cell Dimensions with CELLPADDING

As you will soon discover, just about every aspect of a table's appearance has an author-definable setting. You can even determine the amount of spacing above, below, and around each cell's contents by applying a number-of-pixels value to the CELLPADDING attribute. The following HTML sets this value to 30:

```
<HTML>
<HEAD>
```

```
<TITLE>Table Rendered with 30-Pixel Cell
Widths</TITLE>
</HEAD>
<BODY>
<TABLE CELLPADDING=30>
<CAPTION>"Example Changing Cell Wall
Dimensions."</CAPTION>
<TR>
    <TH>Column I</TH> <TH>Column II</TH> <TH>Column
III</TH>
</TR>
<TR>
    <TD>Center 1-1</TD> <TD>Center 1-2</TD>
<TD>Center 1-3</TD>
</TR>
<TR>
    <TD>Right 2-1</TD> <TD>Right 2-2</TD> <TD>Right
2-3</TD>
</TR>
</TABLE>
</BODY>
</HTML>
```

Figure 5.6 renders the newly padded cell's dimensions.

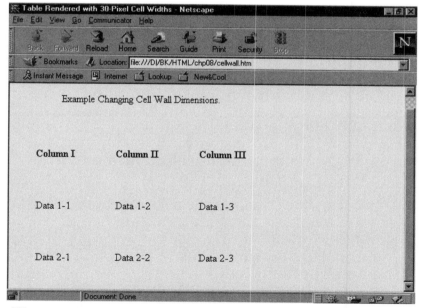

Figure 5-6: *Using the CELLPADDING attribute to change cell content spacing.*

Figure 5.6 also demonstrates the visual impact of a borderless table, which takes on the appearance of columnar data lists.

CELLSPACING, FRAME, RULES, and WIDTH Attributes

Another approach to table data spacing is to use the CELLSPACING attribute. Unlike CELLPADDING, which defines the number of pixels surrounding the cell's contents, CELLPADDING defines the number of pixels *between* each cell wall, as in

```
<TABLE CELLSPACING=5>
```

The table WIDTH attribute allows you to set the width of the entire table, defined in number of pixels or a percentage of the window's dimensions, as in

```
<TABLE WIDTH="50%">
```

The RULES attribute defines which inner borders of the table to render. The syntax is

```
<TABLE RULES="TYPES"
```

Table 5.2 lists the legal available RULE types.

Table 5–2: *RULES Types and Descriptions*

Type	Description
NONE	Does not render any internal borders.
GROUPS	Renders horizontal borders between all table groups. (Note: Groups are defined by the THEAD, TBODY, TFOOT, and COLGROUP tags.)
ROWS	Renders only horizontal borders between all table rows.
COLS	Renders only vertical borders between all table columns.
ALL	Renders both horizontal and vertical borders between all table cells.

Similar to RULES, the FRAME attribute describes how the outer border of the table is rendered. The FRAME attribute is more diverse than the BORDER attribute. The syntax looks like

```
<TABLE FRAME="TYPE">
```

Table 5.3 lists the available FRAME TYPEs.

Table 5–3: *FRAME Types and Descriptions*

Type	Description
VOID	Does not render any outer border.
ABOVE	Renders only the top outer border.
BELOW	Renders only the bottom outer border.
HSIDES	Renders the top and bottom outer borders only.
LHS	Renders only the left-hand side outer border.
RHS	Renders only the right-hand side outer border.
VSIDES	Renders only the left and right outer borders.
BOX	Renders an outer border on all sides of the table frame.
BORDER	Same as BOX.

Adding Color and Image with Internet Explorer's BORDERCOLOR, BGCOLOR, BACKGROUND, using <COLGROUP>

Just as you would certainly rather view a color television image than a black and white one, your Internet Explorer Web page visitors will prefer viewing more flavorful tables if they are rendered in color. But first a rule on color selection. All professional graphic artists know the cardinal rule is to limit the number of colors in a graphic display to three! Any more than this becomes visually confusing and detracts from the intended impact provided by a good color scheme.

One of the best uses for color is within a table. When a table contains many columns and numerous rows of data, it becomes difficult when scanning extreme right and bottom cells, far from their row and column headings, to know what data goes with which label. Simply highlighting alternate rows or columns in a different color eliminates this grid confusion.

Using <COLGROUP> and BGCOLOR

In order to effect a row-by-row attribute change, you first need to define column groups. Each column group you define can contain its own unique set of attributes, in this case, background color. The <COLGROUP> tag has the following attributes: ALIGN, CHAR, CHAROFF, VALIGN, SPAN, and WIDTH. The following HTML example combines <COLGROUP> and BGCOLOR:

```
<HTML>
<HEAD>
<TITLE>Candy-Striped Column Highlighting</TITLE>
</HEAD>
<BODY>
<TABLE BORDER=15>
<COLGROUP ALIGN=CENTER>
<COLGROUP SPAN=3 ALIGN=LEFT>
<COLGROUP SPAN=2 ALIGN=RIGHT BGCOLOR="GRAY">
<CAPTION ALIGN=TOP>Visually Separating Columns with
Color</CAPTION>
<TR><TH><TH COLSPAN=3>Internal<TH COLSPAN=2>External
<TR><TH><TH>Modems<TH>28K<TH>36K<TH>36K<TH>56K
<TR><TH>Card<TD><TD>2<TD>1<TD>0<TD >2
<TR><TH>Board<TD>1<TD>1<TD>0<TD>1<TD>0
<TD><TH>Sales<TD>0<TD>0<TD>0<TD>1<TD>1
<TR><TH>Quantity<BR>On Order<TD>0<TD>2<TD>0<TD>0<TD>0
</TABLE>
</BODY>
</HTML>
```

Figure 5.7 demonstrates how column highlighting helps separate rows and columns of information.

Of course, on a color display, changing the BORDERCOLOR can help attract the end-user's eye to the entire table. The following HTML change demonstrates how easy this is

```
<TABLE BORDER="15" BORDERCOLOR="BLUE">
```

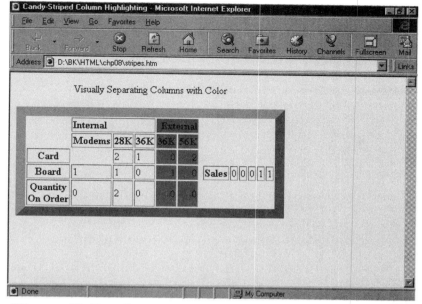

Figure 5–7: *Separating columns of information with color highlighting.*

Changing a Table's BACKGROUND

Cell background enhancements aren't just limited to colors. Using the BACKGROUND attribute inside a <TABLE>, </TABLE> definition allows you to paint each cell with a graphics image.

```
<HTML>
<HEAD>
<TITLE>Candy-Striped Column Highlighting</TITLE>
</HEAD>
<BODY  TEXT="WHITE">
<TABLE BORDER="15"
BACKGROUND="d:\bk\html\chp08\Firework.jpg">
<COLGROUP ALIGN=CENTER>
<COLGROUP SPAN=3 ALIGN=LEFT>
<COLGROUP SPAN=2 ALIGN=RIGHT BGCOLOR="GRAY">
<TR><TH><TH COLSPAN=3>Internal<TH COLSPAN=2>External
<TR><TH><TH>Modems<TH>28K<TH>36K<TH>36K<TH>56K
<TR><TH>Card<TD><TD>2<TD>1<TD>0<TD >2
<TR><TH>Board<TD>1<TD>1<TD>0<TD>1<TD>0
<TD><TH>Sales<TD>0<TD>0<TD>0<TD>1<TD>1
<TR><TH>Quantity<BR>On Order<TD>0<TD>2<TD>0<TD>0<TD>0
```

```
</TABLE>
</BODY>
</HTML>
```

Figure 5.8 renders the table with a slightly more explosive background.

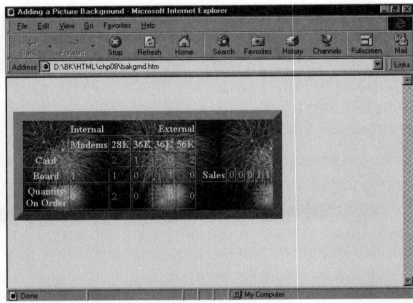

Figure 5-8: *Adding visual impact with a table BACKGROUND image.*

Loading Tables from Right to Left with <DIR>

The direction in which way a table's contents are rendered is specified by the DIR attribute for the <TABLE>, </TABLE> tag pair. For a left-to-right table (the default), column one is on the left side of the table and row one is at the top. For a right-to-left table, column one is one the right side and row one is at the top.

Similarly, for left-to-right tables (the default), extra row cells are added to the right of the table, and for right-to-left tables, extra cells are added to the left side. When set for the <TABLE> tag, the DIR attribute also affects the direction of text within table cells. To specify a right-to-left table, set the DIR attribute as follows:

```
<TABLE DIR="RTL">
```

```
…Table contents go here…
</TABLE>
```

Should you need to change the direction of text within an individual cell, you use the DIR attribute within the tag that defines the cell itself.

Table Footers

The HTML table tags <THEAD>, <TFOOT>, and <TBODY> allow you to group table rows into a head, foot, and one or more body sections. This allows browsers to scroll through table contents separately from their head and foot sections. When long tables are printed, the head and foot information may be repeated on each page that contains table data.

The <TFOOT> tag must always appear before the <TBODY> tag and be nested inside the <TABLE>, </TABLE> tag pair in order for the browser to display the footer before receiving all of the rows of data. The following summarizes which tags are required and which may be omitted:

- The start tags for THEAD and TFOOT are required when the head and foot sections are present, respectively, but the corresponding end tags may always be safely omitted.
- The TBODY start tag is always required except when the table contains only one body and no head or foot sections. The TBODY end tag may always be safely omitted.

The following example demonstrates how to break your HTML table into a header, footer, and body sections:

```
<TABLE>
   <THEAD>
      …header information goes here…
   </THEAD>
   <TFOOT>
      …footer information here…
   </TFOOT>
   <TBODY>
      …finally the table body here…
   </TBODY>
</TABLE>
```

Spoken Tables with AXIS and AXES

The HTML attributes AXIS and AXES allow you to enhance a table's visual presentation by adding an auditory component and if you know that your Web page might be viewed by the visually impaired, to have the tables rendered using the latest in speech- and Braille-based technologies. In the following example table, the value of the AXES attribute is set to reference the corresponding header cell for that column:

```
<TABLE BORDER="10" SUMMARY="Manufacturer, Number in
stock, product, is backordered.">
<CAPTION>Quantity of Instock-Items.</CAPTION>
<TR>
    <TH ID="t1">Manufacturer</TH>
    <TH ID="t2">Instock</TH>
    <TH ID="t3" ABBR="Product">Type of Product</TH>
    <TH ID="t4">Backordered?</TH>
<TR>
    <TD AXES="t1">USRobotics</TD>
    <TD AXES="t2">11</TD>
    <TD AXES="t3">56K Modems</TD>
    <TD AXES="t4">Yes</TD>
<TR>
    <TD AXES="t1">Toshiba Am.</TD>
    <TD AXES="t2">15</TD>
    <TD AXES="t3">Techra</TD>
    <TD AXES="t4">Yes</TD>
</TABLE>
```

This markup could be rendered to speech as

```
Caption: Quanity of Instock-Items
Summary: Manufacturer, Number, product, is backo-
rdered.

Name: US Robotics,    Instock: 11,    Product: Modems,
Backordered?: Yes
Name: Toshiba Am.,    Instock: 15,    Product: Techra,
Backordered?: Yes
```

Note how the header *Type of Product* is abbreviated to *Product* using the ABBR attribute. In the absence of the AXES attribute, a browser may choose to search for an ordered list of headers using one of the following methods.

- Row headers are found inserted in the table in the order they appear, for example, the leftmost headers are found inserted before the header to the right, or column headers are found inserted after corresponding row headers in the order they appear in the table, and the topmost header is found inserted before the header below it.

- Using a left-to-right cell position scan order to detect header cells (the search is canceled whenever the table extent is reached or a data cell is found after a header cell).

- Using an upward column search for header cell information (the search is canceled whenever the table extent is reached or a data cell is found after a header cell).

- When a cell contains both the <TD> tag and AXIS attribute, the cell is treated as acting as a <TH> tagged cell.

- When a header cell contains the AXES attribute, the header is referenced by this attribute and is inserted into the list, stopping the directional search.

HTML Table Example

The following example HTML renders a portion of Appendix D using grouped rows and columns. It is an excellent example from which to clone or base your own meaningful tables.

```
<HTML>
<HEAD>
<TITLE>Attribute Name</TITLE>
</HEAD>
<BODY>

<TABLE BORDER CELLSPACING=1 CELLPADDING=7 WIDTH=583>
<CAPTION>Portion of Appendix D</CAPTION>

<TH BGCOLOR="GRAY"><FONT FACE="Arial,Times New Roman"
SIZE=4><P>Attribute Name</FONT>
<TH BGCOLOR="GRAY"><FONT FACE="Arial,Times New Roman"
SIZE=4><P>Related Elements</FONT>
<TH BGCOLOR="GRAY"><FONT FACE="Arial,Times New Roman"
SIZE=4><P>Note</FONT>

<TR><TD WIDTH="27%" VALIGN="TOP">
<FONT FACE="Arial,Times New Roman"
SIZE=3><P><B>abbr</B></FONT></TD>
<TD WIDTH="29%" VALIGN="TOP">
<FONT FACE="Times,Times New Roman" SIZE=2><P>TD</P>
```

```
<P>TH</FONT></TD>
<TD WIDTH="44%" VALIGN="TOP">
<FONT FACE="Times,Times New Roman"
SIZE=2><P>Abbreviation used for header.</FONT></TD>
</TR>

<TR BGCOLOR="GRAY"><TD WIDTH="27%" VALIGN="TOP">
<FONT FACE="Arial,Times New Roman"
SIZE=3><P><B>accept-charset</B></FONT></TD>
<TD WIDTH="29%" VALIGN="TOP">
<FONT FACE="Times,Times New Roman"
SIZE=2><P>FORM</FONT></TD>
<TD WIDTH="44%" VALIGN="TOP">
<FONT FACE="Times,Times New Roman"
SIZE=2><P>Character sets that are
supported.</FONT></TD>
</TR>

<TR><TD WIDTH="27%" VALIGN="TOP">
<FONT FACE="Arial,Times New Roman"
SIZE=3><P><B>accept</B></FONT></TD>
<TD WIDTH="29%" VALIGN="TOP">
<FONT FACE="Times,Times New Roman"
SIZE=2><P>INPUT</FONT></TD>
<TD WIDTH="44%" VALIGN="TOP">
<FONT FACE="Times,Times New Roman" SIZE=2><P>MIME
types available for file uploading.</FONT></TD>
</TR>

<TR BGCOLOR="GRAY"><TD WIDTH="27%" VALIGN="TOP">
<FONT FACE="Arial,Times New Roman"
SIZE=3><P><B>accesskey</B></FONT></TD>
<TD WIDTH="29%" VALIGN="TOP">
<FONT FACE="Times,Times New Roman" SIZE=2><P>A</P>
<P>AREA</P>
<P>BUTTON</P>
<P>INPUT</P>
<P>LABEL</P>
<P>LEGEND</FONT></TD>
<TD WIDTH="44%" VALIGN="TOP">
<FONT FACE="Times,Times New Roman" SIZE=2><P>Key
character accessibility.</FONT></TD>
</TR>

<TR><TD WIDTH="27%" VALIGN="TOP">
<FONT FACE="Arial,Times New Roman"
SIZE=3><P><B>action</B></FONT></TD>
<TD WIDTH="29%" VALIGN="TOP">
<FONT FACE="Times,Times New Roman"
SIZE=2><P>FORM</FONT></TD>
<TD WIDTH="44%" VALIGN="TOP">
```

```
<FONT FACE="Times,Times New Roman" SIZE=2><P>Provides
information for the server-side form
handler.</FONT></TD>
</TR>

</TABLE>

</BODY>
</HTML>
```

Figure 5.9 shows the resulting table using many of the common table elements discussed in this chapter. You will notice from the HTML document that lengthy table creation is a painstaking endeavor since you must manually enter detailed HTML and data elements for each row and column.

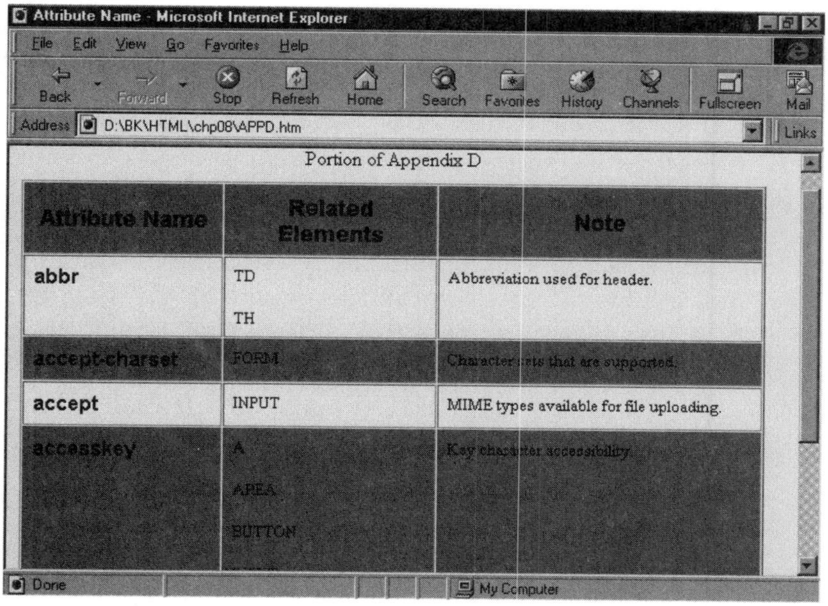

Figure 5–9: *Portion of a table.*

Links and Anchors

From the very beginning HTML authors have enjoyed the convenience of HTML's conventional publishing idioms for rich text and structured Web page design. However, what is unique to HTML versus other markup languages is its ability to incorporate hypertext and interactive documents. This chapter looks deeper into the link or hyperlink, the basic hypertext construct. A link is a connection from one Web resource to another. While this idea is very straightforward in design, it is the link that has been one of the, if not the, most important end user–friendly feature generating the tremendous popularity of Web surfing.

Technically speaking, a link has two ends, or ancestors, along with an associated direction. The source anchor is located on the originating HTML document and points to the destination anchor. The destination can include any type of browser-aware resource such as a text document, graphic image, sound bite, video stream, or even a program.

The <A>nchor element is the gateway for adding hyperlinks to almost any document type. Hyperlinks are not just limited to text. You can also use images as hyperlinks by placing the image between the <A> and </A> anchor tags in the same way you would place text.

Tag Description

The <A>nchor tag is used to define both the source and destination of a hypertext link. Frequently used attributes include HREF, NAME, REL, REV, COORDS, SHAPE, and TITLE. The <LINK> element specifies the current document's relationship with other documents. However, it is rarely used because it requires properly defined values which, as yet, haven't been fully determined.

Using the ANCHOR Elements

HTML provides two elements for defining and using links: the <LINK> and <A> elements along with the HREF, NAME, REV, REL, COORDS, SHAPE, and TITLE attributes. Each, of course, has its own syntax, for example, <LINK>. Note: <LINK> can only appear in the <HEAD> of an HTML document, while <A> may be placed anywhere in the <BODY>.

Browsers process the referenced link in different ways depending on the resource type. In some instances the browser opens a new document window; in others it may actually launch a separate program to handle the resource. However, most browsers render an <A>nchor-flagged element by underlining the reference indicating the presence of the link. If the <A> anchor reference uses the NAME attribute, the reference defines an anchor that is probably accessed by other links. HTML allows the <A>nchor reference to use both the HREF and NAME attributes at the same time.

CORRECT <A>NCHOR NAMES

HTML <A>nchor names have a set of rules all their own. First, they must be unique within the defining document and remember, they are case insensitive so Section1 and SECTION1 do not qualify. The following example is illegal with respect to uniqueness since the two names are the same except for case:

```
<A NAME="Section1">...>/A>
<A NAME="SECTION1">...>/A>
```

Second, <A> anchor name comparisons between fragment URL identifiers and <A> anchor names must be executed to generate an identical pair. For example, the following example is correct, using the rules of string matching:

```
<A HREF="#Section1">...>/A>

...additional document goes here...

<A HREF="Section1">...>/A>
```

This next example highlights some of the peculiarities in various browsers, since some will consider the example HTML a match, others will not. Note, however, that the example is technically legal HTML.

```
<A NAME="#Section1">...>/A>

...additional document goes here...

<A HREF="Section1">...>/A>
```

While on the subject of <A> anchor rules, here's one more, <A>nchors may not be nested. The following example demonstrates an illegal attempt at putting an <A>nchor within another <A> anchor reference:

```
<A NAME="GG1 Locator" HREF="gg1usasl">First Anchor
<A NAME="GG1 East Coast" HREF="gg1ec.html">Nested
Anchor
</A></A>
```

Using \<A> anchor with the HREF Attribute

The most frequent use for an HTML link is to access another resource on the Internet. The following HTML example contains three links. The first accesses a fellow hobbyist's Web site, the second references a hobby-related sales brochure, and the third anchor attaches to a JPG image file.

```
<HTML>
<HEAD>
<TITLE>Using HyperText Links</TITLE>
</HEAD>
<BODY>
<H1>Using HyperText Links</H1>
A Friend's Web-site <A
HREF="www.myhome.com/jim/index.html"></A>.<BR>
For Catalog Info see <A HREF="www.myhome.com/jim/cat-
alog.html"></A>.<BR>
My Favorite GG1 image <A
HREF="www.myhome.com/jim/gg1.gif"></A><BR>.<BR>
</BODY>
</HTML>
```

By clicking with the mouse, using keyboard input, or nowadays using voice commands, users activate the link allowing them to visit these resources (see Figure 5.10). Note that an attribute in each source anchor specifies the address of the destination anchor with a URL. Sometimes the destination anchor of a link is an element within the source HTML document. In this case the destination anchor is given an anchor name and any URL addressing this anchor must include the name as its fragment identifier.

A destination anchor must include either an \<A>nchor element (naming it with the ID attribute), or by any other element (naming with the ID attribute), for example, an HTML author could easily create a catalog whose entries link to header elements within the document as in

```
<BODY>
<H1>GG1's Past and Presant</H1>
<A HREF="#Past">GG1s of Yesteryear</A><BR>
<A HREF="#Presant">Where are GG1s Today?</A><BR>
<A HREF="#Presant.1">An Original Pensy GG1</A><BR>
…and so on with detailed catalog information here…
…remainder of body goes here…
```

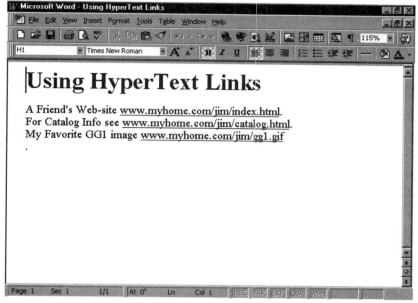

Figure 5–10: *Creating Web-site links with the <A>nchor HREF attribute.*

```
<H2><A name="Past">GG1 Conductor Tells All</A></H2>
…confessions of train conductor…
<H2><A name="Presant">Across the US</A></H2>
…Nation-wide info goes here…
<H3><A name="Presant.1">East Coast Locations</A></H2>
…East Coast info goes here…
```

However, HTML anchor elements also allow the author to actually make the header elements the anchors. Many HTML authors prefer the more streamlined version seen next:

```
<BODY>
<H1>GG1s Past and Presant</H1>
<A HREF="#Past">GG1s of Yesteryear</A><BR>
<A HREF="#Presant">Where are GG1s Today?</A><BR>
<A HREF="#Presant.1">An Original Pensy GG1</A><BR>
…and so on with detailed catalog information here…
…remainder of body goes here…
<H2 id="Past">GG1 Conductor Tells All</H2>
…confessions of train conductor…
<H2 id="Presant">Across the US</H2>
…nation-wide info goes here…
<H3 id="Presant">East Coast Locations</H3>
…East Coast info goes here…
```

Using <A> anchors with TITLE Attributes

You use the <A> anchor element to specify a relationship between the current, or source, document and another resource. Although the link referenced has no content, the relationships it defines may be recognized and rendered by the browser. <A>nchor is frequently used in conjunction with the TITLE attribute to add information about the nature of a link. How the browser interprets the resource depends on its content type. The reference might be rendered as a tooltip, it may play a background theme, or even speak the information out loud. The following example demonstrates the syntax for using the TITLE attribute:

```
<BODY>
...the main body goes here...
For further information see
<A HREF="../GG1Begin.html" TITLE="GG1
Background">History</A>.
To see your first GG1<A HREF="../gg1jpgs/gg1-1.jpg"
   TITLE="JPEG image of the original GG1">Pensy
GG1</A>
</BODY>
```

Using the <A> anchor ID Attribute

Another way to create an anchor is to use the ID attribute within the start tag of any element. The following HTML example begins by attaching an ID to an H2 element:

```
<BODY>
If you are interested in GG1 use today see GG1s Today
<A HREF="#GG1Today">GG1s Today</A>.
...defined elsewhere within the document...
<H2 ID="GG1Today">GG1s Today</H2>
...or generate a backwards reference with...
If you think the past was interesting see GG1s Today
<A HREF="#GG1Today">GG1s Today</A> for an update.
</BODY>
```

The GG1Today anchor is linked to the <A HREF="#GG1Today"> element. The ID name attributes share the same name space, so once again the rule of uniqueness applies. This means that the following HTML document is illegal:

```
<BODY>
<A HREF="#GG1Today">...</A>
...some document goes here...
<H1 ID="GG1Today">
...more HTML text...
<A NAME="GG1Today"></A>
</BODY>
```

HTML specifies that the NAME attribute may contain entities, for example, numeric character references in either decimal or hexadecimal, or named character references. For these reasons the following are legal NAME attributes: Dýrst is a valid name, as is Dýrst. Note, however, that the ID attribute can not contain entities.

A Word about URL Paths

You always want to set up your HTML document so that your links work properly. In HTML, path information is always defined with a URL. Relative URLs are resolved according to a base URL, which may come from a variety of sources. By simply including a BASE element you define the starting point for all further relative URL references. Remember that the BASE tag must be present within the <HEAD> section of an HTML document, for example,

```
<HTML>
  <HEAD>
    <TITLE>GG1 Catalog</TITLE>
    <BASE
HREF="http://www.myservice.com/GG1/cover.html">
  </HEAD>

  <BODY>
    Take a look at this powerful electric train
engine
      <A HREF="../GG1jpgs/GG1.jpg">The Original</A>!
  </BODY>
</HTML>
```

The relative address /GG1jpgs/GG1.jpg is actually parsed as

Error! Reference source not found.

Forward and Backward Links

While linking within an HTML document makes for easy table and index creation, the most frequent use for a link is to reference another Web source. However, you can also use links to create forward or backward link relationships by including a link type. For example, examine the following HTML text:

```
<HEAD>
...header HTML goes here...
<TITLE>GG1s in the 1950s</TITLE>
<LINK REL="PREV" HREF="GG11940.html">
<LINK REL="NEXT" HREF="GG11960.html">
</HEAD>
```

Notice the use of the REL link type attribute for the first HREF of PREV and the second one of NEXT. Links defined with a LINK element are not rendered with the document's contents, although some browsers may render them in other ways using navigation tools.

This next example uses GIF images to make the link selection a little more visual in appearance:

```
<HTML>
<HEAD>
<TITLE>Using GIF Images with Links</TITLE>
</HEAD>
<BODY>
<P>Simply click <BRE>
on the appropriate button<BR>
to move forward or backward<BR>
through the links.</P>
<A HREF="page1.html">
<IMG SRC="c:\html\chp05\Back_up.gif">
</A>
<A HREF="page3.html">
<IMG SRC="c:\html\chp05\Forw_up.gif">
</A>
</BODY>
</HTML>
```

Notice that the HREF values are set to logically relate to each arrow's visual image as seen in Figure 5.11.

The solution, illustrated in Figure 5.11, to activating an HTML's links is the preferred approach whenever the end user does not necessarily need to know the details of a link address.

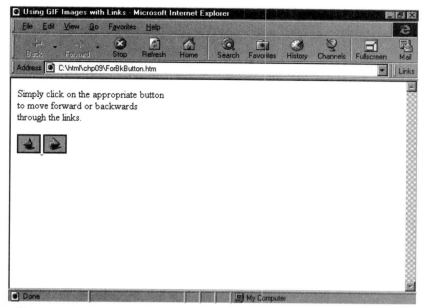

Figure 5–11: *Associating GIF images with links.*

Link Types

Link types are defined by the values you supply to the REL and REV attributes. (Note: Link types may not contain any whitespace and are case insensitive.) They are interpreted by browsers and search engines in a variety of ways. Both attributes may be specified in the same element start tag. Authors may use the following recognized link types, listed here with their conventional interpretations.

Table 5.4 lists the common link types.

Table 5–4: *Link Types Used with LINK REL and REV Attributes*

Alternate	The alternate link type defines alternate versions for the HTML document containing the link. You can use the ALTERNATE and LANG attributes to infer multilanguage translations of the source document, or in conjunction with the MEDIA attribute to provide access to alternate multimedia formats.

Table 5–4: *Link Types Used with LINK REL and REV Attributes (Continued)*

Appendix	Indicates that the link is to an appendix for the source HTML document.
Bookmark	Indicates that the link is to a referencing bookmark. Bookmarks are frequently used as entry gateways into larger compositions with the source document containing multiple bookmarks streamlining content access. Bookmarks can be labeled with a TITLE attribute.
Chapter	Defines the referenced text as being a chapter of the source document.
Contents or ToC	Defines the referenced text as containing a table of contents.
Copyright	Defines the referenced text as containing copyright information.
Glossary	Defines the referenced text as containing a glossary of terms pertaining to the current document.
Help	Defines the referenced text in a help format frequently containing more LINKs to additional resource materials.
Index	Defines the referenced text as a resource containing an index for the source document.
Next	Indicates that the referenced text follows some logical progression of the main topic. Some browsers may choose to preload the next document, thereby streamlining download time.
Prev or Previous	Defines the referenced text as logically preceding the current HTML resource.
Section	Defines the referenced text as a file containing a section of a larger work.
Start	Defines the referenced text as being the initial HTML resource in a series of documents and directs search engines as to which document is

Table 5–4: *Continued*

147

	considered by the author to be the starting point for the complete work.
Stylesheet	Defines the referenced text as HTML and external style sheet and is used in conjunction with the ALTERNATE LINK type when multiple style sheet options are needed.
Subsection	Defines the referenced text as being a subsection of a larger work.

E-Mail Links Using the MAILTO Attribute

To generate a Web page that allows surfers to easily e-mail the author, try using the <A> anchor tag along with the MAILTO attribute. MAILTO references are not typical links in that they do not lead to another document. Instead MAILTO HREFerences send e-mail to the defined e-mail address. When a browser receives this type of request, it frequently launches a mail program that opens a blank e-mail form with the destination e-mail address automatically entered into the To: field.

The syntax for MAILTO is straightforward. Simply define the HTREF attribute with a legal MAILTO address to cause e-mail to be sent when a link is activated. This next example demonstrates the syntax.

```
<BODY>
…more document goes here…
To order any GG1 material seen here click on the link
<A HREF="MAILTO:GG1Expert@mysubscription.com">GG1
Expert</A>.
</BODY>
```

Multilanguage Links

You know from your experience with Web surfing that many sites contain multilanguage versions for their international surfers. Since both the <A>nchor and <LINK> tags may point to documents written in different languages and using different character sets, the two tags support the CHARSET and LANG attributes. These attributes detail how the browser is to interpret the information at the destination link.

When used properly, both CHARSET and LANG allow browsers to avoid rendering garbage. Instead, they may either locate resources necessary for the correct rendering of the document or, if they cannot locate the resources, they should at least warn the user that the document will be unreadable and explain the cause.

The following HTML example demonstrates a straightforward use of the <LINK> tag and LANG attribute to set up a multilingual presentation:

```
<HEAD>
<LINK LANG="EN" TITLE="English Format"
      REL="alternate"
      HREF="http://USsite.com/page1/index.html">
<LINK LANG="I-CHEROKEE" TITLE="Cherokee Format "
      REL="alternate"
      HREF="http://cherokee.com/page1/index.html">
<LINK LANG="X-PIG-LATIN" TITLE="Fun format"
      REL="alternate"
      HREF="http://kido.com/page1/indexs.html">
</HEAD>
```

Of course, the multidestination format is not strictly limited to text media. The <LINK> tag can also provide a variety of information to search engines, including links to alternate versions of a document, (for example, one designed for different media, for instance, a version especially suited for printing) or access to the starting pages of a collection of documents.

Summary

In this chapter you learned several important HTML concepts involving tables and lists of information, links used for document navigation, and anchors used in image placement. Each one of these elements enables you to visually clarify and enhance the display of JavaScript's screen output. In the next chapter you will learn how to add images to your document syntax, including background image overlays.

CHAPTER 6
WORKING WITH IMAGE MAPS

- Server-Side Maps

- Client-Side Maps

- NCSA File Format

- CERN File Format

Image maps are frequently used in HTML documents. The use of image maps often includes the inclusion of a link array and/or an anchor array that can be manipulated with JavaScript.

With image maps the user can click the mouse on a portion of a graphics image and access information pertaining to that portion of the graphics. The information accessed in this manner can be a simple document, an image stored as a file on the computer, or a specific URL location.

Imagine an HTML document that contains the graphics image of the building layout of a corporate campus. The user could click the

149

mouse on any building to bring up previously saved file information on any particular building. Likewise, imagine an emergency rescue service that uses an image of the human body. Technicians could click the mouse on a nose, ear, foot, or hand to be connected, via a URL, to the physician specializing in that field.

Image maps are divided into two broad techniques; server-side image maps and client-side image maps. Server-side image maps work on most browsers. Their downside is that they place more of the communications burden on the server since it is the server that implements the image map. Client-side image maps have gained increased popularity because the HTML document implements the image map, thus placing less burden on the server. The downside to client-side image maps is that not all browsers support their use.

Server-Side Image Maps

Server-side image maps are accepted everywhere. This fact would generally make them the preferred technique when creating image maps. However, server-side image maps place an additional burden on the server. When the user clicks the mouse on a portion of an image, the browser sends the coordinates of the mouse and the image's name to the server. When the server receives this information, it must examine the image map file and return the URL information to the browser. As a final step, the browser sends its request for the URL location back to the server.

With server-side image maps it is always advisable to include text-based hyperlinks in addition to the URLs supplied by the image map just in case the user's browser is text based. This can be done as a final step in the creation of this portion of the HTML document, after the image map has been completely tested.

In addition to the image map's specifications in the HTML document, server-side image maps require an image, a file specifying the regions where the mouse can be clicked, and a CGI script to process the image map information.

The Image File

The images that are used in server-side image maps can be created with a wide variety of applications such as Microsoft Paint, Microsoft Image Composer, CorelDraw, and so on. It is also possible to use digitized photographs produced by scanners or digital cameras. The main requirement for an image editor is that it be capable of returning coordinate information as the mouse is passed over the various areas of the image. It must also be capable of returning the file in an acceptable format such as the JPG and GIF file formats.

Figure 6.1 shows the first of four rectangular regions used to create an image in Microsoft Image Composer.

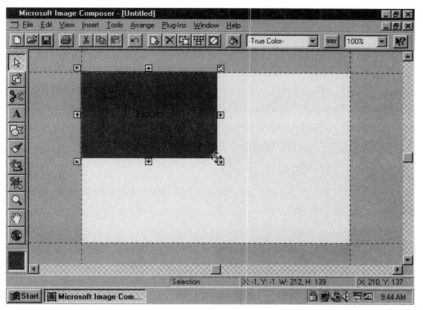

Figure 6–1: *A rectangular area is drawn in the Microsoft Image Composer.*

Notice the coordinate information that is being returned in the lower-right portion of the image editor shown in Figure 6.1. This information will be required in order to identify the various regions in the image where the mouse can be clicked.

Figure 6.2 shows the completed image that will be saved as a file named ImgMap1.jpg.

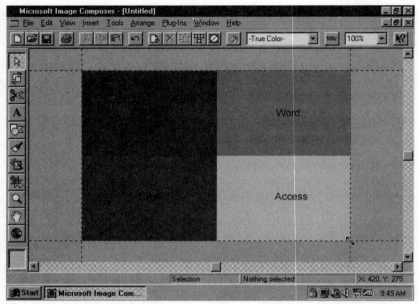

Figure 6–2: *A completed image map image with four rectangular areas.*

The coordinate information for the upper-left and lower-right coordinates is written down for future use as each of the four rectangular areas is placed in the image.

When you create image maps for a document, it should be almost intuitive for a user to know which regions of the image can be clicked on with the mouse.

Image Map MAP Files

The image map MAP file is used to identify the regions where the mouse can be clicked on the image. This is the reason for saving the coordinate information when the image is created in the image editor. There are two formats used for recording this information: the National Center for Supercomputing Applications (NCSA) and Conseil European pour la Recherche Nucleaire (CERN).

NCSA File Format

NCSA image map file format is the de facto standard for most American servers. If you are programming only for this geographic area, the NCSA file format is the one you will use. If you anticipate worldwide communications, consider using the CERN format also.

When developing NCSA image map files, five shapes are acceptable. Rectangles use the rect keyword. Circles use the circle keyword. Polygons use the poly keyword. Points use the point keyword. Defaults, usually an area not covered by a specific region, use the default keyword. The syntax for each shape is straightforward.

```
rect UniqueURL upperleft-x, upperleft-y, lowerright-x,
lowerright-y
circle UniqueURL center-x, center-y, radius
poly UniqueURL x1, y1, x2, y2, .... xn, yn
point UniqueURL x, y
default UniqueURL The following can be a bulleted list
```

In a particular application where each area is a rectangle, the actual code for the NCSA image map might take on this form:

```
rect http://www.microsoft.com/office/ 0, 0, 210, 137
rect http://www.microsoft.com/word/ 211, 0, 420, 137
rect http://www.microsoft.com/excel/ 0, 138, 210, 275
rect http://www.microsoft.com/access/ 211, 138, 420,
275
```

In this example, four rectangular areas are identified in the image. The coordinates are given in pixel units with X increasing as you move from left to right and Y increasing as you move from top to bottom. Recall, these are the numbers returned by the graphics editor when the image was created. Each area is approximately the same size and each, in turn, is used to reference a unique URL location. In this example, the URL locations refer to Microsoft product descriptions.

CERN File Format

The CERN image map file formatting is the de facto standard for most European servers. If you are programming only for this geographic area, the CERN file format is the one you will use. If you anticipate worldwide communications, consider using the NCSA format too.

CERN image map files permit the use of four shapes. Rectangles use the rectangle keyword. Circles use the circle keyword. Polygons use the polygon keyword. Defaults, areas not covered by a specific region, use the default keyword. The syntax for each shape is straight-forward.

```
rectangle (upperleft-x, upperleft-y) (lowerright-x,
lowerright-y) UniqueURL
circle (center-x, center-y) radius UniqueURL
polygon (x1, y1) (x2, y2) .... (xn, yn) UniqueURL
default UniqueURL The following can be a bulleted list
```

The use of the abbreviations rect, circ, poly, and def is also acceptable.

If a particular application uses four rectangular shapes, the actual code for the CERN image map could take on this form:

```
rectangle (0, 0) (210, 137)
http://www.microsoft.com/office/
rectangle (211, 0) (420, 137)
http://www.microsoft.com/word/
rectangle (0, 138) (210, 275)
http://www.microsoft.com/excel/
rectangle (211, 138) (420, 275)
http://www.microsoft.com/access/
```

The coordinates for the four rectangular areas identified in the image are those returned by the image editor. The coordinates are given in pixel units with X increasing as you move from left to right and Y increasing as you move from top to bottom. Each area is approximately the same size and each references a unique URL location. In this case, the URL locations reference the same Microsoft product locations as the NCSA example.

CGI Script

In most cases it is possible to use the default CGI script provided by the server. The CGI script is responsible for reporting the area of the image that was clicked with the mouse and then taking the appropriate action. NCSA servers use the imagemap keyword while CERN servers use the htimage keyword.

The HTML Document

HTML documents can include image maps with relatively simple syntax. Here is an example that can be used with a NCSA server.

```
<A href="/locationURL/imagemapURL">
<IMG src="imagemap.jpg" ismap>
</A>
```

Here *locationURL* points to the CGI script location used to process the mouse click information. The *imagemapURL* references the location of the MAP file holding the coordinate information for the image's various areas. The <A> tag is used to tell the browser where to send the coordinates from the <IMG>. The URL does not directly point to the map.

You are familiar with <IMG> tags from Chapter 4, but this might be the first time you have seen the ismap attribute used. The ismap attribute is used to notify the browser that the image is an image map.

A practical portion of HTML code identifying the example image map could take on the following appearance:

```
<A href="/cgi-bin/imagemap">
<IMG src="ImgMap1.jpg" ismap>
</A>
```

Server-Side Image Map Features

Server-side image maps do not work off-line as their client-side counterparts do. This, of course, is because of the interaction required between the browser and the server.

As you slide the mouse over a server-side image map, only the X,Y coordinate information for the image is returned to the user. With client-side image maps, the actual URL is shown.

You must gain permission from the server to identify your MAP location in its file system. Once this permission is granted, the location of the file can be identified in a manner similar to

```
ImgMap1 : /images/ImgMap1.MAP.
```

Client-Side Image Maps

Client-side image maps, while not as universally supported as server-side image maps, are supported by a very large number of browsers. This fact, coupled with their increased speed and their ability to reduce server traffic, makes them ideal candidates for most image map work.

Client-side image maps, unlike their server-side counterparts, do not place an additional burden on the server since the browser coordinates all interactions between the image area clicked on with the mouse and any associated file or URL.

However, as with server-side image maps, it is always advisable to include text-based hyperlinks in addition to the URLs supplied by the image map just in case the user's browser is text-based. Do this as a final step in the creation of the HTML document, after the image map has been completely tested.

Client-side image maps require an image and the image map's specifications in the HTML document.

The Image File

The images used in client-side image maps are identical to the types of images that can be used in server-side image maps. Create images with applications such as Microsoft Paint, Microsoft Image Composer, CorelDraw, and so on. Recall that the main requirements for image editors is that they be capable of returning coordinate information as the mouse is passed over the various image areas and that they can return the file in an acceptable format. You will find that JPG and GIF file formats are used most frequently.

Keep your image maps as clean and free of "clutter" as possible. Use simple drawing shapes or photographs with intuitive areas for user interaction

The HTML Document

All of the code for processing an image map is contained in the HTML document. Two tags help handle this code: <MAP> and <AREA>.

THE <MAP> TAG

The <MAP> tag identifies the map with a unique name, using the following syntax:

```
<MAP name="mapname">
  .
  .
  .
</MAP>
```

THE <AREA> TAG

The <AREA> tag identifies the areas or hotspots of an image that are associated with a mouse click. The <AREA> tag makes use of several attributes, including shape, coords, nohref and href.

Shape

The shape attribute can be set equal to rect (default), circle, or polygon. The default attribute is used for cases where the mouse is clicked outside any specified areas in the image.

Coords

The coords attribute is used to provide the coordinates of the particular area of the image. The syntax is

```
For a rectangle:
coords=upperleft-x, upperleft-y, lowerright-x,
        lowerright-y

For a circle:
coords=center-x, center-y, radius
```

```
For a polygon:
coords=x1, y1, x2, y2, .... xn, yn
```

In the case of overlapping shapes, the browser resolves the problem by using the first shape listed after the <AREA> tag.

Nohref

The nohref attribute is used to indicate that there is no hyperlink associated with a mouse click in the specified area.

Href

The href attribute is used to specify the URL when the mouse is clicked in the corresponding area of the image.

For example, we created a simple image earlier in this chapter named ImgMap1.jpg. Figure 6.2 shows that this image contains four rectangular areas of approximately the same size. This image information could be included in an HTML document, without the use of JavaScript, by using the <AREA> tag in the following manner:

```
<AREA shape="rect" coords="0, 0, 210, 137"
   href="http://www.microsoft.com/office/">
<AREA shape="rect" coords="211, 0, 420, 137"
   href="http://www.microsoft.com/word/">
<AREA shape="rect" coords="0, 138, 210, 275"
   href="http://www.microsoft.com/excel/">
<AREA shape="rect" coords="211, 138, 420, 275"
   href="http://www.microsoft.com/access/">
```

Recall that the image editor returned the coordinates shown here when the image was created. Each of these rectangles can be considered a hotspot area on the image.

A Complete Client-Side Image Map

If we use the ImgMap1.jpg image file created earlier in this chapter and the code developed in the previous section, it is a fairly easy task to complete a client-side image map application. Examine the following listing:

```
<HTML>

<HEAD>
<TITLE>Client-side imagemap</TITLE>

</HEAD>
```

```
<BODY>

<IMG SRC="ImgMap1.jpg" USEMAP="#firstmap">
<P>You want to go where today?<BR>
<MAP NAME="firstmap">

<AREA SHAPE="rect" COORDS="0, 0, 210, 137"
  HREF="http://www.microsoft.com/office/"
  onMouseOver = "window.status = 'Off to Microsoft
Office';
                  return true"
  onMouseOut = "window.status = ''; return true">

<AREA SHAPE="rect" COORDS="211, 0, 420, 137"
  HREF="http://www.microsoft.com/word/"
  onMouseOver = "window.status = 'Off to Microsoft
Word';
                  return true"
  onMouseOut = "window.status = ''; return true">

<AREA SHAPE="rect" COORDS="0, 138, 210, 275"
  HREF="http://www.microsoft.com/excel/"
  onMouseOver = "window.status = 'Off to Microsoft
Excel';
                  return true"
  onMouseOut = "window.status = ''; return true">

<AREA SHAPE="rect" COORDS="211, 138, 420, 275"
  HREF="http://www.microsoft.com/access/"
  onMouseOver = "window.status = 'Off to Microsoft
Access';
                  return true"
  onMouseOut = "window.status = ''; return true">

</MAP>
</BODY>
</HTML>
```

Figure 6.3 shows this HTML document using the Netscape browser.

As you examine this figure, notice that the mouse pointer is resting over the "Access" portion of the image. When the mouse is over a given rectangular region a mouseOver event occurs. In this case, a little JavaScript code permits the message "Moving to Microsoft Access" to be displayed in the window's status bar region. Can you find it? When the mouse is moved to another region, the appropriate message for that region will be displayed. If this code is

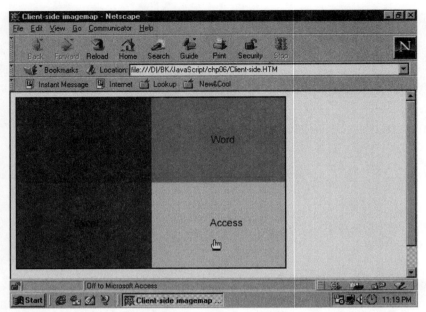

Figure 6–3: *The Netscape browser illustrates our simple client-side image map example.*

removed, the URL for Microsoft's Access page will be shown in the status bar region of the window.

All that remains for this simple application (you didn't forget did you?) is to add the text-based hyperlinks in addition to the URLs supplied by the image map.

Client-Side Image Map Features

Client-side image maps work off-line, unlike their server-side counterparts. This, of course, is because of the browser handles all of the interactions between image areas that are clicked with the mouse and the information that is to be returned.

As you slide the mouse over a client-side image map, the actual URL is shown. Recall that for server-side image maps only the X,Y coordinate information for the image is returned to the user.

If you are concerned about nonsupport issues revolving around client-side image maps, you can provide both client-side and server-side options:

```
<A href="/cgi-bin/images/ImgMap1.map">
<IMG src="/images/ImgMap1.jpg" usemap="#ImgMap1"
ismap>
</A>
```

In this example, if client-side image maps are not supported, a server-side map will be used.

Summary

In this chapter you learned about server-side and client-side image maps. In addition to the advantages and disadvantages of each image map type, you learned the mechanics of adding image maps to your HTML documents. A discussion was also provided for NCSA and CERN image map styles.

CHAPTER 7
WORKING WITH FORMS

- Form Components

- Form Tags

- Form Attributes

- Examples

HTML forms are defined as documents that contain normal content, markup, and combinations of elements called controls. Controls accept and respond to input from the user. This input may be as simple as a button click or menu selection. User input can also include paragraphs of text entered at the keyboard. In order to process this input a CGI script must be placed on the server to handle the form's specific features. (CGI scripting is discussed in Chapter 9.)

Many Web sites are not interactive. For example, personal Web sites hosted by many Internet providers do not allow an interactive capability at all. If you or your company is interested only in disseminating information, then the techniques you have learned to this point are sufficient for your purposes. If your Web site requires inter-active capabilities, you'll want to study this chapter dealing with forms.

JavaScript form object properties can be used in addition to ordinary HTML elements. In Chapter 14, you'll learn how JavaScript can also be used to extended HTML capabilities when dealing with controls, such as buttons, checkboxes, radio buttons, and so on.

HTML Form Components

Forms are created with an opening <FORM> tag and closed with a </FORM> tag. From that point on, forms will be as varied as the purposes for which they were designed. Forms may include combinations of controls, including text entry boxes, push buttons, checkboxes, and so on. The scope of the form's name attribute for any control within a <FORM> is the <FORM> itself.

The <FORM> Tag

The <FORM> element allows several attributes. Table 7.1 lists and briefly describes these attributes.

Table 7–1: <FORM> Element Attributes

Attribute	Description
Accept	A comma-separated list of MIME types that the server will handle.
Accept-charset	Specifies a list of character encodings for input data that are accepted by the server.
Accesskey	Specifies direct keyboard access to form fields.
Action	Specifies a required server-side form handler. Can be an HTTP URL or a mailto URL.
Disabled	Specifies that a form control is initially insensitive.

Table 7–1: *Continued*

165

7   **Working with Forms**

Attribute	Description
Enctype	Used to specify the MIME type encoding for submitting forms. The default value is x-www-form-URLencoded.
Method	HTTP method used to submit the form. Here, GET is the default and appends name/value pairs to the URL given by the action, then sends the new URL to the server. The POST method is the preferred method because it includes name/value pairs in the body of the form rather than in the URL itself.
Onchange	Allows the form provider to verify user-entered data.
Onsubmit	Indicates that the form was submitted.
Onreset	Indicates that the form was reset.
Readonly	Specifies that a form field cannot be changed.
Target	Specifies where the returned data should be sent. This is optional and used by Netscape and the Microsoft Internet Explorer to specify a frame or window.

The most frequently used syntax for sending a form to a program using the HTTP POST method is

```
<FORM action="http://testsite.com/cgi-bin/script.cgi"
method="post">
.
.
.
</FORM>
```

Likewise, the form can be submitted to an e-mail address using the following syntax:

```
<FORM action="mailto:Tango_Tia@SUNYBroome.edu"
method="post">
.
.
.
</FORM>
```

The POST method should be used in most cases. The GET method is the default and is included for backward compatibility with older systems. The GET method passes the information directly to the URL. Information sent in this manner is usually limited to a total of 255 characters. The POST method, on the other hand, sends data as a separate stream to the script. This technique bypasses the limitations of the GET method and allows unlimited amounts of information to be received.

A form can contain a wide variety of controls, but it cannot contain another form. Likewise, forms cannot be nested.

The <INPUT> Tag

The <INPUT> element serves as the starting point for adding things like HTML buttons, checkboxes, and passwords to forms. The syntax for the <INPUT> element is

```
<INPUT type="element_type" name="ref_name">
```

Each type of input is entered as a CGI name/value pair. The element_type defines the field's screen appearance while ref_name represents a keyword referenced by the server's CGI script. The server's CGI script is used to process the form's data.

Table 7.2 lists and briefly describes various <INPUT> types.

Table 7–2: *<INPUT> Element Types*

Input Type	Description
Button	A type of push button with no default behavior.
Checkbox	An on/off type switch. Active when "on." Multiple checkboxes within a group can be checked.
File	Prompts the user for a file name.
Hidden	This input type is not rendered by the user agent. The element's name and value are submitted with the form.
Image	A type of submission push button using a graphical image as the button.
Password	A single-line text entry box that allows text to be entered, but characters are hidden from view with a series of asterisks.

Table 7–2: *Continued*

Input Type	Description
Radio	An on/off type switch. Active when "on." Only one radio button in a group can be set active. Multiple groups are permitted, however.
Reset	A type of push button which, when activated, resets all of the form's controls back to the initial values.
Submit	A type of push button which, when activated, submits the form's contents.
Text	Single-line text entry box.

An attribute name is required for all controls except submit and reset. Table 7.3 lists a variety of new attributes encountered with these <INPUT> types.

Table 7–3: *Input Element Type Attributes*

Attribute	Description
Type	Type of control needed.
Name	Submit as part of the form.
Value	Required for radio buttons and checkboxes.
Checked	Used by radio buttons and checkboxes to indicate selection.
Disable	Control is not available in this context.
Readonly	Used for text and passwords.
Size	Specific to each type of field. For example, size gives the width, in characters, of a text control.
Maxlength	Maximum number of characters for a field.
Src	For fields using images.
Alt	A short description.
Usemap	Use a client-side image map.
Align	Use for vertical or horizontal alignment.

Table 7–3: *Input Element Type Attributes (Continued)*

Attribute	Description
Tabindex	Position in tabbing order.
Accesskey	Accessibility key character.
Onfocus	The element receiving the focus.
Onblur	The element losing the focus.
Onselect	The selected text.
Onchange	The element value was changed.
Accept	List of MIME types for file upload.

You'll learn more about each of these input type elements, their attributes, and how they can be used with JavaScript to enhance your documents in Chapter 14.

The <BUTTON> Tag

The <BUTTON> element allows you to expand types of buttons available for use. This element uses name, value, and type attributes. The name attribute assigns a name to the button while the value attribute assigns a value to the button. The type attribute can be submit, button, or reset. The submit value is used when submitting forms. The reset value is used to reset a form's values. The button value is used to trigger a script.

The syntax for the <BUTTON> element is

```
<BUTTON name="ref_name" value="element_value"
type="element_type">
```

A <BUTTON> element using a submit type whose content is an image is similar to an <INPUT> element that uses an image type, the difference being that <INPUT> renders a *flat* image while <BUTTON> renders a button with relief and an up/down motion when selected.

Here is an example of a <BUTTON> element using a submit type:

```
<BUTTON name="submit_me" value="submit" type"submit">
Send<IMG src="/graphics/doit.jpg" alt="doit">
</BUTTON>
```

In a similar manner a <BUTTON> element using the reset type is like an <INPUT> element using the reset type, but with features like those just described.

The <SELECT> and <OPTION> Tags

The <SELECT> and <OPTION> elements are used together to create a drop-down list. The <SELECT> element uses name, size, and type attributes while the <OPTION> element uses the selected and value attributes. The name attribute assigns a name to the element and is paired with selected values when the form is submitted. The size attribute specifies the number of rows to be rendered. A scrolling mechanism should be used when the number of rows is less than the number of choices. The multiple attribute, when set, will allow multiple selections from the list. The selected attribute is used to identify a selection. The value attribute gives the value to be submitted when the <OPTION> is selected.

Here is a list, or menu, constructed of a <SELECT> element and several <OPTION> elements:

```
<SELECT size="3" name="selectpet">
   <OPTION> Cat </OPTION>
   <OPTION selected> Dog </OPTION>
   <OPTION> Horse </OPTION>
</SELECT>
```

In this example list, three items will be presented since the size attribute was set to three. Dog is selected as the default choice by using the selected attribute.

The <TEXTAREA> Tag

The <TEXTAREA> element is similar to the <INPUT> element using the text type. The main difference is that a text area allows multiple lines of text information to be entered by the user. This element uses the name, rows, and cols attributes. The name attribute assigns a name to the element and is paired with selected values when the form is submitted. The rows attribute identifies the number of lines that are to be visible within the area. Additional lines should be permitted and a scrolling mechanism should be provided. The cols attribute identifies the number of columns that are to be visible within the area. Longer lines should be permitted and a scrolling mechanism should be provided.

Here is an example that sets a 10-row by 40-column text entry area. The area initially contains one line of text.

```
<TEXTAREA name="mystory" rows="10" cols="40">
This is my story:
</TEXTAREA>
<INPUT type="submit" value"sendit">
<INPUT type="reset">
```

If no default text is used, the </TEXTAREA> can immediately follow the <TEXTAREA> element.

The <LABEL> Tag

This element is used to attach information to other control elements. The <LABEL> element uses the for attribute that associates the label with another control. For example, in a <TABLE> you might use the following:

```
<TABLE>
  <TR>
    <TD>
      <LABEL for="city">City Name
      </LABEL>
    <TD>
      <INPUT type="text" name=cityname" id="city">
  <TR>
    <TD>
      <LABEL for="state">State Name
      </LABEL>
    <TD>
      <INPUT type="text" name=statename" id="state">
</TABLE>
```

The for attribute can be used to associate more than one <LABEL> with a control.

The <FIELDSET> and <LEGEND> Tags

The <FIELDSET> element is used to group related controls together. The <LEGEND> element is used to assign a caption to the <FIELD-SET> element.

The <LEGEND> element uses the align attribute to specify the position of the legend with respect to the fieldset. If a value of top is used (the default), the legend is above the fieldset. A value of bottom places the legend below the fieldset. A value of left or right places the legend to the left or right of the fieldset. For example,

```
<FIELDSET>
<LEGEND align="top">Patient Identification</LEGEND>
Social Security Number:
  <INPUT name="social_security" type="text">
  </INPUT>
</FIELDSET>
```

Element Characteristics

There are several ways an active element receives focus from a user. Focus can be achieved with a mouse, keyboard tabbing, or with the use of an access key frequently called a shortcut or accelerator key. The use of a pointing device, such as a mouse, requires no special intervention. The next sections examine tabbing order and access keys. In addition, we'll examine how to disable or make elements read-only.

TABBING ORDER

The tabbing order is set with the tabindex attribute. The tabbing order is the order in which elements receive focus when navigated with the keyboard. The tabbing order can include nested elements. Navigation proceeds with elements with low tabindex values to elements with high tabindex value. Tabindex values need not be sequential. If elements are not provided with tabindex values, they are navigated in the order in which they appear in the HTML document. Disabled elements do not appear in the tabbing order. For example,

```
<INPUT tabindex="2" type="text" name="lastname">
<INPUT tabindex="1" type="text" name="firstname">
<INPUT tabindex="6" type="text" name="state">
<INPUT tabindex="5" type="text" name="city">
```

Here the tabbing order is 1, 2, 5, and 6 or firstname, lastname, city, and state.

ACCESS KEY

An access key is set with the accesskey attribute. The accesskey attribute assigns a single character from the document character set to act as the access key. When an access key is pressed, the identified element receives focus. For example,

```
<LABEL for="lname" accesskey="L">
Last Name
</LABEL>
<INPUT type="text" name="lastname" id="lname">
<LABEL for="fname" accesskey="F">
First Name
</LABEL>
<INPUT type="text" name="firstname" id="fname">
```

Access keys are activated under Windows by using the ALT key in conjunction with the defined access key. Apple systems use the CMD key in conjunction with the defined access key.

DISABLE

When the disable attribute is used with an element, the element will not receive focus. In addition, the element will not be present in the tabbing order and the control's value will not be submitted with the form. The rendering of disabled elements depends upon the user agent, but most frequently the element is "grayed" to indicate that it has been disabled. In the following example, the third element has been disabled.

```
<INPUT tabindex="2" type="text" name="lastname">
<INPUT tabindex="1" type="text" name="firstname">
<INPUT disabled tabindex="6" type="text"
name="state">
<INPUT tabindex="5" type="text" name="city">
```

When the read-only attribute is used with an element and is set, the element prohibits changes. Elements identified as read-only receive focus but cannot be changed. The elements are included in the tabbing order and their values are submitted with the form. For example,

```
<TEXTAREA readonly name="mystory" rows="2" cols="20">
This is my story:
</TEXTAREA>
```

The JavaScript Form Object

The JavaScript form object provides the action, elements[], encoding, method, name, and target properties. The object methods include eval(), reset(), submit(), toString(), and valueof(). The form object uses two event handlers, onReset and onSubmit.

For example, when the onSubmit event handler is activated, it is possible to use various object properties to evaluate and specify locations. For example, the elements[] property can be used to scan a form's input elements, allowing the user to examine, modify, or correct any entries. In a similar manner, the action property can be used to specify where the data is to be sent.

A Simple Form

The following listing produces a complete form for registering a pet for a pet show. The form makes use of many of the elements and attributes discussed in the previous sections. Examine the listing and see if you can determine the reason for the placement of each item.

```
<HTML>
<HEAD>
<TITLE>Pet Registration</TITLE>
<SCRIPT LANGUAGE = "JavaScript">

function SendACopy(datainfo) {
```

```
   infostr = "\nFor a copy of registration data\n"
   infostr += "mailed to your e-mail address,
select\n"
   infostr += "OK, otherwise select Cancel to sub-
mit.\n"

   if (confirm(infostr)) {
      //datainfo.action = "mailto:tango127@epix.net"
      datainfo.action = "mailto:" +
datainfo.email.value
      datainfo.submit()
   }
   else {

   datainfo.action = "http://hoohoo.ncsa.uiuc.edu/cgi-
bin/post-query"
   datit()
   }
}

</SCRIPT>
</HEAD>
<BODY>
<H1>Please complete the following form
<BR>to register your pet</H1>
<HR>
<H3>Information about you:</H3>
<FORM name = "PetRegistration" method="post"
   //action= is defined in the SendACopy() JavaScript
function
   onSubmit="SendACopy(this)">
Your last name: <INPUT type="text" name="lname"
   value = "" maxlength="25" size="18" >
First name: <INPUT type="text" name="fname"
   value = "" maxlength="25" size="18">
<BR>
e-mail Address: <INPUT type="text" name="email"
   value = "" maxlength="25" size="18">
<HR>
<H3>Information about your pet:</H3>
<TABLE>
<TR valign="top">
<TD>Type of pet:
<BR>
<SELECT Name="PetType">
   <OPTION>Cat </OPTION>
   <OPTION selected>Dog </OPTION>
   <OPTION>Horse </OPTION>
   <OPTION>Other </OPTION>
</SELECT>
</TABLE>
<INPUT type="radio" name="sex" value="m">Male
```

```
<INPUT type="radio" name="sex" value="f">Female
<BR>
Pet's breed: <INPUT type="text" name="breed"
  maxlength="20">
<BR>
Please check all that apply to your pet:
<INPUT type="checkbox" name="char"
  value="e">Cropped ears
<INPUT type="checkbox" name="char"
  value="t">Docked tail
<INPUT type="checkbox" name="char"
  value="c">Good with children
<BR>
<H3>Tell us something unique about your pet:</H3>
<TEXTAREA name="info" rows=10 cols=60>
</TEXTAREA>
<HR>
<H3>Thank you for your information -
  your pet will be registered.</H3>
<INPUT type="submit" >
<INPUT type="reset">
</FORM>
</BODY>
</HTML>
```

This form is quite long so Figure 7.1 shows just a portion of a completed registration form.

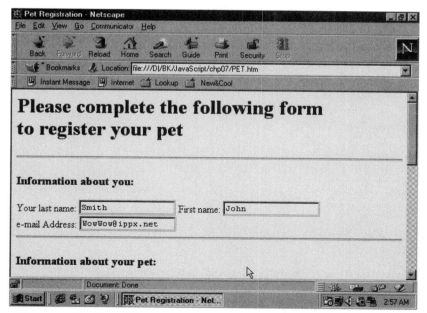

Figure 7–1:   *The upper portion of the Pet Registration form.*

Recall that form design is just one part of the form creation and implementation process. In order to process the form's information there must also be a server-side program. The CGI, or Common Gateway Interface, is the preferred manner of processing form data on the server-side (see Chapter 6).

Happily, however, there is a simple technique that can be used to test the operation of a completed form. We'll discuss that technique in the next section.

Checking Your Form

In the previous section a complete HTML document containing a form was listed. Did you notice that one line in that listing was set in a bold font? Just in case you missed it, here it is:

```
datainfo.action = "http://hoohoo.ncsa.uiuc.edu/
                    cgi-bin/post-query"
```

The NCSA site, identified here, provides a server that will examine data from any submitted form and return the results as an HTML page. Figure 7.2 shows the output returned by the NCSA server.

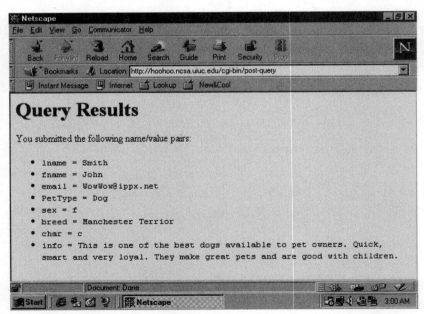

Figure 7–2: *The NCSA server is used to check our form.*

None of the information is saved by the server, but the site is useful when checking initial form operation.

Summary

In this chapter you learned the terms and definitions associated with forms. You also learned that forms often contain normal content, markup, and combinations of elements called controls. Controls used in forms accept and respond to input from the user. You also learned how to develop a complete form and check its operation.

CHAPTER 8

WORKING WITH STYLE SHEETS AND STYLE CONTROL

- Style Sheets
- Cascading Style Sheets
- Properties
- Examples

Style sheets can be used to control both the appearance and layout of an HTML document. Microsoft Windows has pushed HTML developers to require control over font styles and sizes, screen and text colors, and so on. Developers who work in the Windows graphics environment require the same features in their Web page designs that they see in Windows.

HTML was originally developed as a means of presenting scientific *context*. As such, the *presentation* aspect of HTML was chiefly ignored. Many different attempts were put forth to solve the presentation problem. These included using proprietary HTML extensions, converting text to images, using tables for page layout, and so on. Unfortunately, these attempts did not produce uniform results across the industry.

Style Sheet Considerations

The <STYLE> tag was first introduced with HTML 3.2. HTML 4.0 continues to address the style issue by addressing

- Alternative styles and cascading style sheets
- Variations in the placement of style information
- Independence from specific style sheet languages
- Media dependencies
- Performance concerns

In this chapter we'll examine many of these style issues and learn how HTML 4.0 style sheets, along with JavaScript, bring control over the presentation aspects of HTML documents.

This section will address many of the style sheet issues mentioned in the introduction. HTML 4.0 completes the style sheet work initially started in HTML 3.2.

Alternative Styles and Cascading Style Sheets

HTML 4.0 addresses the issue of alternative styles by including provisions for user selectable styles. For example, a user who is visually impaired might prefer a large font style and color in place of the style implemented by the document designers.

HTML 4.0 also permits the use of cascading style sheets or styling information provided by JavaScript. In documents using cascading style sheets, multiple style sheets are combined. For example, a college's computer science department might style documents in a particular manner. When these documents leave the department, they might be styled by the college's style guidelines rather than just those of the computer science department. Cascading style sheets give us that ability. Cascading style sheets have the advantage that individual style sheets can be stored and later reused. When using cascading style sheets, there is an ordered sequence for their use; later style sheets have a higher precedence level than earlier ones. In our earlier example, the computer science department's style sheet would have a lower precedence level than the college's precedence level.

Placement of Style Information

HTML 4.0 allows style sheets to be placed in the HTML document itself or in files separated from the document.

Many developers prefer to place styling instructions at the start of an HTML document. Others prefer to intermix styling elements throughout the body of the document. The disadvantage to this approach is that the styles are uniquely blended with the HTML document itself.

When multiple documents are to use the same styles, it is best to separate the style sheets from the HTML document. This approach makes it easier to manage styles on a site basis, like the college example in the previous section. With this approach you can use HTTP headers to set the style sheets used in any document.

Language and Media Dependencies

HTML 4.0 doesn't require the use of a particular style sheet language. While cascading style sheets (CCSs) are quickly becoming a standard with the major browsers, other style sheet languages are possible as well. Style sheets using JavaScript are one alternative way to include styling in HTML documents.

Developers can also produce documents that are media independent in terms of context. This flexibility permits access to Web pages through a variety of devices including computers with different operating systems, Web-TV, and so on.

Style sheets, on the other hand, usually apply to specific computers or devices. The device would affect the presentation of the document.

Under HTML 4.0, there has been an attempt to allow a specification to be included for a particular media which it addresses. Thus, a style sheet language may specify a computer screen resolution, or whether or not audio capabilities are included.

Performance Issues

If style sheets are held external to the HTML document, there may be performance concerns involving the retrieval and loading of these style sheet files.

Under HTML 4.0, developers can include the rendering instructions within specific HTML elements. This allows the information to be available by the time the element is rendered.

Style Sheet Basics

Style sheet rules can be embedded within the HTML document or in a separate style sheet file. If you are creating CCS style sheets, included as a separate file, the file will use a .css file extension. If you are using JavaScript to implement styling information in a separate file, that file will use a .js file extension.

There are several different ways style sheet information can be provided to a HTML document, as you will see in this section.

The Default Sheet Language

The <META> tag is used to set the default style sheet language for an HTML document. This is needed since the syntax of a style rule belongs to the style sheet language, not the HTML itself.

To set the default language to CSS, the following portion of code should be added to the <HEAD> element of a document. If the language isn't specifically declared, it is assumed to be CCS.

```
<HEAD>
<META name="Content-Style" content="text/css">
.
.
.
</HEAD>
```

If JavaScript is used to provide styling information, this syntax can be used:

```
<HEAD>
<META name="Content-Style" content="text/javascript">
.
.
.
</HEAD>
```

It is also possible to set the default style sheet language with HTTP headers. For example,

```
Content-Style: text/css
```

When two or more style sheet specifications attempt to set the default style sheet language, the last specification takes precedence. HTTP headers are treated as occurring before the <HEAD> element in a document.

Within an HTML document, HTML elements/attributes specify the beginning of style sheet data. The appropriate end tag marks the end of style sheet data, </>. This format is required so that HTML parsers can distinguish HTML code from style sheet rules.

CSS Style Properties

There are a wide variety of style properties that can be specified for use in an HTML document when using CSS style sheets. Table 8.1 provides a list of these properties and a brief description of each.

Table 8–1: CSS Styling Properties

Property	Characteristic	Typical Values
Box	Border	Allows all border values to be set, such as width, style, and color. For example,
		border:10pt solid green
	border-top, border-left, border-bottom, border-right	Sets the style and color of each border surrounding an element. Use *dashed*, *dotted*, *double*, *groove*, *inset*, *outset*, *none*, or *ridged* for the style. For example,
		border-top:blue
	border-top-width, border-left-width, border-bottom-width, border-right-width	Sets the width of each border surrounding an element. Use *thin*, *medium*, or *thick*. Widths can also be specified in ems, percentages, points and so on. For example,
		border-top-width:12pt
	border-width	Sets all four borders at the same time. For example,
		border-width:6pt 8pt 10pt 12pt
	Clear	Used to place an element below any floating element on that side. Use *left*, *right*, or *center*. For example,
		clear:center
	Float	Used to align an element to the *left*, *right*, or *center*. Text wrapping can occur. For example,
		float:right
	Height	Specifies the height of the bounding box. Text boxes contain scrolling bars. Images are scaled to fit the box. A physical value is permitted or *auto* allows automatic allocation of space.

Table 8–1: *Continued*

185

Property	Characteristic	Typical Values
		For example,
		height:auto
	Margin	Allows all four margins to be set at the same time. For example,
		margin: 4em, 4em, 2em, 2em
	margin-top, margin-left, margin-bottom, margin-right	Specify the spacing between adjacent elements. Use a length, percentage or *auto*. For example,
		margin-top:4em; margin-left: 4em; margin-bottom:2em; margin-right:2em.
	Padding	Allows all four padding values to be set at the same time. For example,
		padding:1cm 1cm 0.5cm 0.5cm.
	padding-top, padding-bottom, padding-left, padding-right	Specify the padding between the box and the given elements. Use a length, percentage, or *auto*. For example,
		padding-top:1cm; padding-left: 1cm; padding-bottom:0.5cm; padding-right:0.5cm.
	Width	Specifies the width of the bounding box. Text boxes contain scrolling bars. Images are scaled to fit the box. A physical value is permitted or *auto* allows automatic allocation of space. For example,
		width:auto
Classi-fication	Display	Determines when and how a style element is used. Use *block, inline, list-item,* or *none*. For example,
		display:block
	list-style	Allows list-style -type, -image, and -position to be specified at the same time. For example,

Table 8–1: *CSS Styling Properties (Continued)*

Property	Characteristic	Typical Values
		list-style:circle url(arrow.gif) outside
	list-style-image	Used to specify an image that will replace the normal marker. For example,
		image:url(arrow.gif)
	list-style-position	Used to specify text formatting following the list-item marker. Use *inside* and *outside*. Outside is the default and aligns additional lines with the first character of the original line. Inside aligns additional lines with the item-list marker.
	list-style-type	Used to set marker types for a list. Values can include circle, decimal, disc, lower-alpha, lower-roman, upper-alpha, upper-roman, and none.
	whitespace	Specifies how spaces and line breaks are processed. Use *normal*, *pre*, and *nowrap*. Normal, extra spaces are ignored and breaks are made with ; Pre, all space is left as entered; Nowrap, wrapping done on .
Back-ground	Background	Allows multiple background characteristics to be set at once. The order is -color, -image, -repeat, -attachment, and -position.
	Background-attachment	Used to determine if background image is fixed or can scroll with foreground text. For example,
		background-attachment:url(scroll)
	Background-color	Specifies the background color. Specified by color such as red, green, blue, or by RGB value such as RGB(255,0,0), RGB(0,255,0), RGB(0,0,255), and so on. Hexadecimal values can be used. For example, #FF0000, #00FF00, and #0000FF.

Table 8–1: *Continued*

187

Property	Characteristic	Typical Values
	Background-image	Specifies an image to be displayed on top of a background color. For example, background-image:url(back.jpg)
	Background-position	Specifies an image's starting position. For horizontal, use *left*, *center*, or *right*. For vertical, use *top*, *center*, or *bottom*. Positions can also be given as percentages ranging from 0 to 100%. For example, background-position: center center
	Background-repeat	Specifies if the background should be tiled. Use *repeat-x* to repeat the image in a horizontal line and *repeat-y* to repeat the image in a vertical line. For example, background-repeat:repeat-y
Color	Color	Specifies color of text. Uses same format as background-color.
Font	Font	Permits the font-size, line-height, and font-family to be set at one time.
	font-family	Name of the font family. Families such as arial, courier, roman, and so on are permitted.
	font-size	Font size specified in points, inches, centimeters, pixels, or as a percentage. Point values are the preferred method. Values are expressed, for example, as 12pt, 16pt, 36pt, and so on.
	font-style	Style is used to indicate a *normal*, *italic*, or *bold font*.
	font-variant	Specified as *normal* or *small-caps*. Small-caps are the size of lowercase letters.

Table 8–1: *CSS Styling Properties (Continued)*

Property	Characteristic	Typical Values
	font-weight	Specifies the thickness of a typeface. *Normal*, *bold*, *bolder*, *light*, and so on are allowed. Values from 100 to 900 can also be used.
Measure-ment	Absolute	Use in, *cm*, *mm*, *pt*, or *pc* units. These represent inches, centimeters, millimeters, points, or picas.
	Percentage	Use a numeric value between 0 and 100 relative to a length unit.
	Relative	Use *em*, *ex*, or *px*. The first value represents a typographic term referring to the height of a character; the second value, the height of the letter "x." The third represents measurements in pixels.
Text	line-height	Used to set the leading of a paragraph. Specified in points, inches, centimeters, pixels, or as a percentage
	letter-spacing	Specifies space between letters. See word-spacing below. The value em is the width of the letter "m." Extra space is added between letters with this value. For example, letter-spacing:0.8em
	text-align	Specifies how text is aligned. Use *left*, *right*, *center*, or *justify*. For example, text-align:center
	text-decoration	Allows extra text characteristics such as blinking, strike-through, and so on. For example, text-decoration:blink
	text-indent	Specifies text indenting. Measured in ems or inches as space added to the first line. For example, text-indent:8em

Table 8–1: *Continued*

189

Property	Characteristic	Typical Values
	text-transform	Used to specify capitalization. Use *capitalize* (first letter of each word), *uppercase* (all letters uppercase), *lowercase* (all letters lowercase), and *none* (no capitalization). For example,
		text-transform:capitalize
	vertical-align	Specifies vertical positioning. Use *baseline, bottom, middle, sub, super, text-bottom, text-top, top,* or as a percentage. For example,
		vertical-align:text-top
	word-spacing	Specifies space between words. The value em is the width of the letter "m." The default value is 0em. Another example,
		word-spacing:2em

Many of these properties are incorporated in the example's included in this chapter.

JavaScript Style Properties

JavaScript provides a way to implement many of the same styling properties as CCS. Table 8.2 provides a list of these properties and a brief description of each.

Table 8–2: *JavaScript Styling Properties*

Property Group	Property	Typical Values
Block-Level	align	Sets an element's alignment to *left, right,* or *none.*
	borderColor	Sets the color of each border surrounding an element.

Table 8–2:   *Continued*

Property Group	Property	Typical Values
	borderTopWidth, borderLeftWidth, borderBottom-Width, border-RightWidth borderWidths()	Sets the width of each border surrounding an element. Widths can be specified in ems, percentages, or pixels.
	borderStyle	Sets all four borders at the same time. Use *solid*, *3D*, or *none*.
	clear	Used to place an element below any floating element on that side. Use *left*, *right*, or *both*.
	height	Used to specify the height of an element. Use *length* and *auto*.
	marginBottom marginLeft, marginRight marginTop margins()	Specifies distance between adjacent elements.
	paddingBottom, paddingLeft, paddingRight, paddingTop, padding()	Specifies the space between the border and the contents of the document. Values in ems can be used.
	width	Specify the width of an element. Use *length*, *percentage*, or *auto*.
Classification	display	Determines when and how a style element is used. Use *blocklevel*, *blocklevellist*, or *inline*.
	listStyleType	Allows formatting of list items. Use *circle*, *decimal*, *disc*, *lower-alpha*, *lower-roman*, *none*, *upper-alpha*, or *upper-roman*.

Table 8–2: *Continued*

Property Group	Property	Typical Values
	whiteSpace	Used to specify how whitespace within an element is handled. Use *normal* or *pre*.
Color and Background	backgroundImage	Use the URL to specify the background image of an element.
	color	Specifies an element's text color.
Font	fontFamily	Name of the font family. Families such as arial, courier, roman, and so on are permitted.
	fontSize	Font size specified in points, inches, centimeters, pixels, or as a percentage. Point values are the preferred method. Values are expressed, for example, as 12pt, 16pt, 36pt, and so on.
	fontStyle	Style is used to indicate a *normal*, *italic*, or *bold* font.
Text	lineHeight	Used to set the distance between baselines. Use *length*, *number*, or *percentage*.
	textAlign	Specifies how text is aligned. Use *left*, *right*, *center*, or *justify*.
	textDecoration	Allows extra text characteristics such as blinking, strikethrough, and so on.
	textIndent	Specifies text indenting. Use *length* or *percentage*.
	textTransform	Used to specify capitalization. Use *capitalize* (first letter of each word), *uppercase* (all letters uppercase), *lowercase* (all letters lowercase), and *none* (no capitalization).

Table 8–2: *JavaScript Styling Properties (Continued)*

Property Group	Property	Typical Values
	verticalAlign	Specifies vertical positioning. Use *baseline*, *bottom*, *middle*, *sub*, *super*, *text-bottom*, *text-top*, *top*, or as a percentage.

Many of these JavaScript properties are incorporated in the examples included in this chapter.

In-line Style Information

Adding the style attribute to specific HTML tags creates in-line style sheets. This style information is obtained from the default style sheet language. CSS style declarations use a name:value format. A semicolon separates property declarations.

For example, here is an in-line style that sets the font family, size, and color:

```
<p style="font-family:arial; font-size=16pt;
color:red">
   Setting a font's properties is easy!
</p>
```

It is also possible to use the <SPAN> or the <DIV> tags for in-line styling.

```
<SPAN style="font: arial 16pt">
   Use for short blocks of text.
</SPAN>
<DIV style="font: roman 10pt">
   Use for longer blocks of text.
</DIV>
```

In-line styling is easy to use, especially for shorter HTML documents. Its downfall is that the styling is embedded within the HTML document. Embedding style information makes it nonportable, which certainly defeats the purpose of cascading style sheets.

The <STYLE> Tag

The <STYLE> element is typically used to style whole documents. Style sheet rules are often placed in the document's header. When user agents don't support specific style elements, they must hide the contents of the <STYLE> element. The <STYLE> element often permits a wider variety of rules than the style attribute discussed earlier in the chapter. The <STYLE> element can be used to specify all instances of HTML elements, such as H1, H2, H3 elements, and so on. The <STYLE> element can also be used to style all instances of elements belonging to a class.

An HTML document may contain several H1 and H2 elements. If a border is to be placed around every H1 and H2 element in the document, the <STYLE> element should be used.

```
<HEAD>
  <STYLE type="text/css">
    H1 {border-width:2; border:solid; text-align:cen-
ter}
    H2 {border-width:1;border:dashed; text-
align:left}
  </STYLE>
</HEAD>
```

JavaScript can also be used to set styling within the <STYLE> element.

```
<STYLE>
  tags.H1.color = "red"
  tags.H1.align = "center"
  tags.H1.fontSize = "30 pt"

  tags.H3.color = "blue"

  tags.BODY.fontStyle = "italic"
  tags.BODY.fontSize = "14 pt"
  tags.BODY.backgroundColor = "#00FFFF"
</STYLE>
```

The following example shows how CCS can be used to style all elements in a specific class. Classes behave as a subset of a previously defined declaration. For example,

```
<HEAD>
  <STYLE type="text/css">
    #clasid H1 {border-width:2; border:solid;
    text-align:center}
  </STYLE>
</HEAD>
<BODY>
```

```
<H1 id="classid"> This H1 element is styled. </H1>
<H1 class="anotherclass"> This H1 element is NOT
styled.
</H1>
<H1> This one is NOT affected either. </H1>
</BODY>
```

Many of these styling techniques are used in the example program contained at the end of this chapter.

External Style Sheets

External style sheets exist as documents separated from the HTML document. This gives the developer/user the ability to share the style sheets across a number of documents, sites, and locations. It also has the advantage of being easily modified without affecting the HTML document.

Users are often given the choice of styling. In this case the style sheet is an *alternate* choice. If the user cannot alter a particular style or sheet, it is known as *persistent*. Default style sheets are usually used when loading a document but have the capability of allowing the user to select an alternative style sheet.

The <LINK> tag is used to incorporate an external style sheet. The href attribute identifies the location of the style sheet. The rel attribute is used to indicate if it is persistent or alternate. Set rel="stylesheet" for persistent and use rel="alternate stylesheet" for alternate. The title attribute can be used to change the style sheet from persistent to default.

Here is an example using two external style sheets:

```
<LINK href="CompSheet.css" rel="alternate stylesheet">
<LINK href="CollSheet.css" rel="stylesheet">
```

The first style sheet is a alternate style sheet that might be used by a computer science department. The second style sheet is persistent and might be used by the entire college.

If two alternate style sheets share the same title, they will both be applied when that style is activated. For example,

```
<LINK href="CollSheet1.css" title="header"
  rel="alternate stylesheet">
<LINK href="CollSheet2.css" title="header"
  rel="alternate stylesheet">
```

The <META> element can be used to set the default style for an HTML document. For example,

```
<HEAD>
<META http-equiv="Default-Style" content="header">

</HEAD>

<LINK href="CollSheet1.css" title="header"
  rel="alternate stylesheet">
<LINK href="CollSheet2.css" title="header"
  rel="alternate stylesheet">
```

In a similar manner, a media attribute can be used to specify different media such as screen, printing, speech, and so on.

```
<LINK href="CollScreen.css" media="screen"
rel="stylesheet">
<LINK href="CollPrint.css" media="print"
rel="stylesheet">
```

HTML Document Styling Examples

In the following example we'll borrow the pet registration HTML document from the previous chapter. This document involved a form for pet registration but didn't contain any styling. In this example, named `Register.htm`, we'll create a cascading style sheet and save it as an external file. This external style sheet will then be brought into the HTML document. The development of this initial HTML document was discussed in the previous chapter.

Styling Register.htm

This example uses an external JavaScript file that contains styling information. The external file containing the style sheet is named mystyle.js and exists at the same location as Register.htm. Here are the contents of the mystyle.js file. The mystyle.js file is a simple text file that can contain any amount of styling needed for your documents.

```
tags.H1.color = "red"
tags.H1.align = "center"
tags.H1.fontSize = "30 pt"
```

```
tags.H3.color = "blue"

tags.BODY.fontStyle = "italic"
tags.BODY.fontSize = "14 pt"
tags.BODY.backgroundColor = "#00FFFF"
```

If you prefer, a CCS style sheet can be used. Here is equivalent CCS code:

```
<STYLE type="text/css">
  BR {}
  H1 {font-size:30pt; text-align:center; color:red}
  H3 {color:blue}
  BODY {font-size:14pt; font-style:italic;
        background: #00FFFF}
</STYLE>
```

The mystyle.js file is brought into the Register.htm file with just a small portion of code, shown next.

```
<HTML>
<HEAD>
<TITLE>Pet Registration</TITLE>

<LINK href = "mystyle.js"
      type="text/javascript"
      rel = "stylesheet">

<SCRIPT LANGUAGE = "JavaScript">
function SendACopy(datainfo) {

   infostr = "\nFor a copy of registration data\n"
   infostr += "mailed to your e-mail address,
select\n"
   infostr += "OK, otherwise select Cancel to sub-
mit.\n"

   if (confirm(infostr)) {
      datainfo.action = "mailto:tango127@epix.net"
      datainfo.action = "mailto:" +
datainfo.email.value
      datainfo.submit()
   }
   else {

   datainfo.action = "http://hoohoo.ncsa.uiuc.edu/cgi-
bin/post-query"
   datainfo.submit()
   }
}
</SCRIPT>
```

```
</HEAD>
<BODY>
<H1>Please complete the following form
<BR>to register your pet</H1>
<HR>
<H3>Information about you:</H3>
<FORM name = "PetRegistration" method="post"
  //action= is defined in SendACopy()
  onSubmit="SendACopy(this)">
Your last name: <INPUT type="text" name="lname"
  value = "" maxlength="25" size="18" >
First name: <INPUT type="text" name="fname"
  value = "" maxlength="25" size="18">
<BR>
e-mail Address: <INPUT type="text" name="email"
  value = "" maxlength="25" size="18">
<HR>
<H3>Information about your pet:</H3>
<TABLE>
<TR valign="top">
<TD>Type of pet:
<BR>
<SELECT Name="PetType">
  <OPTION>Cat </OPTION>
  <OPTION selected>Dog </OPTION>
  <OPTION>Horse </OPTION>
  <OPTION>Other </OPTION>
</SELECT>
</TABLE>
<INPUT type="radio" name="sex" value="m">Male
<INPUT type="radio" name="sex" value="f">Female
<BR>
Pet's breed: <INPUT type="text" name="breed"
  maxlength="20">
<BR>
Please check all that apply to your pet:
<INPUT type="checkbox" name="char"
  value="e">Cropped ears
<INPUT type="checkbox" name="char"
  value="t">Docked tail
<INPUT type="checkbox" name="char"
  value="c">Good with children
<BR>
<H3>Tell us something unique about your pet:</H3>
<TEXTAREA name="info" rows=10 cols=60>
</TEXTAREA>
<HR>
<H3>Thank you for your information -
  your pet will be registered.</H3>
<INPUT type="submit" >
<INPUT type="reset">
</FORM>
```

```
</BODY>
</HTML>
```

The screen will produce results similar to those shown in Figure 8.1.

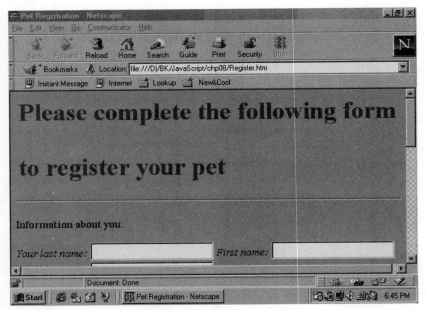

Figure 8–1: *An external JavaScript file provides styling information.*

If you use the CCS style sheet, substitute the following code for the portion of code printed in bold in the previous listing:

```
<LINK href = "mystyle.css"
      rel = "stylesheet"
      type = "text/css">
```

Summary

In this chapter you learned the terms and definitions associated with HTML style sheets. At this point you should understand how style sheets can add power and a professional touch to your documents. You also learned how JavaScript can be incorporated into documents using style sheets to provide additional programming capabilities.

CHAPTER 9
THE CGI CONNECTION

- Web Servers

- HTML Documents

- CGI Script

You learned in Chapter 7 that communications between a client-side HTML document and a server-side program require uploading an application to the server. In this manner, information can be sent from the HTML document to the server. Once the server receives the information and processes it, the information can be collected in a database and used for future reference.

Server-side applications of this sort are written according to Common Gateway Interface (CGI) requirements. These applications handle the communications linkage between the client and server sides.

Two languages have emerged as the de facto languages for CGI scripts: Perl and C/C++. The example we have included in this chapter is a C programming example, but you should also consider scripting in Perl. There are a number of Perl runtime compilers available for free on the Web for your use.

Also recall from Chapter 7 that the GET and POST request methods must be processed differently. We strongly recommend the POST method, and our example in this chapter assumes this method.

There are whole books devoted just to the topic of CGI scripting. These books cover a wide range of topics including communication problems, scripting tips and techniques, and so on. One of the best books we have seen dealing with both Perl and C scripting is *CGI How-To* by Asbury, Mathews, Sol, and Greer. The Waite Group Press published this book in 1996. You'll want to consider a book such as this if your scripting needs require complex parsing or database needs.

Web Servers

If you have been developing HTML documents, you realize that many of these documents are just client-side documents that allow browsing through various pages of text, images, sounds, and so on.

If you are developing applications for your personal use, your Internet provider may allow you to create a personal Web page on the server with no additional monthly charge. When this is possible, you'll be given your own site address and your friends and relations can connect to this address to view your home page. Basically, you create your HTML document on your computer and then upload the document to the server. Personal Web pages, such as this, are great if your want to show friends pictures of your new baby or the progress of a house under construction. What is missing here in the simple Web page is the ability to form a two-way communication between the client and server. In order to form two-way communication you will have to have the ability to upload CGI scripts to the server. Most personal Web sites will not provide this capability for free.

If you are interested in obtaining information from users viewing your HTML document, such as information returned by a form that you have created, you will probably have to establish a commercial account. You will have to pay monthly charges to open and maintain a commercial account, but with it comes the ability to collect data from users. If you read the ads in computer magazines, such as *PC Magazine*, you'll find advertisements from dozens of commercial Web site providers willing to offer monthly Web accounts for as little as $17.95 per month. On the other hand, if you work for a large corporation or educational institution, you'll find that the ability to upload CGI code already exists. Find someone in the computer center who can assist you in creating an account and uploading your CGI scripts.

If you want to simply test a form as you develop it, you can access the NCSA site discussed in Chapter 7. Use the following code in your HTML document:

```
<FORM method="post"
      action="http://hoohoo.ncsa.uiuc.edu/cgi-bin/post-
query">
```

This site provides a server using a script that will examine data from any submitted form and return the results as an HTML page. None of the information is saved, but the site is useful when checking initial form operation.

Personal Web Servers

If you don't have easy access to a server for uploading and testing CGI scripts, we highly recommend using a personal Web server. A personal Web server allows you to create a server that can be accessed by a single computer or a small group of computers on an intranet.

Microsoft FrontPage will install a personal Web server during the installation of the product. If you save your HTML document in the home page location using the name default.htm, the personal Web server will allow you to communicate with a CGI script. The CGI script is compiled and placed in the cgi-bin subdirectory of the personal Web server. All you will need to do is specify this location in your HTML document.

Developing a Simple Example

In the following example, we'll borrow the pet registration document developed originally in Chapter 7 and then modified in Chapter 8.

Next, we'll write a CGI script in C that will allow us to intercept data returned by the form when the submit button is clicked. Believe us when we tell you that CGI scripting can become much more complicated than our simple example. The reason is that the form often returns information that can be intercepted as a command-line argument by the script. The data received is in the form of a single string that must be parsed and decoded. Decoding is required because the string contains "+" symbols instead of spaces. Also, "&" symbols are used to separate key-value pairs. Other special symbols are also used.

Figure 9.1 shows a string of raw data returned by the pet registration form in key-value form.

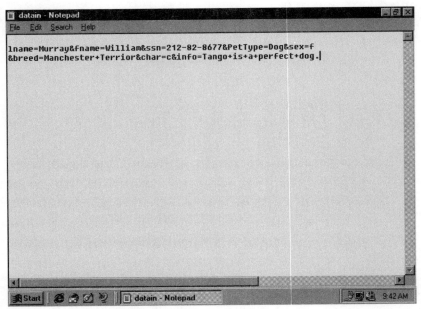

Figure 9–1: *Form information is returned as a long string with special symbols representing spaces and key-value separators.*

In the next section we'll show you how to intercept this string and perform some simple parsing and decoding.

The HTML Document

The following listing contains the HTML pet registration document completed in Chapter 8. A small change has been made to the form submission line. This change is printed in a bold font. The action method indicates that the script file, DataIn.exe, is located in the server's cgi-bin subdirectory.

Here is the external JavaScript file that contains styling information for the project. The external style file is named mystyle.js and exists at the same location as the document file. The mystyle.js file is a simple text file that can contain any amount of styling needed for your documents.

```
tags.H1.color = "red"
tags.H1.align = "center"
tags.H1.fontSize = "30 pt"

tags.H3.color = "blue"

tags.BODY.fontStyle = "italic"
tags.BODY.fontSize = "14 pt"
tags.BODY.backgroundColor = "#00FFFF"
```

The document file is named default.htm if you are experimenting with the Microsoft personal Web server provided by FrontPage. This code contains several modified lines, which are shown in a bold font. The code you enter on these lines will depend upon how locations are specified on your personal server.

```
<HTML>
<HEAD>
<TITLE>Pet Registration</TITLE>

<LINK href = "mystyle.js"
      type="text/javascript"
      rel = "stylesheet">
```

204

```
<SCRIPT LANGUAGE = "JavaScript">
function SendACopy(datainfo) {

  infostr = "\nFor a copy of registration data\n"
  infostr += "mailed to your e-mail address,
select\n"
  infostr += "OK, otherwise select Cancel to sub-
mit.\n"

  if (confirm(infostr)) {
    datainfo.action = "mailto:tango217@pix.net"
    datainfo.action = "mailto:" +
datainfo.email.value    datainfo.submit()
  }
  else {
  datainfo.method = "post"
  datainfo.action = "http:/cgi-bin/datain.exe"
  datainfo.submit()
  }
}
</SCRIPT>

</HEAD>
<BODY>
<H1>Please complete the following form
<BR>to register your pet</H1>
<HR>
<H3>Information about you:</H3>
<FORM name = "PetRegistration" method="post"
  //action= is defined in SendACopy()
  onSubmit="SendACopy(this)">
Your last name: <INPUT type="text" name="lname"
  value = "" maxlength="25" size="18" >
First name: <INPUT type="text" name="fname"
  value = "" maxlength="25" size="18">
<BR>
e-mail Address: <INPUT type="text" name="email"
  value = "" maxlength="25" size="18">
<HR>
<H3>Information about your pet:</H3>
<TABLE>
<TR valign="top">
<TD>Type of pet:
<BR>
<SELECT Name="PetType">
  <OPTION>Cat </OPTION>
  <OPTION selected>Dog </OPTION>
  <OPTION>Horse </OPTION>
  <OPTION>Other </OPTION>
</SELECT>
</TABLE>
<INPUT type="radio" name="sex" value="m">Male
```

```
<INPUT type="radio" name="sex" value="f">Female
<BR>
Pet's breed: <INPUT type="text" name="breed"
   maxlength="20">
<BR>
Please check all that apply to your pet:
<INPUT type="checkbox" name="char"
   value="e">Cropped ears
<INPUT type="checkbox" name="char"
   value="t">Docked tail
<INPUT type="checkbox" name="char"
   value="c">Good with children
<BR>
<H3>Tell us something unique about your pet:</H3>
<TEXTAREA name="info" rows=10 cols=60>
</TEXTAREA>
<HR>
<H3>Thank you for your information -
   your pet will be registered.</H3>
<INPUT type="submit" >
<INPUT type="reset">
</FORM>
</BODY>
</HTML>
```

As you examine the listing, notice that there are several names that will be used as key names when information is returned. For example, lname, fname, ssn, and so on are used as key names. You might have noticed these key names when you examined Figure 9.1. They were actually embedded in the string.

The CGI script developed in the next section will intercept this string of data, parse it, and remove embedded "+" and "&" symbols.

The CGI Script

The C program developed in this section is quite simple. The simplicity is important in order to focus on the minimum CGI script code needed to intercept and parse data returned by the HTML document. The script file assumes a POST data return and performs no real error checking.

Name this CGI script file DataIn.c. When you compile the application with your C compiler, make sure you place the executable (.exe) file in the cgi-bin subdirectory of the personal Web server.

```c
/* DataIn.c is an application that serves as a
 *  CGI script for intercepting, parsing and
 *  removing '+' and '&' symbols before
 *  printing key-value pairs.
 */

#include <stdio.h>
#include <stdlib.h>
#include <string.h>

void GetInfo(char **);

void main(int argc, char *argv[])
{
   char *info;
   char searchTokens[] = "+&";
   char *startOfNextToken;

   /*required CGI header*/
   printf("Content-type: text/plain\n\n\n");

   printf("Parsed key-value pairs:\n\n\n");

   GetInfo(&info);
   startOfNextToken = strtok(info, searchTokens);
   while (startOfNextToken != NULL) {
     printf(" %s\n", startOfNextToken);
     startOfNextToken = strtok(NULL, searchTokens);
   }
}

void GetInfo(char **tempStr)
{
   char *infoStr;
   int infoLen;
   int i;

   infoLen = atoi(getenv("CONTENT_LENGTH"));
   infoStr = (char *) malloc(sizeof(char) * (infoLen +
1));

   i = 0;
   while(i < infoLen)  {
     infoStr[i++] = fgetc(stdin);
   }
   infoStr[i] = '\0';

   *tempStr = infoStr;
}
```

A call to the GetInfo() function returns a string of key-value pairs that are parsed using the strtok() function. The strtok() function allows the string to be scanned for "+" and "&" characters. As the original string is scanned, a substring named *startofNextToken* is created. This string represents the characters from the previous token to the next token; in other words, all of the characters from the previous "+" or "&" symbol to the next. A while loop controls the number of times a substring is created and printed.

The GetInfo() function contains a number of features that should be discussed. First, the getenv() function obtains the length of the information passed to the application via *argc* and *argv*. This information is used to determine the size of a memory buffer for the string. The standard malloc() function is used for this purpose. The string of information is built, one character at a time, using a while loop and the fgetc() function.

Figure 9.2 shows the resulting output with the same data as used in Figure 9.1.

Once you have learned how to parse information, you are ready to intercept information in a database or spreadsheet.

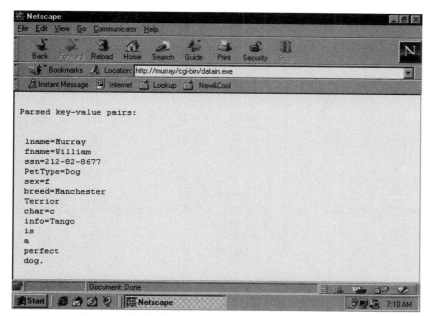

Figure 9–2: *A CGI script parses a string of data returned by the HTML form.*

Summary

In this chapter you have learned that server-side applications are written according to Common Gateway Interface (CGI) requirements and handle the communications linkage between the client and server sides. CGI scripts are commonly written in Perl or C/C++. The example program in this chapter was written in C.

This chapter was designed to illustrate the fundamentals of scripting and to complement the work done earlier in Chapters 7 and 8. In order to become proficient in writing CGI scripts you will need a book devoted entirely to that topic.

PART THREE

Javascript Fundamentals

In Part Three you'll learn the fundamentals of the JavaScript programming language. If you have programmed in another language, you'll find many familiar programming concepts in JavaScript. You'll find that JavaScript allows you to expand from traditional procedure-oriented language concepts to the exciting world of object-oriented programming. In this section, you'll find that new object-oriented programming concepts, such as objects, events, and methods, are carefully integrated along with traditional procedure-oriented concepts. All are presented at a pace that you can master as you move from chapter to chapter.

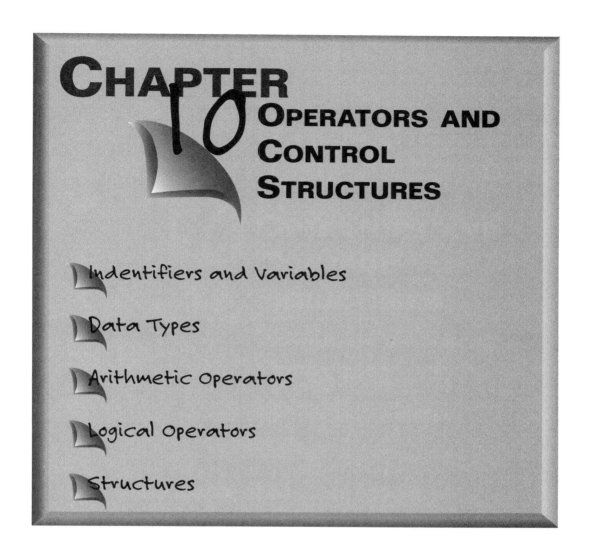

CHAPTER 10
OPERATORS AND CONTROL STRUCTURES

- Indentifiers and Variables
- Data Types
- Arithmetic Operators
- Logical Operators
- Structures

Chapters 1 through 9 reviewed the fundamentals necessary to understand the HTML elements necessary to create the hosting document for a JavaScript. Chapters 10 through 15 detail the syntax and logic used in writing and using the JavaScript language. As with any other programming language introduction, this first chapter officially dedicated to JavaScript syntax begins with a discussion of the standard data types, operators, and control structures provided by this exciting new language.

Rules for Identifiers

Identifiers are the alphanumeric names you give to your variables and functions. The rules for legal JavaScript identifiers are identical to those used by C and C++. In JavaScript, a variable must begin with either an upper- or lowercase letter (A, a...Z, z) or the underscore character (_). The remaining characters can consist of letters, digits (0...9), or the underscore character. Examples of legal identifiers look like

```
lastname
LastName
last_name
Last_Name
_MyProc
record1
```

The key to successful identifier selections revolves around consistency in style—always. Also, like C and C++, identifiers are cAsE-sEnSiTiVe! This means that if you define an identifer as *LastName* but forget and try to reference the variable *lastname* within your JavaScript, the interpreter will not be able to find a symbol-table match.

Specifying a Variable's Data Type

Hold on to your hats for this one—in JavaScript you do *not* specify a variable's data type! Not only do you not specify a variable's type but also throughout a JavaScript program, the data type(s) you store in the same variable may change. For example, a variable may start out holding a string, then an integer, next a floating-point value, and finally a logical true or false with the JavaScript interpreter taking care of each conversion type. Needless to say this feature has its definite good and bad points. For example, whenever you want to enter the decimal ASCII value of a character and then next view it as a character, great, but there are also times when this automatic conversion process can lead to incorrect results. The section entitled Rules for Conversions later in the chapter explains these delicacies.

Standard Data Types

JavaScript includes the necessary plethora of data types for all your programming needs, namely,

- Integer
- Floating point
- Boolean
- String

JavaScript also supports complex types such as arrays and objects. However, unlike most of the other computer languages you have used in the past, you do not declare a variable's type. Instead, the type of a variable is implicitly discerned from the surrounding syntax. Since a single variable may contain multiple data type assignments throughout a JavaScript, it is the last type assigned to a variable that determines its successive use. For example, if a variable is assigned a floating-point value, then floating-point operations become legal for the variable's use. However, if the same variable is next assigned a string literal, legal operations for the variable switch to string manipulations.

Integers

JavaScript supports three integer formats: decimal (base ten), hexadecimal (base sixteen), and the less used octal (base eight). The JavaScript interpreter effortlessly converts from one data type to another, as needed, in all numerical expressions. For example, in a mixed-mode calculation involving integer and floating-point data types, JavaScript permutes the integer data value to a floating-point equivalent to complete the evaluation of the expression.

While you need no reminders on how to use decimal values, remember that to flag the JavaScript interpreter to the fact a hexadecimal value is being expressed, you precede the value with a 0x, or 0X. This is necessary since hexadecimal values can start with the letters A,a…F,f which look more like the beginning of a variable name instead of a numeric value. To distinguish a decimal 7 from an octal 7,

JavaScript requires a preceding 0. Therefore a 7 is viewed as a decimal 7, while a 07 is viewed as an octal 7. Also, remember that the octal number system only contains the values 0 through 7! The following program and associated figure (Figure 10.1) illustrate the use of integers.

```
<HTML><HEAD><TITLE>Using Integers in a JavaScript
Program</TITLE ></HEAD> <BODY>
<SCRIPT LANGUAGE="JavaScript" >
<!--
document.write("Integer - 3 + 5 = ")
document.write(3 + 5)
document.write("<BR>")
document.write("Octal - 07 + 01 = ")
document.write(07 + 01)
document.write("<BR>")
document.write("Hexadecimal - 0xF + 0x1 = ")
document.write(0xF + 0x1)
document.write("<BR><BR>")
document.write("NOTICE: all calculations are con-
verted to decimal!")
// -- >
</SCRIPT>
</BODY>
</HTML>
```

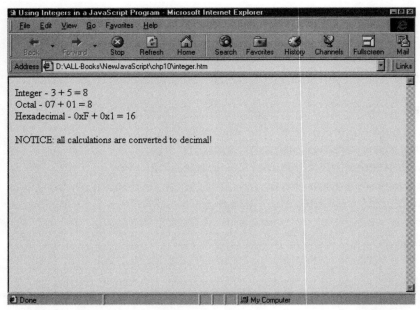

Figure 10–1: *Using JavaScript decimal, octal, and hexadecimal data types.*

Notice in particular that the octal and hexadecimal examples, while returning the correct numeric results, did not display those results in the equivalent base.

Floating Point

JavaScript provides the floating-point data type for the representation of additional precision or large values. Floating-point values must include either a decimal point (.) or an exponent expressed with either a lower- or uppercase e (e or E). The following list illustrates the proper syntax:

```
3.14159
-7.1
+6.
2e10
2E10
-10e-5
.1
```

As you can see from the examples, floating-point values may contain an initial integer, followed by an optional decimal point and fraction, or followed by an optional exponent along with its associated exponent value. Notice too that the intial integer and/or integer exponent value(s) may be signed as positive or negative. The following program demonstrates JavaScript's output interpretation of these internal representations:

```
<HTML><HEAD><TITLE>Using Floating-point in a JavaScript
Program</TITLE></HEAD>
<BODY>
<SCRIPT LANGUAGE="JavaScript">
<!--
document.write("3.14159 = ")
document.write(3.14159)
document.write("<BR>")
document.write("-7.1 = ")
document.write(-7.1)
document.write("<BR>")
document.write("+6. = ")
document.write(+6.)
document.write("<BR>")
document.write("2e10 = ")
document.write(2e10)
document.write("<BR>")
document.write("2E10 = ")
```

```
document.write(2E10)
document.write("<BR>")
document.write("-10e-5 = ")
document.write(-10e-5)
document.write("<BR>")
document.write(".1 = ")
document.write(.1)
// -->
</SCRIPT>
</BODY>
</HTML>
```

Figure 10.2 displays the relationship between internally specified precisions versus output display formatting.

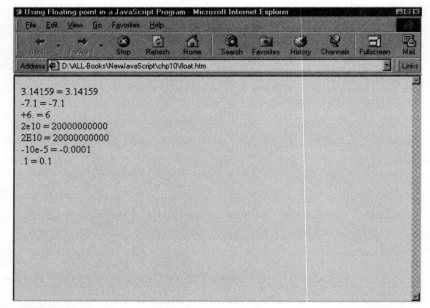

Figure 10–2: Output display interpretation of floating-point values.

Boolean

JavaScript, just like the latest ANSI C/C++ compliant compilers, provides programmers with the logical Boolean data type. Boolean variables may only contain the values *true* or *false*. As does C/C++, JavaScript interprets these values as the integer 1 for *true* and 0 for *false* and allows you to use variables of the Boolean type with several different operators. The following program highlights this legal blend:

```
<HTML>
<HEAD>
<TITLE>Using Boolean values in a JavaScript
Program</TITLE>
</HEAD>
<BODY>
<SCRIPT LANGUAGE="JavaScript">
<! --
document.write("true + 1 = ")
document.write(true + 1)
document.write("<BR>")
document.write("false + 1 = ")
document.write(false + 1)
// -->
</SCRIPT>
</BODY>
</HTML>
```

In Figure 10.3 notice *true* equates to the inter 1, and *false* as 0.

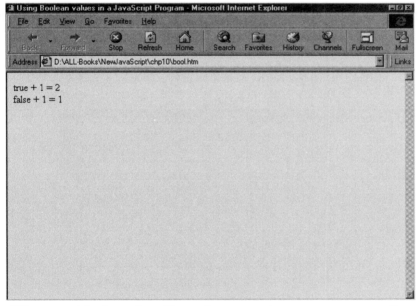

Figure 10–3: *JavaScript's integral interpretations of true and false.*

Strings

JavaScript strings are any sequence of zero or more characters that are enclosed in either a pair of double quotes ("...") or single quote ('...') marks. Nesting quotations within a string (when the string is delimited by matching double quotes), or including single hypens (when the string is single quote delimited) requires the use of the backslash symbol (\) before the nested offender. The following program illustrates this necessity:

```
<HTML>
<HEAD>
<TITLE>Using Strings in a JavaScript Program</TITLE>
</HEAD>
<BODY>
<SCRIPT LANGUAGE="JavaScript">
<!--
document.write("Double quote, \"within double quote
\"<BR>")
document.write("Single quote, 'within double
quote'<BR>")
document.write('Single quote, \'within single
quote\'<BR>')
document.write('Double quote, "within single quote"')
// -->
</SCRIPT>
</BODY>
</HTML>
```

Figure 10.4 enumerates the four possible combinations of the two string delimiter formats.

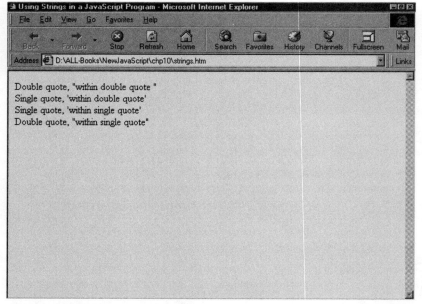

Figure 10–4:   Using combinations of string single and double quote delimiters.

While it is true that JavaScript strings may include the familiar C/C++ control formats seen in Table 10.1, they are not interpreted properly when used for screen output.

Table 10–1: *JavaScript String Control Formats*

Control Format	Description
\n	new line
\t	horizontal tab
\r	carriage return
\b	backspace
\f	form feed

However, even though the control formats misbehave when sent to the display screen, they do work as anticipated when outputting strings to external files and this explains why they are an integral part of the JavaScript language. The following program highlights which control formats do and do not output properly when used exclusively for screen interaction:

```
<HTML>
<HEAD>
<TITLE>Using String Control Formats in a JavaScript
Program</TITLE>
<PRE>
<SCRIPT LANGUAGE="JavaScript">
<!--
document.write("The new line control format \nworks
fine!\n")
document.write("The tab control format \t works
fine!\n")
document.write("However the backspace \bbuck-
eyes!\n")
document.write("The form feed does too \f\n")
document.write("And the carriage return \r behaves
like a new line")// --></SCRIPT>
</PRE>
</BODY>
</HTML>
```

As you are viewing the resulting screen output in Figure 10.5, remember that the inclusion of these control format codes is to maintain external file output compatibility with other programming languages that may need to input JavaScript-generated data.

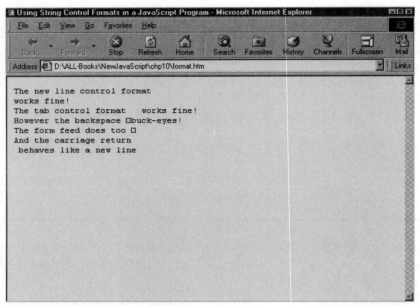

Figure 10–5: *Caution when using control formats on screen string output.*

Understanding Data Type Conversions

If you have been following the coded examples in this chapter, you are aware that there is a significant difference between numeric values as they are represented within your JavaScript versus their output formats and interpretations. In addition, since JavaScript automatically converts values from one data type to another when they are used in an expression, you need to understand the process.

When JavaScript evaluates an expression, it parses the expression into its component unary (operators applied to one operand) and binary (operators applied to two operands) expressions based upon the order of operator precedence (which operator *binds* first). It then evaluates the component unary and binary expressions. In mixed data-type-mode operations, JavaScript will attempt to use the following operator precedence rules (listed from highest priority to lowest). JavaScript will attempt to perform string operations first; floating point, second; integer operators, third; followed by logical operators, which have the lowest priority. The following program demonstrates these principles along with a review of the numeric interpretations of *true* and *false* Boolean data types, and the three different interpretations of the value *null*.

```
<HTML>
<HEAD>
<TITLE>Understanding Data Type Conversions</TITLE>
<SCRIPT LANGUAGE-"JavaScript">
<!--
string_value = "string"
numeric_string_value = "3.14159"
integer_value = 10
float_value = 1.2
Boolean_true_value = true
Boolean_false_value = false
null_value = null
document.write("string_value + integer_value = ")
document.write(string_value + integer_value)
document.write("<BR>")
document.write("integer_value + float_value = ")
document.write(integer_value + float_value)
document.write("<BR>")
document.write("float_value + Boolean_true_value = ")
document.write(float_value + Boolean_true_value)
document.write("<BR>")
document.write("string_value + null_value = ")
document.write(string_value + null_value)
document.write("<BR>")
document.write("integer_value + null_value = ")
document.write(integer_value + null_value)
document.write("<BR>")
document.write("Boolean_false_value + null_value = ")
document.write(Boolean_false_value + null_value)
// -->
</SCRIPT>
</BODY>
</HTML>
```

Figure 10.6 displays the interesting results. If JavaScript cannot convert a value to a type that is valid for an operation, it will generate a *runtime error*. This typically happens if a conversion from a string value to a numerical or logical value is required and the string value does not represent a value of the target type. In the next chapter you will learn about JavaScript's explicit data type conversions functions for those circumstances where autoconversions generate incorrect precisions or formats.

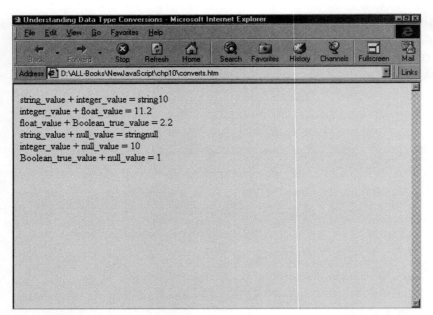

Figure 10–6: *JavaScript's autoconversion of data types.*

Operators

JavaScript provides the anticipated set of standard operators. These include

- Arithmetic
- Logical
- Relational
- Bit manipulation
- String
- Assignment and combinational
- Conditional

The following sections detail their use along with a review of operator precedence levels which will enable you to *know* which operator binds (kicks-in) first.

Arithmetic

Table 10.2 lists the seven JavaScript arithmetic operators, which coincidentally look exactly like their C/C++ counterparts.

Table 10–2: *Arithmetic Operators*

Arithmetic Operator	Definition
+	addition
-	subtraction
*	multiplication
/	division
%	modulus
++	increment (pre- and postfix forms)
−−	decrement (pre- and postfix forms)

The first four arithmetic operators are standard fare, however modulus (%) may be new to you. Modulus calculates the *remainder* of dividing two integer values. Also, increment (++) and decrement (−−) are somewhat unique operators in that they automatically increment or decrement an integer variable by 1 but they have two formats as in *integer_value++* (postfix form) and *++integer_value* (prefix form). The difference has to do with *when* the addition takes place. The first form (postfix form) says to use the original value of *integer_value* in the related expression, and *then* add 1. The second syntax (prefix form) says to increment *integer_value* by 1 *first* and then use the *incremented* value in the related expression.

Logical

JavaScript provides three logical operators: logical and (&&), logical or (||), and the logical not (!). You use JavaScript logical operators to perform Boolean operations on Boolean operands.

Relational

Table 10.3 enumerates the six JavaScript relational operators. Relational operators determine whether two values are equal to or greater/lesser than one another.

Table 10–3: *Relational Operators*

Relational Operator	Definition
==	equality
!=	nonequality
<	less than
<=	less than or equal
>	greater than
>=	greater than or equal

Bit Manipulation

You use the bit manipulation operators to manipulate the binary representation of a value. Table 10.4 lists JavaScript's six bit manipulation operators.

Table 10–4: *Bit Manipulation Operators*

Bit Manipulation Operator	Definition
&	bitwise AND
|	bitwise OR
^	EXCLUSIVE OR
<<	left shift
>>	right shift
>>>	zero-fill right shift

String

Under the current implementation of JavaScript there is only one string operator, the string concatenation operator (+).

Assignment and Combinational

Table 10.5 lists both the assignment and combinational operators available to you. The assignment operator is straightforward in meaning and usage; however, the combinational operators may be new to you.

Combinational operators are formed by combining the assignment operator with one of the other standard operators available in JavaScript. These combinations are more than simple shorthand or alternate syntax abbreviations. Combinational expressions parse into more efficient (fewer) statements than their longhand equivalents. For example,

```
running_total = running_total + current_value
```

when rewritten using the conditional form looks like

```
running_total += current_value
```

requiring fewer machine code instructions to execute.

If you are new to conditional operator use, here's a clue as to when you can rewrite a longhand form expression with a conditional. Anytime you see the same variable name on *both sides* of an assignment statement, remove the variable's use on the right-hand side of the assignment operator and move the second operator, within the expression, right in front of the assignment operator

Table 10–5: *Assignment and Combinational Operators*

Assignment and Combinational Operator	Definition
=	assignment
+=	combinational addition
-=	combinational subtraction

Table 10–5: *Assignment and Combinational Operators (Continued)*

Assignment and Combinational Operator	Definition
*=	combinational multiplication
/=	combinational division
%=	combinational modulus
<<=	combinational left shift
>>=	combinational right shift
>>>=	combinational zero-fill right shift
&=	combinational bitwise AND
|=	combinational bitwise OR
^=	combinational bitwise EXCLUSIVE OR

Conditional

Originating in the C/C++ languages, the conditional operator (?:) is a shorthand syntax substitution for a simple one-line if-else statement. The syntax for the conditional operator looks like

```
( test expression ) ? if_true_expression_action :
if_false_expression_action
```

With experience, when used properly, you will learn to prefer these one-liners over their four-line nested if-else counterparts.

Precedence

Table 10.6 groups JavaScript operators from highest priority to lowest. The only time this information is needed is when you begin combining operators within the same expression and wish to guarantee that the appropriate meaning is inferred.

Table 10–6: *Operator Precedence Levels*

Operator Group	Precedence Level
()	1 or highest precedence
!, ~, ++, −, - (unary)	2
*, /, %	3
+, -	4
<<, >>, >>>	5
<, <=, >, >=	6
==, !=	7
&	8
^	9
|	10
&&	11
||	12
?=	13
=, +=, -=, *=, /=, %=, <<=, >>=, >>>=, &=, ^=, |=	14 or lowest precedence

Control Structures

Control structures, sometimes called logic control statements, fall into two categories: single execution and repetitive execution. Examples of single-execution statements include

- data declarations
- assignment statements
- if and if-else statements
- switch-case statements

- break statements
- continue statements
- function calls
- return statements
- member function or method calls

Examples of repetitive-execution statements include

- while loops
- do while loops
- for loops
- with

The following section briskly covers those statement types familiar to all programming languages by giving a simple generic syntax example and details only those statement types that are less common or unavailable in older high-level languages such as Pascal, Fortran, COBOL, and PL/I.

Data Declarations

JavaScript data declarations follow the standard form:

```
legal_identifier = valid_data_type_value
```

Assignment Statements

Assignment statements use the straightforward assignment operator (=) or any of the combinational forms (+=, -=, ...). Remember, however, that the combinational forms have a lower operator precedence than simple assignment (=).

if and if-else Statements

if or **if-else** statements follow the similar C/C++ syntax only without the semicolon. The obvious syntax looks like

```
if(boolean_test_expression)
   statement_to_execute
or
if(boolean_test_expression)
   statement_to_execute_if_true
else
   statement_to_execute_if_false
```

Switch Statements

The **switch-case** statement requires a little explanation since it is not as automatic as many selection statements available in other high-level languages. This nuance revolves around the selective use of the **break** keyword. First the generic syntax for **switch-case** statements:

```
switch(integral_value) {
   case actual_integral_value1: [action1a]
                                [action1b...n]
                                [break]
   case actual_integral_value2: [action2a]
                                [action2b...n]
                                [break]
   case actual_integral_valuen: [actionna]
                                [actionnb...n]
                                [break]

   [default]: [default_actiona]
              [default_actionn]
}
```

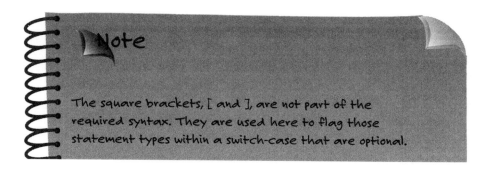

Note

The square brackets, [and], are not part of the required syntax. They are used here to flag those statement types within a switch-case that are optional.

But first, a correct logical review of how selection case statements should be entered. You should always pretest the **switch-case**'s *integral_value* to make certain that it indeed *matches* one of the *actual_integral_values*. This is necessary since once you enter a **switch-case** an *action* **will be taken** whether or not a match is truly found!

If you are *not* going to pretest the *integral_value* prior to entering the statement, then your **switch-case** should professionally include the **default** case to *catch* any *integral_value* falling through the enumerated **case**s.

In addition, some languages, Pascal for example, have powerful **case** syntax *not* available in JavaScript. For example, Pascal allows a case to be a subrange, or set using the two following types of syntax: 'a'..'z' or ['A', 'E', 'I', 'O', 'U']. The equivalent translation into an appropriate JavaScript program would instead use a selective nonuse of the **break** statement along with the drop-through feature of JavaScript's **switch-case** statements, as in

```
case 'a': no_action
case'b': no_action
  .
  .
  .
case'z':action_to_take_for_all_as_to_zs
or
case 'A': no_action
case 'E': no_action
  .
  .
  .
case 'U':action_to_take_for_all_vowels
```

These examples are a nice introduction to the use of **break** statements within a **switch-case**, since it is their presence or absence that causes the execution flow to jump out of the **switch-case** control statement and continue on with the remaining algorithm.

break Statement

The **break** statement has two uses in JavaScript. The first you have seen already in the **switch-case** statement. Here **break** forces the exit from the executed matching **case**. The second use for **break** is to exit a loop before the loop's normal control statement determines the iterations are complete. The following example demonstrates this use:

```
value = 5
while( value < 20 ) {
  value *= 5
  if(value = 25)
    break
}
```

You should only use this exit option for special cases, not as an excuse to implement a poorly designed Boolean test expression!

continue Statement

The **continue** statement works identically to **break** except for one significant difference. If a **break** statement is encountered within a loop structure, the **break** causes the respective loop to stop iterating. Instead, had a **continue** been encountered, only the *current iteration* would be terminated, causing all statements within the loop, but below the **continue,** to be ignored. However, **continue** would *not* circumvent a check of the loop's normal Boolean test condition and could therefore still allow the loop to iterate sucessively.

Function and Method Calls

JavaScript function calls and member function or method calls are identical to those found in C/C++ and many other object-oriented languages. To call a function you simply use its name followed by the optional actual argument list:

```
call_my_function([optional_formal_argument_list])
```

The syntax for a method call looks like

```
object_name.object_method([optional_formal_argument_list
])
```

and use the period (.) member operator to select the associated method.

return Statement

In the case where a function or method has been defined to return a value, the subroutine's body must terminate with a **return** statement, as in

```
my_function([formal_argument_list]) {
   function_body_statements
   return value
}
```

while and do-while Loops

JavaScript **while** and **do-while** syntax is straightforward:

```
while(boolean_test_expression) {
    action_statement(s)
}
```

or

```
do {
   action_statement(s)

while(boolean_test_expression)
```

for Loop

The **for** statement syntax by itself is obvious and looks like

```
for(initialization_statement; boolean_test_condition;
update_control_value) {
   action_statement(s)
}
```

However, JavaScript incorporates a **for..in** syntax that is rather unique. The **for..in** statement is similar to a **for** statement in that it repeatedly executes a set of statements. However, instead of iterating the statements based on the *boolean_test_condition*, it executes the statements for all properties that are defined for an object. The syntax looks like

```
for(variable in object){
   action_statement(s)
}
```

Look at this next example:

```
for(object_properties in student_record)
   document.write(object_properties+<"BR">)
```

First, don't be upset by the missing squiggly-bracket pairs ({,}). These are only necessary when the loop body contains more than one executable statement. Had the *student_record* properties of *student_ID*, *student_Name*, and *student_Address* been defined, the **for** loop would cause the following text to be written to the current document:

```
student_ID
student_Name
student_Address
```

with Statement

If you know the Pascal language, you will be right at home with the JavaScript **with** statement. This shorthand syntax option allows you to do away with repetitive naming of an object when accessing its members. The syntax looks like

```
with(variable_name) {
   action_statement(s)
}
```

For example, when accessing the **document.write()** method, you could eliminate the need to constantly retype the object name *document* by beginning the statement sequence with

```
with(document) {
   write(...)
   write(...)
   write(...)
```

Summary

In Chapters 10 through 15 you begin to learn the syntax and logic of the JavaScript language. In this beginning JavaScript chapter, as with any formal introduction to a computer language, you learned about JavaScript's standard data types, operators, and control structures provided by this exciting new language. In the next chapter you will see how similar the use of JavaScript functions is to other programming languages, along with an introduction to objects.

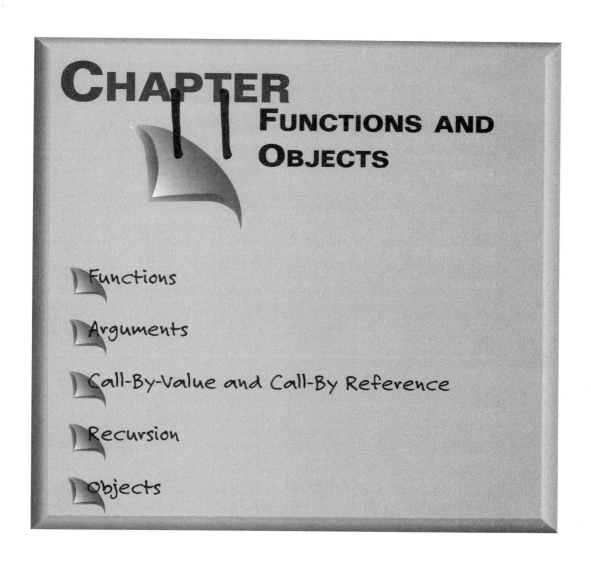

CHAPTER 11
FUNCTIONS AND OBJECTS

- Functions

- Arguments

- Call-By-Value and Call-By Reference

- Recursion

- Objects

If you have done any high-level language programming at all, you are already familiar with the syntactical and logical use of functions. However, you could be quite new to the syntax and concepts involved with objects. The good news is that objects don't give you anything you didn't already have as a programmer—just a more robust syntax. If this last statement weren't true, then you'd have to go out and buy a new computer architecture to run object-oriented programs, and you don't!

Functions

In any good introductory programming course you discuss the topic of subroutines, in particular procedures and functions. Though initially confusing, you eventually understand the subtle differences between the two types of coding. Well, hang on, you may be surprised to find out how JavaScript handles this topic.

Definition

Subroutines allow you to localize a logically related set of statements and variable declarations for the purposes of modularity, ease in coding, ease in modification, and code and data hiding (to minimize side effects). Most importantly they allow you to break a large problem down into simpler steps. Lastly, properly written subroutines are reusable from program to program, eliminating the coding/debugging phases altogether for the sake of efficiency. JavaScript, like C/C++, has only the latter category of subroutine—the function. Unlike procedures, which can be passed from zero to many arguments and return from zero to several values, functions *always* return one value. The syntax for a JavaScript function looks like

```
function function_identifier(formal_argument_list) {
    function_body   code for function...
}
```

The *function_identifier* follows the rules for all legal JavaScript identifiers, meaning the function's name must begin with an upper- or lowercase letter, or the underscore. The remaining characters can include more alphanumeric symbols and additional underscores. JavaScript is cAsE-sEnSiTiVe, so take care to remember *exactly* how you defined your function so that when you use it later on in your program, the interpreter can find it! The *formal_argument_list* passed to the function appears in parentheses and is separated by commas.

Defining Function Arguments

JavaScript has a straightforward method for dealing with the actual arguments passed to a function. JavaScript creates two properties available within the called function: *function_identifier.arguments* and *function_identifier.arguments.length*. The first property is an array with an entry for each argument. The second property identifies the number of array entries. This approach is similar to C++'s ellipsis operator (...) which allows you to define a function with a variable length *formal_argument_list*.

The following function demonstrates how you would pass a product description, called *product_name*, to a function for formatted output:

```
function printProduct(product_name) {
   document.write("<HR>Today's Special is <B><I>");
   document.write(product_.name);
   document.write("</B></I><HR>");
}
```

Calling Functions

JavaScript can call functions with either variables or literal actual arguments. If you have been following along in the text, the above function *printProduct()* could be called with the literal *"Sun Glasses"* as in

```
printProduct("Sun Glasses");
```

or with a previously defined variable as in:

```
var a_product = "Sun Glasses";
printProduct(a_product);
```

Call-by-Value or Call-by-Reference

Most programming languages allow you specify how a variable is passed to a subroutine. The term call-by-value indicates that a copy of the variable's contents is being passed. This means that any change to the value made in the subroutine will *not* be reflected in the calling routine.

The term call-by-reference indicates that the calling routine is passing the *address* of the variable, not a copy of its contents. This approach allows the subroutine to change the variable's contents with an associated change reflected back in the calling routine. JavaScript uses call-by-value. To accomplish the equivalent call-by-reference syntax you need to use another approach (see discussion below on external versus internal scope).

Returning Data

When a function needs to return a value to the calling routine, you simply insert a **return** statement before terminating the function body definition. The following example returns the cube of a value:

```
function cubeIt(integer_value) {
   return integer_value * integer_value *
integer_value;
}
```

Notice that the **return** statement itself can actually execute a statement. This approach avoids the necessity of declaring a temporary local variable to store the intermediate result and then passing its contents to the calling routine as in

```
function cubeIt(integer_value) {
   var tempResult = integer_value * integer_value *
integer_value;
   return tempResult;
}
```

External versus Internal Scope

Any variable declared outside all functions is said to be at the *external level* and is global in scope to the entire JavaScript. Variables declared inside functions are said to be at the internal level and are local in scope.

Whenever a calling routine wishes to pass a variable to a function and have the function return the variable with updated contents, the variable needs to be declared at the external level. Otherwise, the default passing convention is call-by-value which precludes a called subroutine from changing and returning an updated variable.

The following examples highlight the difference between call-by-value and call-by-reference. The first program passes an integer to the function printit() call-by-value.

```
<HTML>
<HEAD>
<TITLE>Call-By-Value</TITLE>
<SCRIPT LANGUAGE="JavaScript">
<!- hide from non-JavaScript aware browsers
//printit() defined
function printit(integer_value) {
  integer_value++
  document.write("From inside printit() = ")

  document.write(integer_value,"<BR>")
}
// stop hiding from non-JavaScript aware browsers
</SCRIPT>
</HEAD>
<BODY>
<SCRIPT LANGUAGE="JavaScript">
<!- hide from non-JavaScript aware browsers
var integer_value = 10
printit(integer_value)
document.write("From inside script = ")
document.write(integer_value)
// stop hiding from non-JavaScript aware browsers
</SCRIPT>
</BODY>
</HTML>
```

The output from this program looks similar to Figure 11.1.

Clearly, *integer_value* was incremented within the function *printit()*, as in *integer_ value*++; however the "script" section does *not* reflect this update. When you want your function to return an updated value, you rewrite the algorithm to look like

```
<HTML><HEAD><TITLE>Call-By-Reference</TITLE><SCRIPT
LANGUAGE="JavaScript"><!- hide from non-JavaScript
aware browsers
//printit() defined
function printit(integer_value) {
  integer_value++
  document.write("From inside printit() = ")
  document.write(integer_value,"<BR>")
// return the incremented value
  return ++integer_value++
}
// stop hiding from non-JavaScript aware browsers
</SCRIPT>
```

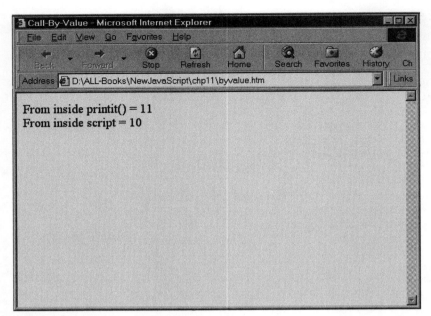

Figure 11–1: *Call-by-value output.*

```
</HEAD>
<BODY>
<SCRIPT LANGUAGE="JavaScript">
<!— hide from non-JavaScript aware browsers
integer_value = 10
//store the updated returned value
integer_value = printit(integer_value)
document.write("From inside script = ")
document.write(integer_value)
// stop hiding from non-JavaScript aware browsers
</SCRIPT>
</BODY>
</HTML>
```

The updated output now resembles Figure 11.2.

Recursion Definition: See Recursion

JavaScript supports the concept of a function calling itself, known as *recursion*. Recursive algorithms, while nebulous to trace the first time you encounter them, lend themselves to very clean solutions to unique types of problems such as binary tree traversals. The syntax for

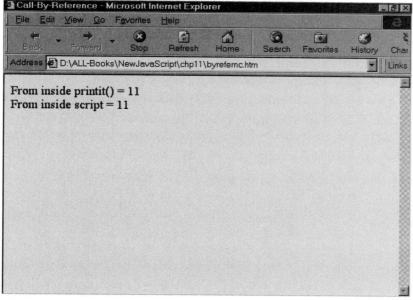

Figure 11–2: *Passing back function-updated values.*

creating a recursive algorithm is reviewed here using the proverbial *recursive_factorial()* example.

```
function recursive_factorial(x) {
  if(x>1) {
    return x * recursive_factorial(x-1)
  }
  else
    return x
  }
}
```

Objects

Object-oriented technology isn't some new temporary phase pro-gramming languages are going through just to push more "product." Object-oriented syntax and logic allow you to define, share, and use bulletproof code that performs meaningful tasks.

Definition

The simplest way to define an object is to think of a logically related set of data declarations and functions, syntactically bundled together, to do one thing. For example, in Microsoft Windows, you have a scroll bar object. This object contains data declarations to hold information like the scroll bar's current screen coordinates, maximum, and minimum, the increment to use when the user clicks on the arrow, where the thumb is, and so on.

However, a scroll bar is more than just a screen graphic—it has some horsepower, such as knowing when the user has clicked on it, redrawing the thumb if moved, resizing the entire scroll bar if the user reshapes the bounding window, along with updating the program's workspace. So, getting back to the definition of an object, the scroll bar object has a data declaration component, called *member data*, and functionality which is encapsulated in functions called *member functions* or *methods*.

Instantiation and Instances

In a procedural language such as C, you would say the following statement

```
int integer_value:
```

was *declaring* the integer variable *integer_value*. In a similar grammar, but using object-oriented terminology, the following JavaScript statement

```
currentDate = new Date();
```

is *instantiating* the object *instance currentDate*. What was called *declaring* is now called *instantiating* and what was a variable is now an instance. Since objects are usually dynamically created, the term instance carries with it the idea of a snapshot in time, or temporary, a good analogy for the persistence of memory objects.

Data Encapsulation

Sometimes referred to as data hiding, data encapsulation is that layer of interpreter/compiler protection provided by declaring variables at the internal level, inside a function. This syntax prevents any stray statements external to the subroutine from accessing the variable's contents. This same principle holds true for the members of an object in most object-oriented languages such as C++ and Ada. Unfortunately, JavaScript does *not* support this robust feature, meaning all object members are visible throughout the program.

Inheritance

Another concept associated with object-oriented syntax and logic design is the idea of inheritance. Here the programmer defines an object and then begins a second object description, with the second inheriting all of the previously defined members of the first. Some languages, like C++, support multiple inheritance, where a child object inherits members from two different parent objects. Other languages, like Java, support only single inheritance. Once again, JavaScript leaves this feature out.

Polymorphism

Linked with the idea of inheritance is a compiler's polymorphic capabilities. When inheritance is possible, child objects inherit parent object members with the same member names. When you call a method that exists by the same name in several derived objects, the compiler's ability to know which one you actually want is its polymorphic ability. JavaScript of course does not need this since it does not support object inheritance.

Constructors

A constructor is an optional object method that has a unique syntax and logical use. Logically, constructors are used to initialize an object's member data. Syntactically, JavaScript, like many other object-oriented languages, requires that the method's name *match* the name of the object. The final distinction between a normal object method and an object's constructor is that a constructor is never *directly* called. Instead, the constructor method is automatically invoked whenever the object itself is instantiated.

Method Overloading

Method overloading allows a programmer to reuse the name of a method within an object's formal definition. This is most frequently applied to the constructor method. Since constructors are logically responsible for initializing an object's member data, overload constructors typically have progressively longer formal argument lists providing several options for instantiating an object—based on how much the program knows about the object's data ahead of time.

new, delete, and typeof

The operators **new**, **delete**, and **typeof** are discussed in this chapter since they are most closely associated with the definition and use of objects.

new

You can use the **new** operator to create an instance of a user-defined object type or of one of the predefined object types: Array, Boolean, Date, Function, Object, Option, RegExp, or String. Use **new** as follows:

```
objectIdentifier = new objectType ( param1 [,param2]
...[,paramN] )
```

delete

The **delete** operator deletes an object's property or an element at a specified index in an array. Its syntax is

```
delete objectIdentifier.property
delete objectIdentifier[index]
delete property
```

where *objectIdentifier* is the name of an object, *property* is an existing property, and *index* is an integral value representing the location of an element in an array. The third example syntax is legal only within the scope of a **with** statement. If the deletion succeeds, the **delete** operator sets the property or element to undefined.

typeof

The **typeof** operator is used in one of two forms:

- typeof (operand)

or

- typeof operand

The **typeof** operator returns a string indicating the type of the unevaluated *operand*. *Operand* is the string, variable, keyword, or object for which the type is to be returned. The parentheses are optional. Suppose you define the following variables:

```
var someFunction = new Function("argument")
var name="George"
var size=10
var aDate=new Date()
```

The **typeof** operator returns the following results for these variables:

```
typeof someFunction is object
typeof shape name is string
typeof name size is number
typeof aDate is object
typeof undeclaredIdentifier is undefined
```

For the keywords null and true, the **typeof** operator returns the following results:

```
typeof null is object
typeof true is boolean
```

For a number or string, the **typeof** operator returns the following results:

```
typeof 55 is number
typeof 'Now is the time...' is string
```

For property values, the **typeof** operator returns the type of value the property contains:

```
typeof document.lastModified is string
typeof window.length is number
typeof Math.LN10 is number
```

For methods and functions, the **typeof** operator returns results as follows:

```
typeof printit is function
typeof sumit is function
typeof translate is function
typeof myobject.methodname is function
```

For predefined objects, the **typeof** operator returns results as follows:

```
typeof Date is function
typeof Function is function
typeof Math is function
typeof Option is function
typeof String is function
```

Standard JavaScript Objects

JavaScript ships with Boolean, Date, **String**, **Math**, Regular Expression, and Navigator objects. These general-purpose object types support frequently used operations. (**Date**, **Math**, and **Navigator** objects are introduced here but are covered extensively in their own chapters, 16 and 21, respectively.)

Boolean

Use the predefined **Boolean** object when you need to convert a non-Boolean value to a Boolean value. You can use the **Boolean** object any place JavaScript expects a primitive **Boolean** value. JavaScript returns the primitive value of the **Boolean** object by automatically invoking the valueOf() method. To create a **Boolean** object:

```
booleanObjectName = new Boolean(value)
```

booleanObjectName is either the name of a new object or a property of an existing object. When using Boolean properties, *booleanObjectName* is either the name of an existing Boolean object or a property of an existing object. *value* is the initial value of the **Boolean** object. The value is converted to a **Boolean** value, if necessary. If *value* is omitted or is 0, null, false, or the empty string "", the object has an initial value of false. All other values, including the string "false," create an object with an initial value of true. The following examples create Boolean objects:

```
falseBoolean = new Boolean(false)
trueBoolean = new Boolean(true)
```

Date

Overloaded constructor methods allow the same constructor name to be repeatedly defined within the object, with each *overloaded* version specifying unique formal argument lists. This allows the user/program to instantiate an object with varying degrees of foreknowledge about the current instance's state. Table 11.1 lists all of the **Date** object constructors methods available to a JavaScript for setting and querying every aspect of month, day, date, year, hour, seconds, and time zone.

Table 11–1: *Date Constructors*

Date Constructor	Definition
Date()	Instantiates a Date object containing the current date and time.

Table 11–1:   Date Constructors   (Continued)

Date Constructor	Definition
Date(*date_string*)	Instantiates a **Date** object with the *date_string* specified in the format, "*month day, year hours:minutes:seconds.*"
Date(*year, month, day*)	Instantiates a **Date** object initialized to the specified *year*, *month*, and *day*.
Date(*year, month, day, hours, minutes, seconds*)	Instantiates a **Date** object initialized to the specified *year*, *month*, *day*, *hours*, *minutes*, and *seconds*.

```
<HTML>
<HEAD>
<TITLE>Using Overloaded Date Constructors</TITLE>
</HEAD>
<BODY>
<SCRIPT LANGUAGE="JavaScript">
<!--
currentDate = new Date()
document.write("currentDate = ",currentDate,"<BR>")
stringDate = new Date("January 10, 1999 12:0:0")
document.write("stringDate = ",stringDate,"<BR>")
ymdDate = new Date (1999, 2, 2)
document.write("ymdDate = ",ymdDate,"<BR>")
ymdhmsDate = new Date(1999, 3, 3, 12, 20, 20)
document.write("ymdhmsDate = ",ymdhmsDate)
// -->
</SCRIPT>
</BODY>
</HTML>
```

The output from the JavaScript program is seen in Figure 11.3.

Table 11.2 lists all of the **Date** object methods available to a JavaScript for setting and querying every aspect of month, day, date, year, hour, seconds, and time zone.

Table 11–2:   Date Methods

Date Method	Definition
getDate()	Returns the day of the month.

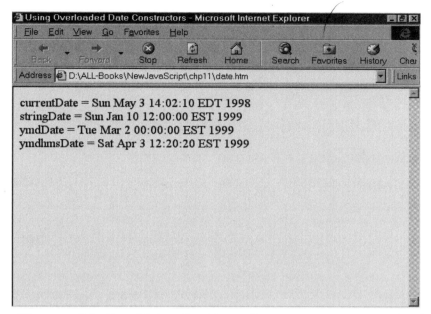

Figure 11–3: Using the three Date constructor methods.

Table 11–2: (Continued)

Date Method	Definition
getDay()	Returns the current day of the week.
getMonth()	Returns the current month.
getYear()	Returns the current year.
getHours()	Returns the hour of the day.
getMinutes()	Returns the number of minutes into the day.
getSeconds()	Returns the number of seconds.
getTime()	Returns the current time.
getTimeZoneOffset()	Returns, in minutes, the current time zone offset.
parse()	Returns elapsed milliseconds since 12:00 midnight, January 1, 1970– local time.
setDate(integer_value)	Sets the day of the month.

Table 11–2: (Continued)

Date Method	Definition
setMonth(integer_value)	Sets the current month.
setYear(integer_value)	Sets the current year.
setHours(integer_value)	Sets the hour of the day.
setMinutes(integer_value)	Sets the minutes.
setSecondsf(integer_value)	Sets the seconds.
setTime(integer_value)	Sets the time of day.
toGMTString()	Maps the current date to a string in Greenwich Mean Time (GMT) format.
toLocalString()	Maps the current date to a string in locale time format (regional format).
UTC()	Returns elapsed milliseconds, in Universal Coordinated Time (UCT), since January 1, 1970 GMT.

Math

The **Math** object definition begins with the constants defined in Table 11.3. The standard set of **Math** object methods are listed in Table 11.4. See Chapter 16 for an in-depth use of the **Math** object.

Table 11–3: Math Methods

Math Constant	Definition
E	Euler's constant.
LN2	Natural logarithm of 2.
LN10	Natural logarithm of 10.
LOG2E	Base 2 logarithm of E.
LOG10E	LOG10E Base 10 logarithm of E.

Table 11-3: *Math Methods* *(Continued)*

Math Constant	Definition
PI	The constant PI.
SQRT1_2	Square root of _.
SQRT2	Square root of 2.

Table 11-4: *Math Methods*

Math Method	Definition
abs(x)	Returns the absolute value of x.
acos(x)	Returns the arc cosine of x in radians.
asin(x)	Returns the arc sine of x in radians.
atan(x)	Returns the arc tangent of x in radians.
atan2(x,y)	Returns the angle of the polar coordinate corresponding to (x,y).
ceil(x)	Returns the least integer greater than or equal to x.
cos(x)	Returns the cosine of x.
exp(x)	Returns e^x.
floor(x)	Returns the greatest integer less than or equal to x.
log(x)	Returns the natural logarithm of x.
max(x,y)	Returns the larger of the two x or y.
min(x,y)	Returns the smaller of the two x or y.
pow(x,y)	Returns x^y.
random()	Returns a random number between 0 and 1.
round(x)	Returns x rounded to the closest integer.
sin(x)	Returns the sine of x.
sqrt(x)	Returns the square root of x.

Table 11–4: *Math Methods (Continued)*

Math Method	Definition
tan(*x*)	Returns the tangent of *x*.

String

The **String** object methods listed in Table 11.5 illustrate JavaScript's rich assortment of text manipulation routines including font, color, size, case change, and substring operations. Chapter 15 discusses **String** objects in detail.

Table 11–5: *String Methods*

String Method	Definition
anchor(*anchor_ID*)	Displays the *anchor*_ID as a hypertext anchor.
big()	Outputs the string with the big HTML attribute.
blink()	Outputs the string with the blink HTML attribute.
bold()	Outputs the string with the bold HTML attribute.
charAt(*index*)	Returns a string containing a character at the specified index of the string.
fixed()	Outputs a string using the teletype HTML tag.
fontcolor(*color*)	Outputs a string in the specified color.
fontsize(*size*)	Ouputs a string in the specified font size (1 to 7).
indexOf(*match_string*)	Returns the index position of the first string matching *match_string*. Returns

Table 11–5: *String Methods* *(Continued)*

String Method	Definition
	a −1 when no match is found.
indexOf(*match_string, start_index*)	Identical to previous method except that *start_index* allows you to specify where the match search begins.
italics()	Outputs a string using the italics HTML attribute.
lastIndexOf(*match_pattern*)	Returns the index position of the last string matching match_string. Returns a −1 when no match is found.
lastIndexOf(*match_string, start_index*)	Identical to previous method except that *start_index* allows you to specify where the match search begins.
link(*href*)	Outputs a string as a hypertext link to the *href* URL specified.
small()	Outputs a string using the small HTML attribute.
split(*split_char*)	Splits a string into substrings based on the *split_char*.
strike()	Outputs a string using the strike HTML attribute.
sub()	Outputs a string using the subscript HTML attribute.
sup()	Outputs a string using the superscript HTML attribute.
subString(*start_index, end_index*)	Outputs a substring from a string starting at *start_index* and ending at *end_index*.
toLowerCase()	Returns a copy of the string converted to all lowercase.
toUpperCase()	Returns a copy of the string converted to all uppercase.

Regular Expressions

You use regular expressions to match character pattern combinations in strings. In JavaScript, regular expressions are also objects. For example, to search for all occurrences of "abc" in a string, you create a pattern consisting of "abc" and use the pattern to search for its match in a string. Regular expression patterns can be constructed using either object initializers (for example, /abc/) or the **RegExp** constructor function [for example, re = new RegExp("abc")]. These patterns are used with the match, replace, search, and split methods of **String** objects.

CREATING A REGULAR EXPRESSION

JavaScript allows you to construct a regular expression in one of two ways, using an object initializer, as in

```
RegularExpression = /ab+c/
```

Object initializers provide compilation of the regular expression when the script is evaluated. When the regular expression will remain constant, use this for better performance.

The second approach to constructing a regular expression is to call the constructor function of the **RegExp** object, as in

```
RegularExpression = new RegExp("ab+c")
```

Using the constructor function provides runtime compilation of the regular expression. Use the constructor function when you know the regular expression pattern will be changing, or you don't know the pattern and are getting it from another source, such as user input. Once you have a defined regular expression, if the regular expression is used throughout the script and if its source changes, you can use the compile method to compile a new regular expression for efficient reuse.

You create a regular expression pattern using simple characters, such as /abc/, or a combination of simple and special characters, such as /a*bc/.

Using Simple Patterns

Simple patterns are constructed of characters for which you want to find a direct match. For example, the pattern /ABC/ searches for character combinations in strings only when the characters "ABC" occur together in exactly that order. Such a match would succeed in the strings "The ABCs of Nutrition."

Special Searches

When the search for a match requires finding one or more x's, or finding whitespace, the pattern includes special characters. For example, the pattern /a*bc/ searches for any character combination in which any number of "a's" (0 or more) is followed by "b" and then immediately followed by "c." In the string "aaaabaabcbbbbcdec," the pattern matches the substring "aabc." Table 11.6 provides a complete list and description of the special characters that can be used in regular expressions.

Table 11–6: *Special Characters in Regular eExpressions*

Character	Meaning
\	Indicates that the next character is special and not interpreted literally. For example, /b/ matches the character "b." By placing a backslash in front of b, that is, by using /\b/, the character becomes special to mean match a word boundary. Or, * is a special character that means 0 or more occurrences of the preceding character should be matched; for example, /b*/ means match 0 or more b's. To match * literally, precede it with a backslash; for example, /b*/ matches "b*."

Table 11–6: *Special Characters in Regular Expressions (Continued)*

Character	Meaning
^	Searches for beginning of input or line. For example, /^T/ does not match the "T" in "a Thesis A" but does match it in "The thesis."
$	Searches for end of input or line. For example, /g$/ does not match the "g" in "gingham," but does match it in "plug."
*	Searches for the preceding character 0 or more times. For example, /go*/ matches "goooo" in "A gooooey mess" and "goo" in "A good girl," but nothing in "A boat sank."
+	Searches for the preceding character 1 or more times. Equivalent to {1,}. For example, /a+/ matches the "a" in "Sandy" and all the a's in "Raaaaaaaid!"
?	Searches for the preceding character 0 or 1 time. For example, /e?le?/ matches the "el'" in "angel" and the "le" in "angle."
.	The decimal point matches any single character except the newline character. For example, /.n/ matches "an" and "on" in "nay, an apple is on the tree," but not "nay."
(x)	Searches for "x" and remembers the match. For example, /(foo)/ matches and remembers "foo" in "foo bar." The matched substring can be recalled from the resulting array's elements [1], ..., [n], or from the predefined RegExp object's properties $1, ..., $9.
x|y	Searches for either "x" or "y." For example, /black|white/ matches "black" in "black car" and "white" in "white car."
{n}	Where n is a positive integer. Matches exactly n occurrences of the preceding character. For example, /a{2}/ doesn't match the "a" in "candy," but it matches all of the a's in "caandy," and the first two a's in "caaandy."
{n,}	Where n is a positive integer. Searches for at least n occurrences of the preceding character. For example,

Table 11–6: (Continued)

257

11 Finctions and Objects

Character	Meaning
	/a{2,} doesn't match the "a" in "candy" but matches all of the a's in "Saandy" and in "Raaaaaaaid!"
{n,m}	Where n and m are positive integers. Searches for at least n and at most m occurrences of the preceding character. For example, /a{1,3}/ matches nothing in "Sndy," the "a" in "candy," the first two a's in "Saandy," and the first three a's in "Raaaaaaaid!" Notice that when matching "Raaaaaaaid!" the match is "aaa," even though the original string had more a's in it.
[xyz]	A character set. Searches for any one of the enclosed characters. You can specify a range of characters by using a hyphen. For example, [abcd] is the same as [a-c]. They match the "b'" in "brisket" and the "c" in "ache."
[^xyz]	A negated or complemented character set. That is, it searches for anything that is not enclosed in the brackets. You can specify a range of characters by using a hyphen. For example, [^abc] is the same as [^a-c]. They initially match "r" in "brisket" and "h" in "chop."
[\b]	Searches for a backspace. (Not to be confused with \b.)
\b	Searches for a word boundary, such as a space. (Not to be confused with [\b].) For example, /\bn\w/ matches the "no" in "noonday";/\wy\b/ matches the "ly" in "possibly yesterday."
\B	Searches for a nonword boundary. For example, /\w\Bn/ matches "on" in "noonday," and /y\B\w/ matches "ye" in "possibly yesterday."
\cX	Where X is a control character. Searches for a control character in a string. For example, /\cM/ matches control-M in a string.
\d	Searches for a digit character. Equivalent to [0-9]. For example, /\d/ or /[0-9]/ matches "2" in "B2 is the suite number."

Table 11–6: *Special Characters in Regular Expressions (Continued)*

Character	Meaning
\D	Searches for any nondigit character. Equivalent to [^0-9]. For example, /\D/ or /[^0-9]/ matches "B" in "B2 is the suite number."
\f	Searches for a form feed.
\n	Searches for a line feed.
\r	Searches for a carriage return.
\s	Searches for a single whitespace character, including space, tab, form feed, line feed. Equivalent to [\f\n\r\t\v]. For example, /\s\w*/ matches " bar" in "foo bar."
\S	Searches for a single character other than whitespace. Equivalent to [^ \f\n\r\t\v]. For example, /\S/\w* matches "foo" in "foo bar."
\t	Searches for a tab.
\v	Searches for a vertical tab.
\w	Searches for any alphanumeric character including the underscore. Equivalent to [A-Za-z0-9_]. For example, /\w/ matches "a" in "apple," "5" in "$5.28," and "3" in "3D."
\W	Searches for any nonword character. Equivalent to [^A-Za-z0-9_]. For example, /\W/ or /[^$A-Za-z0-9_]/ matches "%" in "50%."
\n	Where n is a positive integer. A back reference to the last substring matching the n parenthetical in the regular expression (counting left parentheses). For example, /apple(,)\sorange\1/ matches "apple, orange," in "apple, orange, cherry, peach." A more complete example follows this table. Note: If the number of left parentheses is less than the number specified in \n, the \n is taken as an octal escape as described in the next row.
\ooctal\xhex	Where \ooctal is an octal escape value or \xhex is a hexadecimal escape value. Allows you to embed ASCII codes into regular expressions.

Navigator Object

The term *navigator object* applies to client-side JavaScript objects and differentiates them from user-defined server-side objects. When you load a document in the Navigator browser, it creates a number of JavaScript objects with property values based on the HTML in the document along with additional application-specific information. These objects form the object hierarchy seen in Figure 11.4.

When viewing the Navigator object hierarchy, each object's descendants or children are considered properties of the object. For example, Layer is a property of *document* and is referenced using the member dot operator as *document.Layer*.

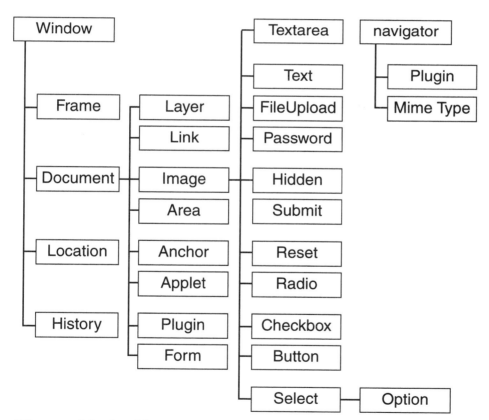

Figure 11–4:   *Navigator object hierarchy.*

For each window you create, Navigator creates the following standard set of objects:

navigator — containing the Navigator name and version, the plug-ins installed, and the MIME types suported by the client.

window — containing the properties that apply to the entire window. This top-level *window* object is created for each child window in a frame document.

document — has properties based on the current content of the document, for example, the title, color, anchors, links, and forms.

location — URL-based properties.

history — URL-based properties list of sites previously visited.

Reflection refers to the relationship between JavaScript object properties and their supporting counterpart with your HTML document. JavaScript uses a one-to-one, top-down, display relationship between your HTML elements and their display formats. For example, the following HTML FORM contains several text-input elements:

```
<FORM NAME="address">
<INPUT TYPE ="text" name = "firstName" size = 35>
<INPUT TYPE="text" name = "phone" size = 12>
```

After the form is defined, your JavaScript program can use these form elements:

```
document.address.firstName
document.address.phone
```

Suppose you want to print the values of each object within your JavaScript. You would simply write

```
<SCRIPT>
document.write(document.address.firstName.value)
document.write(document.address.phone.value)
</SCRIPT>
```

In these examples the HTML *firstName* and *phone* elements are reflected in their counterpart JavaScript object's *document.address .firstName* and *document.address.phone*. However, remember there is an order to these events. If you tried to execute the previous two statements above their definitions in the HTML document, you would get an error, since the objects do not exist yet in Navigator. The Navigator object is discussed in detail in Chapter 21.

Using Objects

Normally, an object-oriented solution to a programming problem requires a ground-up design philosophy change over the procedural solution. In an object-oriented world objects are usually based on or derived from previously defined objects, inferring a base/parent/root to child or subclass family structure.

For example, a tire company database would revolve around a *parent_tire* object with common member data, such as *tire_diameter*, *tire_cost*, *tire_materials*, *tire_quantity*, and common methods, such as *howManyInStock()*, and *showTire()*. This base/parent/root object would then pass these members into actual objects that would be instantiated, such as *snowTire*, *rainTire*, *allSeasonTire*, and so on, with each child object adding its own set of member data, and inherited method code updates as needed.

If you are new to the world of object-oriented programming, the good news is that JavaScript does *not* support this syntax. Instead, JavaScript uses a syntax that resembles object-oriented technologies but in reality works more like a procedural language. In this sense, then, you would approach the solution to your programming problem in JavaScript the way you would in most older high-level languages by breaking a large problem down into smaller, more easily managed steps. The only difference is that the standalone functions you would have conceived in a procedural language will syntactically morph into member functions or method syntax.

Although JavaScript does not provide all of the features of full object-oriented programming languages, such as C++, it does provide a suite of object-based features that are specially tailored to browser and server scripting.

Properties

JavaScript properties are used to access the data values contained in an object. Properties, by default, can be updated as well as read, although some properties of the predefined JavaScript objects are marked read-only. Accessing an object's properties involves using the object's name, followed by the period member operator (.) and then the property name, as in

```
objectIdentifier.objectProperty
```

For example, the foreground color of the current Web document is defined by the **fgColor document** object. If you wanted to alter the color used to render text to the display monitor, you would use the following syntax:

```
document.fgColor="blue"
```

The following JavaScript demonstrates this approach:

```
<HTML>
<HEAD>
<TITLE>Changing Text fgColor Property</TITLE>
</HEAD>
<BODY>
<H1>RGB Text Colors</H1>
<FORM>
<P><INPUT TYPE="BUTTON" NAME="RED" VALUE="Red"
   ONCLICK='document.fgColor="red"'>
<INPUT TYPE="BUTTON" NAME="GREEN" VALUE="Green"
   ONCLICK='document.fgColor="green"'>
<INPUT TYPE="BUTTON" NAME="BLUE" VALUE="Blue"
   ONCLICK='document.fgColor="blue"'></P>
document.write("<BR>The color chosen is: = ", docu-
ment.fgColor)
</FORM>
</BODY>
</HTML>
```

Figure 11.5 displays the resulting output.

Invoking Methods

You access an object's member functions, or methods, with the same member operator used for object properties or data members. The syntax looks like

```
objectIdentifier.objectMethod([optional_argument_list])
```

When the *optional_argument_list* is included, individual arguments are separated by commas.

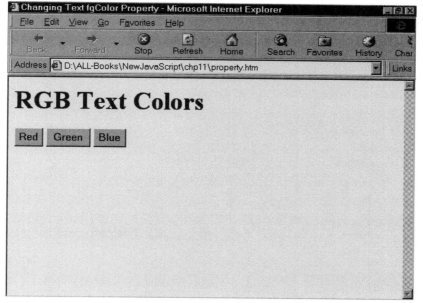

Figure 11–5: *Setting the document.fgColor property.*

A Complete Example

The following example uses many of the concepts discussed in this chapter to create an object-oriented mail-order request. Following this complete program listing, the discussion sections break the algorithm down into its required components.

```
<HTML>
<HEAD>
<TITLE>Interactive Mail Order</TITLE>
<SCRIPT LANGUAGE="JavaScript"
<!-- hide from non-JavaScript aware browsers
// displayOrder method definition
function displayOrder() {
   document.write("<H1>OnLine Merchants Thanks You for
your " + "order!" + ì</H1><HR><PRE>")
document.write("Customer Name: " + this.name +
"<BR>")
document.write("Product Ordered:  " + this.product +
"<BR>")
document.write("Product Cost: " + this.cost + "<BR>")
document.write("</PRE>")
}
//mailOrder object definition
function mailOrder() {
```

```
    this.name=prompt("Please Enter Your Name: ",
"name")
    this.product=prompt("Please Enter Product Name: ",
"product")
    this.cost=prompt("Please Enter Product Cost: ",
"cost")
    this.displayOrder.displayOrder
}
anOrder = new mailOrder()
// --> end hide from non-JavaScript aware browsers
</SCRIPT>
</HEAD>
<BODY>
<SCRIPT LANGUAGE="JavaScript">
<!-- hide from non-JavaScript aware browsers
anOrder.displayOrder();
// --> end hide from non-JavaScript aware brtowsers
</SCRIPT>
</BODY>
</HTML>
```

The formal description of the mailOrder object begins with an object description:

```
//mailOrder object definition
function mailOrder() {
    this.name=prompt("Please Enter Your Name: ",
"name")
    this.product=prompt("Please Enter Product Name: ",
"product")
    this.cost=prompt("Please Enter Product Cost: ",
"cost")
    this.displayOrder.displayOrder
}
```

that interactively prompts the user for *name, product,* and *cost* data members (see Figures 11.6, 11.7, and 11.8), and the *displayOrder* method.

Notice the use of the **this** pointer. **this** is a JavaScript keyword that represents the memory address, or alias, of the object currently in scope.

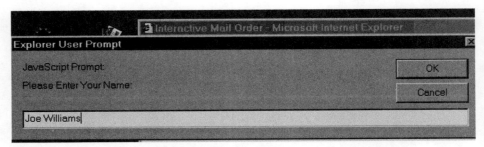

Figure 11-6: *JavaScript prompting for customer name.*

Figure 11–7:   *JavaScript prompting for product.*

```
// displayOrder method definition
function displayOrder() {

   document.write("<H1>OnLine Merchants Thanks You for
your " + "order!" + ì</H1><HR><PRE>")
document.write("Customer Name: " + this.name +
"<BR>")
document.write("Product Ordered:  " + this.product +
"<BR>")
document.write("Product Cost: " + this.cost + "<BR>")
document.write("</PRE>")
}
```

Of course, defining a *mailOrder* object and *displayOrder()* method does not *instantiate* an actual memory object. To do this your JavaScript needs to make a call to the **new** operator:

```
anOrder = new mailOrder()
```

This statement actually places into memory a *mailOrder* object by the name *anOrder* and launches the interactive input mode.

Display output is generated with the following statement:

```
anOrder.displayOrder();
```

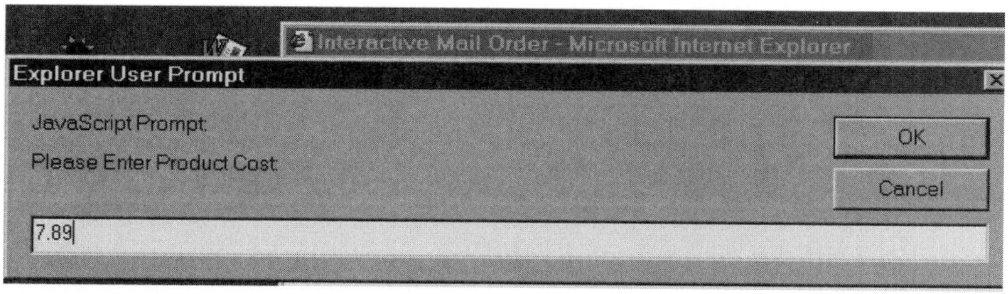

Figure 11–8:   *JavaScript prompting for cost.*

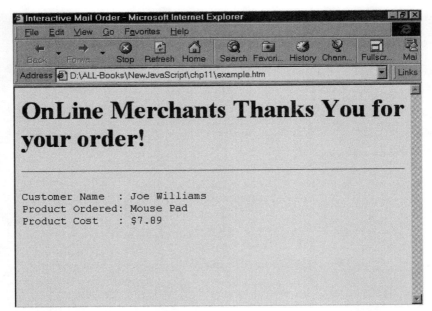

Figure 11–9: *Interactively entered product information.*

which outputs the interactively entered product information to the user for verification (see Figure 11.9).

Summary

In this chapter you learned the "good news"–that objects don't give you anything you didn't already have as a programmer, just a more robust syntax. You now understand the fundamental concepts involved with declaring and using objects and the simpler high-level language, such as the use of JavaScript functions. The next chapter will illustrate how you associate some interactive responses to objects via JavaScript events.

CHAPTER 12 EVENTS

- Events
- Responding to Events
- Event Handlers
- Event Objects
- Object Properties

Welcome to the world of push-button programming! Well, almost! Today's programming languages are much more automated than ever before. With robust, powerful objects pulled into your program with a single line of code and event-driven algorithms, code shells are almost self-generating.

If you've ever used an older high-level language such as Pascal and tried to add a mouse interface, you know what it is like to write brute-force code in Assembly Language, assemble the file, write the Pascal driver, compile it, and then hopefully link everything together to get it working. Well, today's languages assume you want to use the mouse and provide internal routines to report this information.

However, JavaScript, for example, goes much further and ties mouse-movement reports into more useful information. Back to the Pascal/Assembly Language example. Once you had the mouse recognized by the Pascal driver, you still had to write subroutines to check the reported mouse coordinates against an application-specific set of screen coordinates to know if the user was over anything of program interest. JavaScript combines these frequently needed capabilities into what are called events.

What Are Events?

Events are reported actions generated by the user. Events are triggered by your browser and include information on when a page has finished loading, when the user is entering data in a form, or clicking on a control—such as a radio button or checkbox. All of this automation makes for much easier algorithm design.

In a way, you can imagine first using a paint program to generate the visual image for a Web page, including titles, menus, lists, hotlinks, forms, and images. With the Web page "painted," you can, as the artist turned programmer, simply say, "Now all I have to do is decide what I want my program to do when the user moves the mouse over..., or clicks on... ." It's that easy!

Examples of signaled actions include when a user clicks on a hypertext link, changes data in a form entry field, or when a page finishes loading. A complete list of the events available in JavaScript appears in Table 12.1.

Table 12–1: *JavaScript Events*

JavaScript Event	Description
abort	Generated by user canceling a load image command.
blur	Generated when the input focus is removed from a form element or focus is removed from a window.
change	Generated when the value of a form field is changed by the user.

Table 12–1: *JavaScript Events   (Continued)*

JavaScript Event	Description
click	Generated when the user clicks on a form or link element.
dragdrop	Generated when the user drops an object onto the browser window, such as dropping a file on the browser window.
error	Generated when an error occurs during the loading of a document or image.
focus	Generated when input focus is applied to a window or form element.
keydown	When user depresses a key.
keyup	When user releases a key.
load	Generated when a page is loaded into the browser.
mousedown	When user depresses a mouse button.
mousemove	When user moves the mouse.
mouseout	Generated when the user positions the mouse pointer off a clickable area or link.
mouseover	Generated when the user moves the pointer over a hypertext link.
mouseup	When user releases a mouse button.
move	When the user or script moves a window.
reset	Generated when the user clears a form using the Reset button.
resize	When the user or script resizes a window.
select	Generated when the user clicks on a form element.
submit	Generated when the user clicks on the Submit Form button.
unload	Generated when the user exits a page.

Responding to Events

Once a JavaScript has received a flagged event, it uses an *event handler* to process the user's action. Event handlers are scripts, in the form of attributes of specific HTML tags, which you as the programmer can write. The syntax for an event handler looks like

```
<HTML ATTRIBUTES eventHandler="JavaScript code">
```

Usually the *JavaScript code* is a call to a function defined in the header of the document or a single JavaScript command. However, any JavaScript statement, method, or function may appear inside the quotation marks of the *eventHandler*. While syntactically legal, the code style of placing an entire *eventHandler*'s code within the *JavaScript code* makes for a difficult program to view or modify and is not recommended. It also easily precludes the reuse of the *JavaScript code* in other programs. Table 12.2 lists the HTML attributes and their associated JavaScript events.

Table 12–2: HTML Attributes and Associated JavaScript Events

HTML Tag(/s)	JavaScript Event	Description
<A>...</A>	click	Generated when user clicks on a hotlink.
	mouseOver	Generated when the user moves the mouse over the hotlink.
	mouseOut	Generated when the user moves the mouse from over the hotlink.
<IMG>	abort	Generated when the user aborts an image load.
	error	Generated when there is a problem loading an image.
	load	Generated when the user has loaded and displayed an image.

HTML Tag(/s)	JavaScript Event	Description
<AREA>	mouseOver	Generated when the mouse is moved over an area of an image map.
	mouseOut	Generated when the mouse is moved outside an image map.
<BODY>... </BODY>	blur	Generated when the document loses the input focus.
	error	Generated when an error occurs when loading a document.
	focus	Generated when a document receives the input focus.
	load	Generated when the document is finished loading.
	unload	Generated when the user exits the document.
<FRAMESET>... </FRAMESET>	blur	Generated when a frame loses the input focus.
	error	Generated when an error occurs loading a frame set.
	focus	Generated when a frame set receives the input focus.
	load	Generated when a frame set has finished loading.
	unload	Generated when the user exits a frame set.
<FRAME>... </FRAME>	blur	Generated when a frame loses the input focus.

Table 12–2: HTML Attributes and Associated JavaScript Events   (Continued)

HTML Tag(/s)	JavaScript Event	Description
	focus	Generated when a frame receives the input focus.
<FORM>... </FORM>	submit	Generated when a form is submitted by the user.
	reset	Generated when the user resets a form.
<INPUT TYPE= "text">	blur	Generated when a text field loses the input focus.
	focus	Generated when a text field receives the input focus.
	change	Generated when a text field is modified and loses the input focus.
	select	Generated when the mouse moves over a text field.
<TEXTAREA>... </TEXTAREA>	blur	Generated when a text area loses the input focus.
	focus	Generated when a text area receives the input focus.
	change	Generated when a text area is changed and loses the input focus.
	select	Generated when the text is selected within the text area.
<INPUT TYPE= "button">	click	Generated when a button is depressed.
<INPUT TYPE= "submit">	click	Generated when a submit button is depressed.

Table 12–2: *HTML Attributes and Associated JavaScript Events (Continued)*

HTML Tag(/s)	JavaScript Event	Description
<INPUT TYPE= "reset">	click	Generated when a reset button is depressed.
<INPUT TYPE= "radio">	click	Generated when a radio button is depressed.
<<INPUT TYPE= "checkbox">		Generated when a check box is clicked.
<SELECT>... </SELECT>	blur	Generated when a selection element loses the input focus.
	focus	Generated when a selection element receives the input focus.
	change	Generated when a selection element is changed and loses the input focus.

Each JavaScript event is processed by one or more of the event handlers listed in Table 12.3.

Table 12–3: *JavaScript Controls and Related Event Handlers*

JavaScript Control	Available Event Handler(s)
Button element	onClick
Checkbox	onClick
Clickable image	onMouseOver, onMouseOut
Document	onLoad, onUnload, onBlur, onFocus, OnResize
Form	onSubmit, onReset
Framesets	onBlur, onFocus
Hypertext link	onClick, onMouseOver, onMouseOut

Table 12–3: *JavaScript Controls and Related Event Handlers*

JavaScript Control	Available Event Handler(s)
Image	onLoad, onError, onAbort
Radio button	onClick
Reset button	onClick
Selection list	onBlur, onChange, OnFocus
Submit button	onClick
Text elements	onBlur, onChange, onFocus, onSelect, onDblClick
Textarea element	onBlur, onChange, onFocus, onSelect
Window	onLoad, onUnload, onBlur, onFocus

Your First In-line Event Handler

Two of the simplest and most frequently used JavaScript event handlers are the **onLoad** and **onUnload**. The **load** event is generated whenever a page has completed loading. An **unload** event is automatically generated whenever the user exits the page. The **onLoad** and **onUnload** events are set as attributes to the HTML BODY tag. The following HTML document uses this syntax to automatically cause the browser to output two messages (see Figures 12.1 and 12.2).

```
<HTML>
<HEAD>
<TITLE>Using onLoad and onUnload Event
Handlers</TITLE>
<BODY onLoad="alert('Hello World!');"
      onUnload="alert('Have a GREAT day!');"
</BODY>
</HTML>
```

Table 12.4 describes the event handlers available in JavaScript.

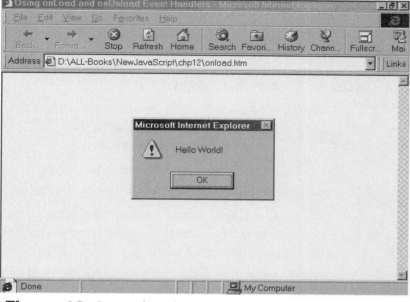

Figure 12–1: *onLoad event handler.*

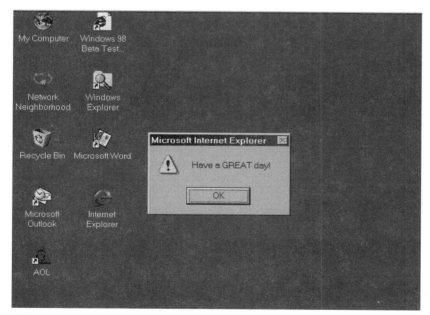

Figure 12–2: *onUnload event handler.*

Table 12–4: *JavaScript Event Handlers*

JavaScript Attribute	Description
onAbort	Identifies code to be executed when the loading of an image is aborted.
onBlur	Identifies code to be executed when a document, text field, text area, selection, or frame set loses the input focus.
onChange	Identifies code to be executed when a text field, text area, or selection is changed.
onClick	Identifies code to be executed when a button (radio, reset, checkbox, submit), link, or image is clicked.
onDragDrop	Identifies code to be executed when an object is dropped onto the browser window, such as dropping a file on the browser window.
onError	Identifies code to be executed when an error occurs.
onFocus	Identifies code to be executed when a document, text field, text area, selection, or frame set receives the input focus.
onKeyDown	Identifies code to be executed when user depresses a key.
onKeyPress	Identifies code to be executed when user presses or holds down a key.
onKeyUp	Identifies code to be executed when user releases a key.
onLoad	Identifies code to be executed when a document, image, or frame set is loaded.
onMouseDown	Identifies code to be executed when user depresses a mouse button.
onMouseMove	Identifies code to be executed when user moves the mouse.
onMouseOut	Identifies code to be executed when the mouse moves out of a link or image.

Table 12–4: *JavaScript Event Handlers*   *(Continued)*

277

Events

12

JavaScript Attribute	Description
onMouseOver	Identifies code to be executed when the mouse is moved over a link or image.
onMouseUp	Identifies code to be executed when user releas a mouse button.
onMove	Identifies code to be executed when user or script moves a window.
onReset	Identifies code to be executed when a reset button is depressed.
onResize	Identifies code to be executed when user or script resizes a window.
onSelect	Identifies code to be executed when when text is selected within a text field or area.
onSubmit	Identifies code to be executed when the submit form button is depressed.
onUnload	Identifies code to be executed when the user exits a document or frame set.

Methods for Creating Event Handlers

Today's popular browsers support two basic event handler methods:

- Those based on an HTML attribute
- Those using an event property

This example improves upon the simple approach used in the previous HTML document by incorporating a function to process an **onClick** event handler script in the body of the tag (see Figure 12.3).

```
<HTML>
<HEAD>
<TITLE>Your First onClick Event Handler
Function</TITLE>
```

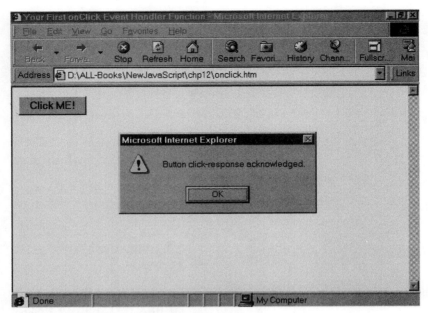

Figure 12–3: onClick button response.

```
<SCRIPT LANGUAGE="JavaScript">
<!-- hide from non-JavaScript aware browsers

function FirstAlert() {
   alert("Button click-response acknowledged.");
}

// --> stop hiding from non-JavaScript aware browsers
</SCRIPT>
</HEAD>

<BODY>

<FORM NAME="aForm">
<INPUT TYPE="button" NAME="aButton" VALUE="Click ME!"
onClick="FirstAlert()">
</FORM>

</BODY>
</HTML>
```

A second approach used in assigning a function to a specific event
handler is to use an assignment to an object's event handler property
as in this next example:

```
<HTML>

<HEAD>
```

```
<TITLE>Your First onClick Event Handler
Reference</TITLE>

<SCRIPT LANGUAGE="JavaScript">
<!-- hide from non-JavaScript aware browsers

function FirstAlert() {
  alert("Button click-response acknowledged.");
}

// --> stop hiding from non-JavaScript aware browsers
</SCRIPT>
</HEAD>

<BODY>

<FORM NAME="aForm">
  <p><INPUT TYPE="button" NAME="aButton" VALUE="Click
ME!">
</FORM>


<SCRIPT LANGUAGE="JavaScript">
<!-- hide from non-JavaScript aware browsers

document.aForm.aButton.onclick = FirstAlert;

// -->
</SCRIPT>

</BODY>
</HTML>
```

Internet Explorer 4.0 Explicit Event Handler Scripts

The following section highlights the exclusive approach used by Internet Explorer 4.0's *explicit event handler scripts*. An explicit event handler script is an ordinary script that executes only when a specific event occurs for a given object. The problem with the following algorithm

```
<SCRIPT LANGUAGE="JavaScript" EVENT="onclick" FOR="doc-
ument">
<!--

alert("Clike ME!");
```

```
// -->
</SCRIPT>
```

is that the alert dialog box pops up immediately when you load the page. However with Internet Explorer 4.0x, the script is executed only when a click event EVENT="onclick" occurs for the **document** object FOR="document." Notice that the EVENT attribute gets an event handler, not an event. When dealing with a button's event handler, the script must be placed within the form, unless the button has a unique identifier:

```
<FORM>
<INPUT TYPE="button" NAME="aButton" VALUE="Click
ME!">
<SCRIPT LANGUAGE="JavaScript" EVENT="onclick"
FOR="aButton">
<!--

alert("Button click-response acknowledged.");

// -->
</SCRIPT>
</FORM>
```

For browsers that do not support the EVENT and FOR attributes of the <SCRIPT> tag the code snippet is simply ignored, so the script executes *immediately* when the page loads.

Understanding Event Objects

An event object holds detailed information about an event, such as the type of event, the exact position of the mouse cursor when it occurred, and the object currently under the cursor. Navigator and Explorer 4.0 implement event objects in different ways. Internet Explorer 4.0 uses the **this** object pointer as a property of the window object, so it is specified as window.event. The window object is the default one, so it is not necessary. Thus, the word event simply refers to the event object.

However, under Netscape Navigator 4.0 the event object is passed to the event handler function as an argument if the event handler is specified via the property assignment method. When it is specified as an HTML attribute, you must explicitly provide the event object to the function. The function that processes the event must have a parameter in order to refer to the event object.

Writing a cross-browser event processing function requires the use of a formal argument in order to process a Navigator 4.0's event object. The algorithm also needs to perform an object detection routine to know how to refer to the event object The following example shows how to write a function that is executed when you depress the mouse button:

```
<HTML>

<HEAD>
<TITLE>Explorer and Navigator Event
Processing</TITLE>
</HEAD>

<BODY>


<SCRIPT LANGUAGE="JavaScript">
<!-- hide from non-JavaScript aware browsers

var isNavigator = window.Event ? true : false;

function crossBrowserProcessor(IsNavigatorParam) {
   if (isNavigator) {
      // use IsNavigatorParam
   } else {
      // use "window.event" processor
   }
}

if (isNavigator)
   document.captureEvents(Event.MOUSEMOVE);
   document.onmousedown = crossBrowserProcessor;

// --> stop hiding from non JavaScript aware browsers
</SCRIPT>

</BODY>
</HTML>
```

The conditional statement

```
var isNavigator = window.Event ? true : false;
```

decides which browser is active by seeing if it supports the window.Event object. The critical issue here is actually the single letter *E* in *window.Event*, since it could be *window.event*. Only Internet Explorer 4.0 supports the *e window.event* object that executes only when the event occurs. Navigator 4.0 just supports the *E window.Event* object.

When the variable *isNavigator* evaluates to true, the browser is Navigator 4.0 and the function accesses the event object by referring to the *isNavigatorParam* formal argument:

```
if (isNavigator) {
   // use IsNavigatorParam
} else {
   // use "window.event" processor
}
```

Otherwise, the function should access the event object by specifying its name: event, when an event handler is defined as an HTML attribute, and the event object is explicitly handed to the function

Cross-Browser Event Object Properties

With both Internet Explorer 4.0 and Netscape Navigator 4.0 as equally viable end-user target browsers, writing cross-browser–aware JavaScript event object handlers requires a bit of finesse. Table 12.5 lists the Internet Explorer 4.0 and Netscape Navigator 4.0 equivalent event object properties.

Table 12–5: *Cross-browser Event Object Properties*

Description	Internet Explorer 4.0		Navigator 4.0	
	Property	**Value**	**Property**	**Value**
Defines which keys were pressed when the event occurred.	*altKey* *ctrlKey* *shiftKey*	*Boolean*	*modifiers*	*Event object properties*
Defines the horizontal coordinate of the mouse cursor at the time of the event.	*clientX*	**Integer**	*pageX*	**Integer**
Defines the vertical coordinate of the mouse cursor at the time of the event.	*clientY*	**Integer**	*pageY*	**Integer**

Table 12–5: *Cross-browser Event Object Properties (Continued)*

Description	Internet Explorer 4.0 Property	Value	Navigator 4.0 Property	Value
Defines the horizontal coordinate of the mouse cursor at the time of the event.	**screenX**	**Integer**	**screenX**	**Integer**
Defines the vertical coordinate of the mouse cursor at the time of the event, with respect to the client's screen.	**screenY**	**Integer**	**screenY**	**Integer**
A reference of the object for which the event is intended.	*srcElement*	**Object**	*target*	**Object**
Defines the event type, for example, *mousedown*, *click*, *keypress*. The string represents an event, not an event handler.	**type**	**String**	**type**	**String**
Defines the mouse button or keyboard key code. Certain code values differ from one browser to the next.	*button keyCode*	**Integer**	*which*	**Integer**

Italicized table entries represent properties and data types that are *different* between the two browsers while entries in **bold** represent those properties and data types that are *identical* in each browser. Also, Table 12.5 details only those properties supported by both browsers and that both browsers, while sharing the same property, do *not* share the same property name. For example, both browsers have the *target* property but Internet Explorer 4.0 uses the form *srcElement* property.

Capturing Events in Internet Explorer 4.0

Microsoft's Internet Explorer 4.0 captures an event by an object when the event reaches it instead of using an explicit function for capturing events at the window or document level. If the object doesn't have such an event handler, the event is released. Netscape Navigator 4.0 uses the two methods, captureEvents() and releaseEvents(), to capture and release events.

The equivalent under Internet Explorer 4.0 is to specify an event processing function to capture an event. The following script segment captures all click events that occur on the document:

```
<SCRIPT LANGUAGE="JavaScript">
<!-- hide from non-JavaScript aware browsers

document.onclick = yourFunctionName;

// --> stop hiding from non-JavaScript browsers
</SCRIPT>
```

For example, if you put the following script in your HTML document, an alert dialog box pops up when you click anywhere on the document:

```
<SCRIPT LANGUAGE="JavaScript">
<!-- hide from non-JavaScript aware browsers

function onClicksHandler() {
  alert("Mouse button-response acknowledged.");
}

document.onclick = onClicksHandler;

// --> stop hiding from non-JavaScript aware browsers
</SCRIPT>
```

Turning Off an Event Handler in Internet Explorer 4.0

Without the usual Navigator captureEvents() method to capture events at a high level and the counterpart releaseEvents() method to stop capturing the events, Internet Explorer 4.0 disables event handlers by deleting them! For example, the following statement defines an onclick event handler for the document object:

```
document.onclick = myFunction;
```

However, the next example effectively *turns off* the event handler:

```
document.onclick = null;
```

When the event handler property is assigned the value of *null*, it does not have any function associated with it to process the event. You can also use this approach under Netscape Navigator 4.0.

Canceling Event Processing

There will be times in an interactive session with the user where you may want to cancel an action. You can easily produce this result by writing an event handler that simply returns the Boolean **false**, as in this next example:

```
<FORM NAME="anyForm" ACTION="type">
// ...
<INPUT TYPE="submit" VALUE="submit">
</FORM>

<SCRIPT LANGUAGE="JavaScript">
<!-- hide from non-JavaScript aware browsers.

function cancelFromSubmitAction() {
  return false; // cancel Form Submit
}

document.anyForm.onsubmit = cancelFormSubmitAction;

// --> stop hiding from non-JavaScript aware
browsers.
</SCRIPT>
```

Every object in Internet Explorer 4.0 contains an event.returnValue property that is **true** or **false**. A return value of **false** cancels the default action of the source element of the event. The value of this property takes precedence over values returned by the function, such as through a **return** statement. Here's the previous example using the returnValue property instead of the *cancelFormSubmitAction()* function used in the previous example.

```
<FORM NAME="anyForm" ACTION="type">
.
.
.
<INPUT TYPE="submit" VALUE="submit">
</FORM>

<SCRIPT LANGUAGE="JavaScript">
<!-- hide from non-JavaScript aware browsers.

function cancelFormSubmitAction() {
  window.event.returnValue = false; // cancel event
}

document.myForm.onsubmit = cancelFormSubmitAction;

// --> stop hiding from non-JavaScript aware
browsers.
</SCRIPT>
```

The **returnValue** property is essential for languages that don't support return values. However, JavaScript does support return values, so you should stick with the **return** statement (remember this is an Internet Explorer 4.0 exclusive property).

When to Capture an Event

Netscape Navigator 4.0 uses the captureEvents() method to capture events outside of its intended target (in the window, layer, or document object). For example, the following code segment captures all mousemove events in the document:

```
document.captureEvents(Event.MOUSEMOVE);
document.onmousemove = myFunction;
```

However, Internet Explorer 4.0 uses event bubbling. Here, an event is first directed to the element that initiated the event. Internet

Explorer 4.0 does not use the captureEvents() method, Instead, *you* must make sure it is not executed under Internet Explorer 4.0. The following statements use object detection to define a cross-browser event capturing routine:

```
// under Navigator 4.0
if (window.Event)
  document.captureEvents(Event.MOUSEMOVE);
document.onmousemove = myFunction;
```

Only the second statement is executed on Internet Explorer 4.0 and older browsers.

Automatic Events

One additional programming option provided by JavaScript is the automatic generation of certain types of events. The following list enumerates those user responses that your program can automatically generate:

- blur()
- click()
- focus()
- reset()
- select()
- submit()

These JavaScript methods, used within your program, can fully automate the process of guiding the user through various options, focusing their attention, and even automatically sending completed forms.

Detecting Modifier Keys

Both Internet Explorer 4.0 and Navigator 4.0 have different ways of detecting what modifier keys were pressed down when an event occurred. Netscape Navigator 4.0's modifier keys are reflected in one property: modifiers. This property must be used against a constant property of the event object with the bites AND operator in order to find out which modifier keys were pressed when the event occurred. So the following example,

```
e.modifiers & Event.CTRL_MASK
```

evaluates to a Boolean value indicating the state of the Ctrl key when the event occurred. However, Internet Explorer 4.0 provides a separate property for each modifier key. These properties (alt, ctrl, shift) have a Boolean value, so no operator is required to extract the desired information. Take a look at the following example:

```
<HTML>

<HEAD>
<TITLE>Checking for Ctrl, Alt, and Shift</TITLE>

<SCRIPT LANGUAGE="JavaScript">
<!-- hide from non-JavaScript aware browsers.

var isNavigator = window.Event ? true : false;

function keyCheck(NavParam) {
   if (isNavigator) {
      document.keys.ctrl.checked = NavParam.modifiers &
      Event.CONTROL_MASK;
      document.keys.alt.checked = NavParam.modifiers &
      Event.ALT_MASK;
      document.keys.shft.checked = NavParam.modifiers &
      Event.SHIFT_MASK;
        } else {
            document.keys.ctrl.checked =
window.event.ctrlKey;
            document.keys.alt.checked =
window.event.altKey;
            document.keys.shft.checked =
window.event.shiftKey;
   }
   return false;
}

// --> stop hiding from non-JavaScript aware
browsers.
</SCRIPT>

</HEAD>

<BODY>
```

```
<P>Press Ctrl, Alt, or Shift then ->
<A HREF="javascript:doNothing(0)"
   onMouseDown="return keyCheck(event)"
   onClick="return false">Click ME!</A>.</P>
<FORM NAME="keys">
<INPUT TYPE="checkbox" NAME="ctrl"> Control
<INPUT TYPE="checkbox" NAME="alt"> Alt
<INPUT TYPE="checkbox" NAME="shft"> Shift
</FORM>

</BODY>
</HTML>
```

The output from the program looks like Figure 12.4.

To make certain that a URL link isn't executed, the function doNothing() makes certain no user-defined function is executed. The program begins by using the onmousedown event handler to return the value that is returned by the keyCheck() function, which is false, canceling the default operation of the event. Not canceling the event forces the browser to begin a save document operation when the link was clicked with the Shift key pressed. The onclick event handler was included in a similar manner in order to cancel the click events.

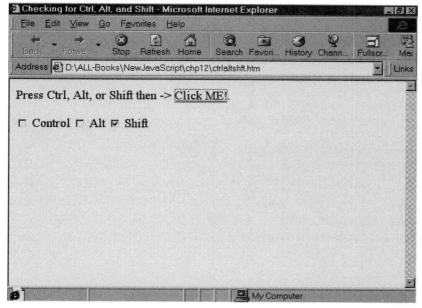

Figure 12–4: *Detecting Ctrl, Alt, and Shift keys.*

With the onmousedown event handler defined as an HTML attribute rather than a JavaScript property, the event handler must explicitly hand the event object to the event processing function. This explains the use of the event object in the event handler script. The keyword event refers to the window.event object in Internet Explorer 4.0x.

Internet Explorer and Netscape Navigator Button Detection

Once again, the two popular browsers approach the subject of button detection in slightly different ways. Internet Explorer 4.0 uses one property to detect what mouse button was pressed and a second property to detect what key was pressed. In Navigator 4.0 one property handles both cases. The following example demonstrates this (see Figure 12.5).

```
<HTML>
<HEAD>
<TITLE>Key Code Processing</TITLE>

<SCRIPT LANGUAGE="JavaScript">
<!-- hide from non-JavaScript aware browsers.

var isNavigator = window.Event ? true : false;

function keyValue(NavParam) {
  if (isNavigator)
     // Using Navigator 4.0
     var KeyCode = NavParam.which
   else
     // Using Internet Explorer 4.0
     if (NavParam.type == "keypress")
        // user entered a character
        var KeyCode = NavParam.keyCode
      else
        var KeyCode = NavParam.button;

  if (NavParam.type == "keypress")
    window.status = "kepressed = " + KeyCode +
                    ", character entered = " +
                    String.fromCharCode(KeyCode)
    else
```

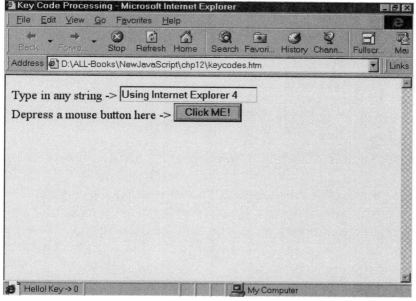

Figure 12–5: Detecting button presses in Internet Explorer 4.0.

```
        window.status = "Hello! The KeyCode is -> " +
KeyCode;
}

// --> stop hiding from non-JavaScript aware
browsers.
</SCRIPT>

</HEAD>

<BODY>

<FORM NAME="Key Code Processing">
Type in any string ->
<INPUT TYPE="text"
        NAME="key"
        SIZE="25"
        onKeyPress="keyValue(event)"><BR>
Depress a mouse button here ->
<INPUT TYPE="button"
        NAME="mouse"
        VALUE="Click ME!"
        onClick="if (isNavigator || window.event)
keyValue(event)">
</FORM>

</BODY>
</HTML>
```

You've already seen how the first conditional (?:) statement determines if this script is being run under Netscape Navigator 4.0 or Internet Explorer 4.0. Since the onclick event handler is supported by *older versions* of NetScape Navigator and Internet Explorer, its script is executed by all JavaScript-enabled browsers. Notice how the if guarantees that the keyValue() function isn't executed unless the user is running the latest versions of these popular browsers. Without the if statement, event handler would generate an error.

Notice (in Figures 12.5 and 12.6) that the code for the primary mouse button differs. In Internet Explorer 4.0 the value is 0, whereas in Navigator 4.0 it is 1. Furthermore, browsers don't let you trap for this user event. Right-clicks in Windows 95 or NT, for example, display a context-sensitive pop-up menu, without passing the event to the page. For this reason your JavaScript doesn't usually check which mouse button the user clicked.

Other differences between the browsers include the Backspace key generating a click event on Navigator, but not on Internet Explorer, and several key values differ. Since the only key codes that differ are infrequently used nonalphanumeric keys, use the String.fromCharCode() to evaluate the code rather than the character itself.

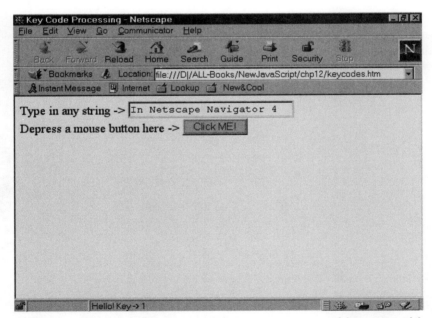

Figure 12–6: *Detecting button presses in Netscape Navigator 4.0.*

Summary

In this chapter you have discovered just how easy it is to add interactivity to an object using JavaScript event handlers, especially since many of the frequently used JavaScript objects come complete with a usable set of previously defined events. In the next chapter you will drop back to a more familiar pace by discussing JavaScript array syntax and usage.

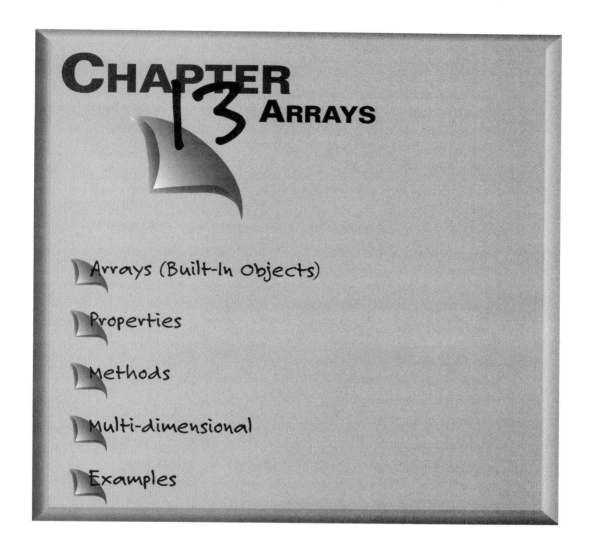

CHAPTER 13 ARRAYS

- Arrays (Built-In Objects)
- Properties
- Methods
- Multi-dimensional
- Examples

Arrays, by definition, are contiguous memory allocations of homogeneous data types. In traditional programming languages they come in two forms: static or dynamic. Static array declarations define arrays whose memory allocation is generated at load time and have a syntax similar to

```
data_type array_name[number_of_elements];
```

This type of array definition allocates a fixed-size memory segment. Dynamic array definitions use the language's dynamic-memory-allocation keyword, usually **new**, as in

```
data_type *array_pointer_name;
```

```
array_pointer_name = new data_type[number_of_elements];
```

The only advantage to this approach is that you can, at runtime, repeatedly execute calls to **new**, creating as many arrays as you need and/or use the identifier *number_of_elements* as a variable, rather than a constant, allowing the user, at runtime, to supply the number of required elements. Either way, you circumvent the fixed size limitation of static array definitions.

With all that said, however, JavaScript breaks the mold. First, JavaScript arrays do *not* necessarily contain homogeneous elements. Second, they are dynamic in nature, by default, meaning you can extend their dimension at runtime with additional assignments!

For a top-down structured programmer trained to use modularization and consistent code structure, this crossover between static/dynamic, pure array element type/record or structured element types appears to be design chaos, but actually it has its advantages.

Arrays as Built-in Objects

JavaScript provides a built-in array object that allows you to create and manipulate arrays in your JavaScript code. Arrays have their own set of properties and methods.

Array Properties

The array property *length* returns the number of elements contained in the array, as in

```
array_name[0]  is  11
array_name[1]  is  22
array_name[2]  is  33
array_name[3]  is  44
```

This array contains four elements.

Array Methods

JavaScript provides three useful routines for manipulating array contents: the *sort()*, *reverse()*, and *join()* methods.

ARRAY SORT() METHOD

One of the operations most frequently applied to array contents is the sort. JavaScript anticipates this need and provides a sort() method. This method allows you to sort arrays in one of two ways. The first syntax involves not specifying an argument when calling the method, as in

```
array_name.sort()
```

This syntax converts the contents of the array to strings and sorts them in alphabetical order.

Unsorted Array

```
array_name[0]  is  Baker
array_name[1]  is  Charlie
array_name[2]  is  Able
array_name[3]  is  1
```

Default Ascending Sort Order

```
array_name[0]  is  1
array_name[1]  is  Able
array_name[2]  is  Baker
array_name[3]  is  Charlie
```

For sort orders other than the default string-type ascending, you will need to define your own comparison method. This comparison method is passed to the sort() method in order to determine the sorting of the array.

The syntax for calling the sort() method looks like

```
array_name.sort( mycompare_method );
```

The following unsorted array

```
array_name[0]  is  10
array_name[1]  is  1
```

```
array_name[2]  is  NAN
array_name[3]  is  4
array_name[4]  is  34
```

when sorted numerically becomes

```
array_name[0]  is  1
array_name[1]  is  4
array_name[2]  is  10
array_name[3]  is  34
array_name[4]  is  NAN
```

mycompare_method() could contain the standard bubble sort–type algorithm which would use the relational operators $<$ or $>$ to compare consecutive array elements, rather than using the JavaScript default mode of converting the contents to their equivalent ASCII values and then performing a sort on the numeric relationships embedded in the ASCII table, which of course could not generate the previous order.

Note

The function mycompare_method() that you write must return an integer in the range 0, >0, or <0. Your algorithm needs to return 0 when the two entries are identical, <0 when in ascending order, and >0 when elements are in descending order.

THE REVERSE() ARRAY SORT METHOD

Once again, if a default, string-type sort suits your needs, JavaScript provides a descending order method called *reverse()*. This method reverses the order of entries in an array. The unsorted array looks like

```
array_name[0]  is  Able
array_name[1]  is  Baker
array_name[2]  is  Charlie
array_name[3]  is  1
```

and reversed becomes

```
array_name[0]  is  Charlie
array_name[1]  is  Baker
array_name[2]  is  Able
array_name[3]  is  1
```

Whenever you have a need to combine array elements, as in the case where successive elements contain recordlike contents, use the array *join()* method. This method returns a string created by joining together, or concatenating, all the entries in the array similar to the Java toString() method.

The syntax for using *join()* looks like

```
array_name.join( [ character_separator ] )
```

where *array_name* is the array whose entries are to be joined together by the *join()* method. The optional *character_separator* parameter allows you to specify the character, or separator, which appears between each of the individual entries in the concatenated string. If a *character_separator* is not supplied, *join()* defaults to using a comma, as in

```
array_name[0]  is  azalea
array_name[1]  is  dogwood
array_name[2]  is  rose
array_name[3]  is  hyacinth
array_name[4]  is  carnation
```

when *join()*ed by default generates the following string

```
"azalea,dogwood,rose,hyacinth,carnation"
```

Alternately,

```
array_name.join('-')
```

with a hyphen generates the following string

```
"azalea-dogwood-rose-hyacinth-carnation"
```

SPECIAL CHARACTERS

The following section lists several of the *special characters* you may need to search for or embed within your strings:

**"hard" space : **

- **&** : &
- **< >** : < >
- **é É** : é É

- -or- **é É** : é É *(you can always use the decimal value of the ISO character set)*
- **À à** : À à **è ì ò ù** : è ì ò ù
- **Â â ô** : Â â ô
- **ç Ç** : ç Ç
- **ñ Ñ** : ñ Ñ
- **ä ë ï ö ü** : ä ë ï ö ü
- **å ø ¶** : **å ø ¶**

Size Limits on JavaScript Array Initialization

JavaScript array objects have a size limit of 256 elements maximum for

```
var array_name = new Array (element1, element2, …, ele-
ment256)
```

Using Arrays

Arrays provide a way to store lists. They are variables that have an *offset* number corresponding to different *elements* in the list.

For example, you may want to store the following list of names: Lexus, BMW, Mercedes, and Lamborghini. You have created an array called *dream_cars*. You could store these names in the array with assignment statements, such as, dream_cars[2]="Mercedes", and dream_cars[0]="Lexus". Then, you could access the array elements by addressing them with their *offset*. For example,

```
    var car_show = ""
    for(var offset=0; offset<dream_cars.length;
++index) {
        car_show += dream_cars[offset]
    }
```

First, this example demonstrates how arrays are always indicted by an *offset* in square brackets following the name. Second, arrays always have a property called *length*, which is the number of elements in the array. Third, the smallest *offset* in an array is always zero. Thus, the largest index in any array is always one less than the number of elements in the array. For example, the largest valid index in an array of length 25 is 24.

Many of the newer programming languages, such as Java and JavaScript, have their roots in C/C++. In the case of C, which is officially a middle-level language, you have a language closer to Assembly Language in origin than to a true high-level language like PL/I, Fortran, and COBOL. In Assembly Language, the name of an array is actually the offset address in memory defining the location of the first array element. The syntax for accessing Assembly Language array elements (actually they are called tables in Assembly Language) is similar to most high-level languages:

```
table_name[offset]
```

This syntax adds the numeric value of *offset* to the address stored in the *table_name* and then references the data at that address. Since the *table_name* already points to the first element, an *offset* value of 0 gets you there. For programmers new to C/C++, Java, and JavaScript, accessing the first element of an array with an *offset* of 0 instead of an *index* of 1 is a bit confusing.

To compound the mapping over from some older high-level language to these newer evolutions, a programmer once accustomed to starting at an *offset* of 0 *forgets* that the last legal *offset* value is *number_of_elements-1!* Where does that get them into trouble? Think of a standard **for** loop construct in Pascal, for example,

```
for(index=1, index <= NUMBER_OF_ELEMENTS,
index=index+1)
begin
   process all array elements
end
```

Translated into C or C++, Java, or JavaScript to the JavaScript newbie might look like

```
for(var index = 0; index <= NUMBER_OF_ELEMENTS;
index++)
ouch!
```

What's wrong with this mapping? Well it starts off gangbusters by changing the starting point from *1* to *0*. However, unlike older high-level language **for** loops which access array elements *to their last*

NUMBER_OF_ELEMENTS value, C/C++/Java and JavaScript must go to *n-1* as in

```
for(var index = 0; index < NUMBER_OF_ELEMENTS; index++)
```

and to be technically correct, why not go all the way and change the identifier *index* to *offset* since that is really what it is. :)

```
for(var offset = 0, offset < NUMBER_OF_ELEMENTS; off-
set++)
```

One final note, the *offset* value is actually an internal calculation based on the current *offset* assigned times the number of bytes occupying each element.

The tricky part about using your own arrays is creating them. In JavaScript an array is a special case of an object, so creating an array is very similar to creating a custom object. Unlike most other computer languages in which you just declare an array, in JavaScript you must have a constructor function for the array and you must use the **new** command in an assignment statement to call the constructor function. To create the array in the example above,

```
function makedream_cars() {
    this.length=4
    this[0] = "Lexus"
    this[1] = "BMW"
    this[2] = "Mercedes"
    this[3] = "Lamborghini"
}

dream_cars = new makedream_cars()
```

You can see in this example that the length property of the array must be set explicitly in the constructor and that the constructor is used to initialize every element in the array.

Object Array Elements

Because an array is a custom object, in addition to being a list of strings or numbers, it can also be a list of objects. That is, each array element can be initialized with a **new** statement to be an object. For example, if each of the names in the example given above had roof_type and a vintage associated with it, then each element may be an object, which is initialized by a constructor function for this object.

This would require the JavaScript to have two constructor functions: one for the array, as in

```
function initializeDreamCarsArray(number_of_cars) {
  this.length = number_of_cars
  for(var offset = 0; offset < number_of_cars; off-
set++) {
    this[offset] = ""
 }
}
```

and one for the objects in the array, as in the example here:

```
function defineA_Car(manufacturer,roof_type,vintage) {
  this.manufacturer = manufacturer
  this.roof_type = roof_type
  this.vintage = vintage
}
  garage = new initializeDreamCarsArray(4)
  garage[0] = new defineA_Car("Lexus","hardtop",1995)
  garage[1] = new defineA_Car("BMW","softtopF",1956)
  garage[2] = new defineA_Car("Mercedes","hard-
top",1963)
  garage[3] = new defineA_Car("Lamborghini","hard-
top",19978)
  document.write(garage[2].vintage+" "+garage[2].manu-
facturer+" a real bute!")
```

In this example, we create an array called *garage*, initialize each element of that array with an object which has three properties, *manufacturer*, *roof_type*, and *vintage*, and then print out two of the properties of one of the objects in the array.

The complete program looks like

```
<HTML>
<HEAD>
<TITLE>Auto-Sales Weekly</TITLE>
<SCRIPT LANGUAGE="JavaScript">
<!— hide from non-JavaScript aware browsers
//array creation routines
function initializeDreamCarsArray(number_of_cars) {
  this.length = number_of_cars
  for(var offset = 0; offset < number_of_cars; off-
set++) {
    this[offset] = ""
 }
}
```

```
function defineA_Car(manufacturer,roof_type,vintage) {
  this.manufacturer = manufacturer
  this.roof_type = roof_type
  this.vintage = vintage
}
// --> stop hiding from non-JavaScript aware browsers
</SCRIPT>
</HEAD>
<BODY>
<SCRIPT LANGUAGE="JavaScript">
<!-- hide from non-JavaScript aware browsers
garage = new initializeDreamCarsArray(4)
garage[0] = new defineA_Car("Lexus","hardtop",1995)
garage[1] = new defineA_Car("BMW","softtopF",1956)
garage[2] = new defineA_Car("Mercedes","hardtop",1963)
garage[3] = new defineA_Car("Lamborghini","hard-
top",1978)
document.write(garage[2].vintage+" "+garage[2].manu-
facturer+" is a real bute!")
// —> stop hiding from non-JavaScript aware browsers
</SCRIPT>
</BODY>
</HTML>
```

The output from the program looks like Figure 13.1.

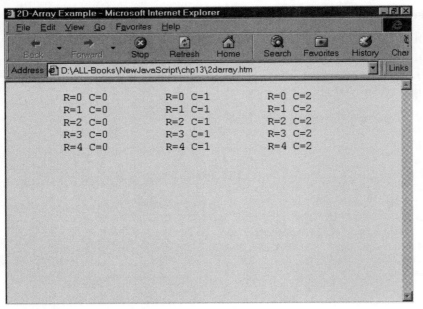

Figure 13–1: *Auto Sales weekly output.*

Two-Dimensional Arrays

An array element can itself be an array. Arrays of arrays are often called two-dimensional arrays because they clearly resemble two-dimensional tables with rows and columns. This next example uses a two-dimensional array. First the array is created; then it is initialized with strings which indicate the current row and column. At this point the entire array is output to the display screen:

```
<HTML>
<HEAD>
<TITLE>2D-Array Example</TITLE>
<SCRIPT LANGUAGE="JavaScript">
<!- hide from non-JavaScript aware browsers
//array creation routines
function createColumns(Rows,Columns) {
 this.length=Rows
 for(var CurrentRow=0; CurrentRow<Rows; CurrentRow++)
{
    this[CurrentRow] = "\t"+"R="+Columns+"
C="+CurrentRow+"\t"
 }
}
function createRows(Rows,Columns) {
  this.length=Rows
  for(var CurrentRow=0; CurrentRow<Rows;
CurrentRow++) {
    this[CurrentRow] = new
createColumns(Columns,CurrentRow)
  }
}
// stop hiding from non-JavaScript aware browsers
</SCRIPT>
</HEAD>
<BODY>
<SCRIPT LANGUAGE="JavaScript">
<!- hide from non-JavaScript aware browsers
_2D_Array = new createRows(5,3)
document.writeln("<pre>")
for(var Row=0;Row<_2D_Array.length;Row++) {
  for(var
Column=0;Column<_2D_Array[Row].length;Column++) {
    document.write(_2D_Array[Row][Column])
  }
  document.write("\n")
```

```
}
document.writeln("</pre>")
// -> stop hiding from non-JavaScript aware browsers
</SCRIPT>
</BODY>
</HTML>
```

The output from the program looks like Figure 13.2.

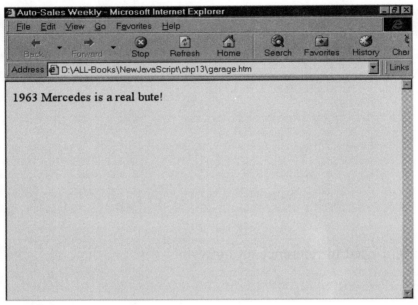

Figure 13–2: *Two-dimensional array output.*

The split() Method

Whenever your JavaScript is sent a stream of information in string format, you can use the *split()* method to perform a substring operation, separating each "word" within the string based on a *split_character*. For example, the string "staples, glue, tacks, folders" could be substringed as in

```
var myString = "staples, glue, tacks, folders"
var myArray = myString.split(" ")
```

which will give the following values:

```
myArray[0] = "staples"
myArray[1] = "glue"
myArray[2] = "tacks"
myArray[3] = "folders"
```

Anchors and links are discussed briefly in this chapter since an array of each is maintained by the JavaScript **document** object (this topic is discussed in greater detail in Chapter 21). Anchors are names of sections of a page, assigned by HTML anchor tags. The **document** object maintains an array of anchors and another array of links, as in

```
<A name="example"></A>
```

In this next example, the links represent hypertext links to URLs or partial URLs, also created by HTML anchor tags, as in

```
<A HREF="arrays.html"></A>
```

Since JavaScript arrays are objects which have a length property, the number of anchors in a document is `document.anchors.length` and the number of links is `document.links.length`. The reference `document.anchors[0]` points to the first anchor object in the document and `document.links[0]` will reference the first link.

Anchor objects do not have any properties or methods, so you will never have a need to reference an individual anchor object. To navigate to a particular anchor, your JavaScript must know its name and then use the `hash` property of the `window.location` object, as in

```
window.location.hash = "example"
```

Summary

While the concept of an array is similar in most high-level languages, in this chapter you have discovered that referencing elements within an array vary among programming languages. In particular, the first element in a JavaScript array is at position 0 not 1! This also translates into a reference change for the last element in the array which goes from a more traditional value of n (n being the number of elements in the array) to n-1.

Simple enough until you either get confused and begin incorrectly declaring your array to be n-1, or, more subtly, forgetting to change statements that use array references of 1 to 10 instead of JavaScript 0 to 9 (for an array of 10 elements). For example, consider test conditions that used to read **while...** <= to the number of array elements (*n*)..., that must now be rewritten **while...**< the number of array elements (*n*-1).

At this point attention now returns to object-oriented programming fundamentals. The next chapter discusses the topic of controls and the various types, such as list boxes, radio buttons, checkboxes, and so on. The good news is that once you learn the terminology, these individual controls are fairly automatic and easy to use.

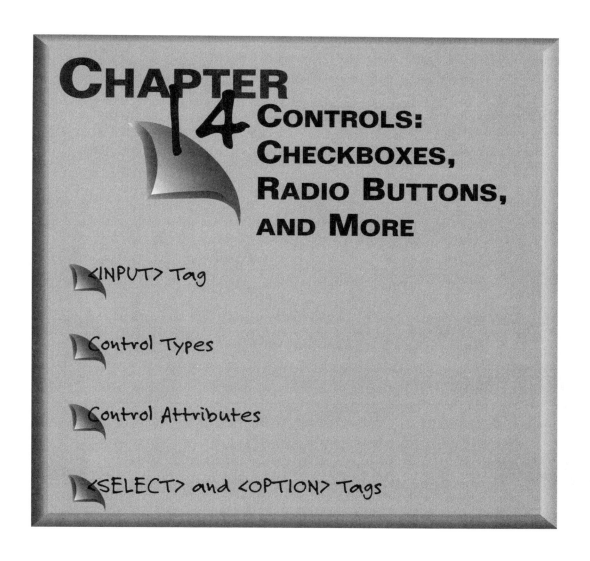

CHAPTER 14

CONTROLS: CHECKBOXES, RADIO BUTTONS, AND MORE

- <INPUT> Tag

- Control Types

- Control Attributes

- <SELECT> and <OPTION> Tags

As you have already learned, HTML forms are defined as documents that contain normal content, markup, and combinations of elements called controls. A variety of controls can be used to accept and respond to input from the user. This input may be as simple as a button click or a menu selection. User input can also include paragraphs of text entered at the keyboard. A server-side CGI script processes information sent to the server, as you learned in Chapter 9.

In this chapter you will learn, in more detail, how to create forms with buttons, text areas, checkboxes, and so on. You'll also see how to interact with many of these controls with simple JavaScript. A form can contain a wide variety of controls, but it cannot contain another form. In other words, forms cannot be nested.

The <INPUT> Tag

The HTML <INPUT> element serves as the starting point for adding buttons, checkboxes, passwords, and so on to a form. The syntax for the <INPUT> element is

```
<INPUT type="element_type" name="ref_name">
```

Each type of input is entered as a CGI name/value pair. The element_type defines the field's screen appearance while ref_name represents a keyword referenced by the server's CGI script. The server's CGI script is used to process the form's data.

Table 14.1 lists and describes various <INPUT> types.

Table 14–1: *<INPUT> Element Types*

Input Type	Description
Button	A type of push button with no default behavior.
Checkbox	An on/off type switch. Active when "on." Multiple checkboxes within a group can be checked.
File	Prompts the user for a file name.
Hidden	The user agent does not render this input type. The element's name and value are submitted with the form.
Image	A type of submission push button using a graphical image as the button.
Password	A single-line text entry box that allows text to be entered, but characters are hidden from view with a series of asterisks.
Radio	An on/off type switch. Active when "on." Only one radio button is a group can be set active. Multiple groups are permitted, however.

Table 14–1: *Continued*

Input Type	Description
Reset	A type of push button which when activated resets all of the form's controls back to the initial values.
Submit	A type of push button which when activated submits the form's contents.
Text	Single-line text entry box.

An attribute name is required for all controls except submit and reset. Table 14.2 lists a variety of new attributes encountered with these <INPUT> types.

Table 14–2: *Input Element Type Attributes*

Attribute	Description
Type	Type of control needed.
Name	Submit as part of the form.
Value	Required for radiobuttons and checkboxes.
Checked	Used by radiobuttons and checkboxes to indicate selection.
Disable	Control is not available in this context.
Readonly	Used for text and passwords.
Size	Specific to each type of field. For example, size gives the width, in characters, of a text control.
Maxlength	Maximum number of characters for a field.
Src	For fields using images.
Alt	A short description.
Usemap	Use a client-side image map.
Align	Use for vertical or horizontal alignment.
Tabindex	Position in tabbing order.
Accesskey	Accessibility key character.
onFocus	The element receiving the focus.

Table 14–2: *Input Element Type Attributes (Continued)*

Attribute	Description
onBlur	The element losing the focus.
onSelect	The selected text.
onChange	The element value was changed.
Accept	List of MIME types for file upload.

In the next sections we'll examine each of the input type elements from Table 14.1 in more detail and see how to interact with many of these types with simple JavaScript.

The Button Type

This type creates a push button with no default behavior. Associating the button with client-side scripts (see Chapter 9) specifies the behavior of the button. These are activated when events pertaining to the button take place, such as a button push. The name of the value attribute is the button's label. In the following portion of code the function named mystart() will be executed when the button is pushed:

```
<INPUT type="button" name="Send" value="Push Me"

        onClick="mystart()">
```

In this example, the mystart() function is a small portion of JavaScript code that responds to the click event.

If you need to reference the name property of this button, use a portion of code similar to this:

```
var NameOfButton = document.forms[0].Send.name
```

The name of the button can be changed by using code similar to this:

```
document.forms[0].Send.name = "NewName"
```

In a similar manner the value property of this button can be returned with the following portion of code:

```
var ValueOfButton = document.forms[0].Send.value
```

The value property can be changed with another small portion of code:

```
document.forms[0].Send.value = "A New Value"
```

The following is a complete HTML document that changes the push button label (value) of the push button from "Push Me" to "Quit."

```
<HTML>
<HEAD>
<TITLE>Test Program</TITLE>
<SCRIPT LANGUAGE="JavaScript">

function mystart() {
   document.forms[0].Send.value = "Quit"
}

</SCRIPT>
</HEAD>
<BODY>
<FORM>
<INPUT type="button" name="Send" value="Push Me"
       onClick="mystart()">
</FORM>
</BODY>
</HTML>
```

The Checkbox Type

The Checkbox type behaves like on on/off switch. This action can represent on/off, true/false, yes/no, and so on. The checkbox is "active" when the switch is on and "inactive" when the switch is off. The checkbox value is submitted with the form when the checkbox is active.

A form may contain multiple checkboxes with the same name attribute. These are considered a group. On submission, each active checkbox in a group sends its name/value pair. This action allows multiple checkboxes to be selected by the user.

Checkboxes are usually small rectangular areas that can contain a check mark or "x" when selected. Checkboxes can use the value and checked attributes.

```
<INPUT type="checkbox" name="Checker"
       value="Interesting" checked
       onClick="CheckInfo()">Check Me In!
```

In this example, the CheckInfo() function is a small portion of JavaScript code that responds to the click event. Using a portion of code similar to this can reference the name property of this checkbox:

```
var NameOfCheck = document.forms[0].Checker.name
```

Using code similar to this can change the name of the checkbox:

```
document.forms[0].Checker.name = "NewName"
```

In a similar manner the value property of this checkbox can be returned with the following portion of code:

```
var ValueOfCheck = document.forms[0].Checker.value
```

The value property can be changed with another small portion of code:

```
document.forms[0].Checker.value = "Not Interesting!"
```

The following is a complete HTML document that accesses the checkbox value. The value was initialized when the checkbox was created.

```
<HTML>
<HEAD>
<TITLE>Test Program</TITLE>
<SCRIPT LANGUAGE="JavaScript">

function CheckInfo() {
   alert(document.forms[0].Checker.value)
}

</SCRIPT>
</HEAD>
<BODY>
<FORM>
<INPUT type="checkbox" name="Checker"
```

```
                value="Interesting" checked
                onClick="CheckInfo()">Check Me In!
</FORM>
</BODY>
</HTML>
```

The checkbox is initially checked since the checked attribute was specified. You might have noted that the checkbox's label is specified in a unique manner. This is because the name and value attributes are used internally. To label a checkbox, simply place the label after the checkbox, as you have seen in the previous example.

The File Type

This type prompts the user for a file name. When the form is submitted, the contents of the file as well as any user input are submitted to the server.

Multiple files should send files in a MIME multipart document.

The Hidden Type

This type is not visible. However, the element's name and value are submitted with the form rendered by the user agent.

This unique text field is frequently used to send information to a CGI script.

For example,

```
<INPUT type="hidden" name="Additional_Information"
         value=""New_Input.html">
```

The Image Type

This type creates a graphical image that is used to represent a submit type button. The value of the src attribute is used to specify the URL of the image. Since it is possible that the image might not be viewable by all users, a text alternative should also be specified with the alt attribute.

When the image is clicked, the form is submitted and the X,Y coordinates of the mouse are passed to the server. The X coordinate increases from left to right and is measured in pixels. The Y coordinate increases from top to bottom and is also measured in pixels. Submitted data is passed as name.x=X coordinate and name.y=Y coordinate using the name attribute.

A possible future extension to image is to add the usemap attribute to <INPUT> for use as a client-side image map when type=image. In this manner the area element corresponding to the mouse location when the image is clicked would be passed to the server.

The Password Type

This type behaves like a single-line text element. However, as each character is entered, it is replaced on the screen with an asterisk. The actual text is submitted by the password control. No actual encoding takes place for the characters typed.

Password fields are frequently used on forms for entering passwords and sensitive information. A password field can use the maxlength, size, and value attributes. For example,

```
<INPUT type="password" name="Social_Security"
       value="" maxlength="9" size="9"
       onChange="GetInfo()">
```

In this example, the maximum length of the information submitted by the user is nine characters. The width of the password control is also set to nine.

Here is a complete HTML document that will allow the user to enter a nine-digit social security number. When the onChange event occurs, a small JavaScript function uses alter() to print the actual data to the screen by accessing the value property.

```
<HTML>
<HEAD>
<TITLE>Test Program</TITLE>
<SCRIPT LANGUAGE="JavaScript">
```

```
function GetInfo() {
  alert(document.forms[0].Social_Security.value)
}

</SCRIPT>
</HEAD>
<BODY>
<FORM>

<INPUT type="password" name="Social_Security"
       value="" maxlength="9" size="9"
       onChange="GetInfo()">

</FORM>
</BODY>
</HTML>
```

It looks like the secret information isn't that secret after all!

The Radio Type

This type behaves like an on/off switch. This action can represent on/off, true/false, yes/no, and so on. The radio button is "active" when the switch is on and "inactive" when the switch is off. The radio button value is submitted with the form when the radio button is active.

A form may contain multiple radio buttons with the same name. These are considered a group. On submission, only one radio button in a group sends its name/value pair. This action allows only a single radio button in a group to be selected by the user. Forms may contain several groups of radio buttons, however.

Radio buttons are similar to checkboxes except that they are usually represented as small round circles. When a radio button is active, a "dot" is placed in the center of the image. Radio buttons can use the name, value, and checked attributes. Here is how to create a single radio button:

```
<INPUT type="radio" name="FamilySize"
       value="" checked onClick="Info()">LARGE
```

The checked attribute identifies this radio button as the default button if it is part of a group.

The following listing is a complete HTML document that accesses one of three radio buttons in a group. The first button is initially checked.

A small JavaScript function alerts the user when a radio button is selected from the group.

```
<HTML>
<HEAD>
<TITLE>Test Program</TITLE>
<SCRIPT LANGUAGE="JavaScript">

function Info() {
   alert("A radio button selection has been made.")
}

</SCRIPT>
</HEAD>
<BODY>
<FORM>

<INPUT type="radio" name="FamilySize"
       value="" checked onClick="Info()">LARGE
<P>
<INPUT type="radio" name="FamilySize"
       value="" onClick="Info()">Medium
<P>
<INPUT type="radio" name="FamilySize"
       value="" onClick="Info()">small

</FORM>
</BODY>
</HTML>
```

You may have noted that the radio button's label behaves in a manner similar to the checkbox control. This is because the name and value attributes are used internally. To label a radio box, simply place the label after the radio button, as in the previous example.

Radio buttons will align themselves horizontally. If a number of buttons are used, the group will wrap to the next line. To force a vertical alignment, use the <P> tag.

The Reset Type

This type allows a form's controls to be reset. When this control is activated by the user, it returns all controls on the form to the initial values specified in the control's value attributes. The name/value pair are not submitted with the form.

```
<INPUT type="reset" value="A New Beginning">
```

The reset button is automatically sized to the text that is entered.

The Submit Type

The submit type allows a form to be submitted to the location given by the action attribute of the parent <FORM>.

Forms may contain multiple submit buttons. Only the active submit button's name/value pair are submitted with the form.

```
<INPUT type="submit" value="New Information">
```

The submit button is automatically sized to the text that is entered.

The Text Type

The text type creates a single-line text entry box. The value that is submitted by a text control is the input text entered by the user.

Text fields are frequently used on forms for entering names, addresses, social security numbers, and so on. A text field can use the maxlength, size, and value attributes. For example,

```
<INPUT type="text" name="Name_Information"
       value="" maxlength="20" size="10"
       onChange="GetNameInfo()">
```

In this example, the maximum length of the information submitted by the user is 20 characters. However, the width of the text control is limited to 10 characters. When more than 10 characters are entered, the control will scroll to accept the remaining characters. Text controls use onBlur, onChange, onFocus, and onSelect to respond to events.

Here is a complete HTML document that will allow the user to enter a 20-character name.

```
<HTML>
<HEAD>
```

```
<TITLE>Test Program</TITLE>
<SCRIPT LANGUAGE="JavaScript">

function GetNameInfo() {
   alert(document.forms[0].Name_Information.value)
}

</SCRIPT>
</HEAD>
<BODY>
<FORM>

<INPUT type="text" name="Name_Information"
       value="" maxlength="20" size="10"
       onChange="GetNameInfo()">

</FORM>
</BODY>
</HTML>
```

When the onChange event occurs, a small JavaScript function uses alert() to print the actual name to the screen by accessing the value property.

The HTML <BUTTON> Tag

The HTML <BUTTON> element allows you to expand types of buttons available for use. This element uses name, value, and type attributes. The name attribute assigns a name to the button while the value attribute assigns a value to the button. The type attribute can be submit, button, or reset. The submit value is used when submitting forms. The reset value is used to reset a form's values. The button value is used to trigger a script.

The syntax for the <BUTTON> element is

```
<BUTTON name="ref_name" value="element_value"
        type="element_type">
```

A <BUTTON> element using a submit type whose content is an image is similar to an <INPUT> element that uses an image type, the difference being that <INPUT> renders a "flat" image while

<BUTTON> renders a button with relief and an up/down motion when selected.

Here is an example of a <BUTTON> element using a submit type:

```
<BUTTON name="submit_me" value="submit" type"submit">
Send<IMG src="/graphics/doit.jpg" alt="doit">
</BUTTON>
```

In a similar manner a <BUTTON> element using the reset type is like an <INPUT> element using the reset type, but with features like those just described.

The HTML <SELECT> and <OPTION> Tags

The <SELECT> and <OPTION> elements are used together to create a drop-down list. The <SELECT> element uses name, size, and type attributes while the <OPTION> element uses the selected and values attributes. The name attribute assigns a name to the element and is paired with selected values when the form is submitted. The size attribute specifies the number of rows to be rendered. A scrolling mechanism should be used when the number of rows is less than the number of choices. The multiple attribute, when set, will allow multiple selections from the list. The selected attribute is used to identify a selection. The value attribute gives the value to be submitted when the <OPTION> is selected.

Here is a list, or menu, constructed of a <SELECT> element and several <OPTION> elements:

```
<SELECT size="3" name="selectinsect">
  <OPTION> Butterfly </OPTION>
  <OPTION selected> Ant </OPTION>
  <OPTION> Lady Bug </OPTION>
</SELECT>
```

In this example list, three items will be presented since the size attribute was set to 3. Ant is selected as the default choice by using the selected attribute.

The HTML <TEXTAREA> Tag

The <TEXTAREA> element is similar to the <INPUT> element using the text type. The main difference is that a text area allows multiple lines of text information to be entered by the user. This element uses the name, rows, and cols attributes. The name attribute assigns a name to the element and is paired with selected values when the form is submitted. The rows attribute identifies the number of lines that are to be visible within the area. Additional lines should be permitted and a scrolling mechanism should be provided. The cols attribute identifies the number of visible columns that are to be visible within the area. Longer lines should be permitted and a scrolling mechanism should be provided.

Here is an example that sets a 10-row by 30-column text entry area:

```
<TEXTAREA name="Story"
          cols = "30" rows = "10"
          onFocus="AddNew()">
```

If no default text is used, the </TEXTAREA> can immediately follow the <TEXTAREA> element. Text areas respond to events that can be handled by onBlur, onChange, onFocus, and onSelect.

Here is a complete HTML document that prints a short story to the text area. When the user clicks the mouse within the text area, the original text is replaced with a single line of text prompting the user to create his or her own short story.

```
<HTML>
<HEAD>
<TITLE>Test Program</TITLE>
<SCRIPT LANGUAGE="JavaScript">

function AddNew() {
  document.forms[0].Story.value = "Once upon a
time..."
}

</SCRIPT>
</HEAD>
<BODY>
<FORM>

<TEXTAREA name="Story"
          cols = "30" rows = "10"
          onFocus="AddNew()">
```

```
        Once upon a time there lived a little black
Manchester
Terrier.  As you might know, Manchester Terriers are
used to hunt rats.  However, having been separated
from
her mother at birth she never learned how to dispatch
rats.  Over time the little dog actually became a
friend
with a group of lucky rats.

        Now click inside of the text area and create
your own
story.
</TEXTAREA>

</FORM>
</BODY>
</HTML>
```

The JavaScript function is triggered when the text area receives focus via a mouse button click.

The HTML <LABEL> Tag

The HTML <LABEL> element is used to attach information to other control elements. The <LABEL> element uses the for attribute to associate the label with another control. For example, in a <TABLE> you might use the following:

```
<TABLE>
  <TR>
    <TD>
      <LABEL for="city">City Name
      </LABEL>
    <TD>
      <INPUT type="text" name=cityname" id="city">
  <TR>
    <TD>
      <LABEL for="state">State Name
      </LABEL>
    <TD>
      <INPUT type="text" name=statename" id="state">
</TABLE>
```

The for attribute can be used to associate more than one <LABEL> with a control.

The HTML <FIELDSET> and <LEGEND> Tags

The <FIELDSET> element is used to group related controls together. The <LEGEND> element is used to assign a caption to the <FIELD-SET> element.

The <LEGEND> element uses the align attribute to specify the position of the legend with respect to the fieldset. If a value of top is used (the default), the legend is above the fieldset. A value of bottom places the legend below the fieldset. A value of left or right places the legend to the left or right of the fieldset. For example,

```
<FIELDSET>
<LEGEND align="top">Patient Identification</LEGEND>
Social Security Number:
  <INPUT name="social_security" type="text">
  </INPUT>
</FIELDSET>
```

Element Characteristics

There are several ways an active element receives focus from a user. Focus can be achieved with a mouse, keyboard tabbing, or with the use of an access key, frequently called a shortcut or accelerator key. The use of a pointing device, such as a mouse, requires no special intervention. In the next sections we'll examine tabbing order and access keys. In addition, we'll examine how to disable or make elements read-only.

Tabbing Order

The tabbing order can be set with the tabindex attribute. The tabbing order is the order in which elements receive focus when navigated with the keyboard. The tabbing order can include nested elements. Navigation proceeds with elements with low tabindex values to elements with high tabindex value. Tabindex values need not be sequential. If elements are not provided with tabindex values, they are navigated in the order in which they appear in the HTML document. Disabled elements do not appear in the tabbing order. For example,

```
<INPUT tabindex="1" type="text" name="lastname">
<INPUT tabindex="2" type="text" name="firstname">
<INPUT tabindex="5" type="text" name="social_secu-
rity">
<INPUT tabindex="4" type="text" name="phone">
```

Here the tabbing order is 1, 2, 4, and 5 or lastname, firstname, phone, and social_security.

Access Key

An access key can be set with the accesskey attribute. The accesskey attribute assigns a single character from the document character set to act as the access key. When an access key is pressed, the identified element receives focus. For example,

```
<LABEL for="lname" accesskey="L">
Last Name
</LABEL>
<INPUT type="text" name="lastname" id="lname">
<LABEL for="fname" accesskey="F">
First Name
</LABEL>
<INPUT type="text" name="firstname" id="fname">
```

Access keys are activated under Windows by using the ALT key in conjunction with the defined access key. Apple systems use the CMD key in conjunction with the defined access key.

Disable

When the disabled attribute is used with an element, the element will not receive focus. In addition, the element will not be present in the tabbing order and the control's value will not be submitted with the form. The rendering of disabled elements depends upon the user agent, but most frequently the element is "grayed" to indicate that it has been disabled.

In the following example, the third element has been disabled:

```
<INPUT tabindex="1" type="text" name="lastname">
<INPUT tabindex="2" type="text" name="firstname">
<INPUT disabled tabindex="5" type="text"
name="social_security">
<INPUT tabindex="4" type="text" name="phone">
```

Read-only

When the read-only attribute is used with an element and is set, the element prohibits changes. Elements identified as read-only receive focus but cannot be changed. The elements are included in the tabbing order and their values are submitted with the form. For example:

```
<TEXTAREA readonly name="mystory" rows="2" cols="20">
This is my story:
</TEXTAREA>
```

Summary

Forms are a key element in HTML documents and JavaScript makes the interaction with form controls very easy. In this chapter you learned how to create forms with buttons, text areas, checkboxes, and so on. You also learned how to interact with these controls with simple JavaScript.

CHAPTER 15 STRINGS

- String Data Type
- String Object
- String Methods
- Conversions
- Examples

The ability to manipulate string information in any language is very important. In JavaScript you'll find that manipulating string and character information is very easy. By definition, a string is simply a collection of individual characters. In JavaScript, a character is handled as if it were a one-character length string. Individual characters in a string can be referenced by using an index value. Like arrays, the first character in a string is assigned an index value of zero.

In this chapter you'll learn how to work with character and string information in JavaScript.

String Data Type and String Object

In JavaScript, a string data type is created with the following syntax:

```
var myStr = "This is my string."
```

An equivalent form is to use single quotes:

```
var myStr = 'This is my string.'
```

The only restriction is that the types of quotes surrounding a string must match. The text between the quotation marks is converted to a string object by JavaScript when needed. To specifically create a string object, use the following syntax:

```
var myStr = new String("This is my string.")
```

Here, *myStr* is the name of the string object. The String() constructor function is responsible for converting the string between quotation marks into a string object.

In the following HTML document a string data type and a string object are created. The typeof() method is used to report the type of each variable.

```
<HTML>
<HEAD>
<TITLE>Test Program</TITLE>
</HEAD>
<BODY>
<SCRIPT LANGUAGE="JavaScript">

var myStr = "This is my first string."
var myStrObj = new String("This is my second
string.")

document.write("This is a " + typeof(myStr) + "<BR>")
document.write("This is an " + typeof(myStrObj) +
"<BR>")

</SCRIPT>
</BODY>
</HTML>
```

The output will appear as

```
This is a string
This is an object
```

Now, add the following lines of code just under the document.write() statements in the previous example:

```
document.write("The string length is: " + myStr.length
+ "<BR>")
document.write("The object length is: " +
myStrObj.length + "<BR>")
```

The output will now appear as

```
This is a string
This is an object
The string length is: 24
The object length is: 25
```

The point of the second exercise is to show that a string data type and string object can successfully use the same properties, such as the length property illustrated in this example.

HTML and the String Object

When text is formatted in HTML, it is contained within a set of tags such as <I>, </I>; <BIG>, </BIG>; or <S>, </S>. Multiple stages of formatting can be achieved by nesting these formatting statements. For example,

```
"<I>
    <BIG>
            <S>TeXt</S>
    </BIG>
</I>"
```

In this HTML statement, the text portion is first italicized, then enlarged, and then a strike through is applied. JavaScript provides similar capabilities.

JavaScript provides a string object type in addition to strings that are created as string data types. The string object type has a variety of methods that can be used to manipulate string objects as well as string data types. Table 15.1 lists the various string object methods.

Table 15–1: *String Object Methods*

name or operation	method
anchor	anchor()
big	big()
blink	blink()
bold	bold()
character at	charAt()
evaluate	eval()
fixed	fixed()
font color	fontcolor()
font size	fontsize()
index of	indexOf()
italics	italics()
last index of	lastIndexOf()
link	link()
small	small()
split	split()
strike	strike()
sub	sub()
substring	substring()
sup	sup()
to lowercase	toLowerCase()
to string	toString()
to uppercase	toUpperCase()
value of	valueOf()

In the following sections we'll investigate some interesting things that can be done with these methods. For example, methods can be used to locate substrings, divide strings, or find characters within a string.

Multiple Methods

As with HTML, multiple format statements can be applied to a string. In JavaScript the general syntax is

```
document.write("TeXt".toLowerCase().bold().fontcolor("gr
een"))
```

String object methods, applied in this fashion, are evaluated from left to right. In this example the string is converted to lowercase, bolded, and printed in a green color.

Location of a Substring

The indexOf() method can be used to find the index value of the first occurrence of a substring within a string.

```
var myStr = "Here is an interesting string."

document.write(myStr.indexOf("in"))
```

In this example, the value of 11 will be returned as the index value. This is because the search string "in" first occurs in the word interesting. The "i" in interesting is at an index position of 11.

You can use the lastIndexOf() method to return the index position of the last occurrence of the search string.

For either method, if an occurrence of the search string does not occur, a –1 value will be returned.

Extracting a Substring

The substring() method can be used to copy a substring from within a string. This method requires the use of two index values as shown in the following portion of code:

```
var myStr = "Here is an interesting string."
```

```
var mySubStr = myStr.substring(11, 22)

document.write(mySubStr)
```

In this example, the value of 11 is the index value of the first character to be returned in the substring. The second value used in the substring() method is the last character to be returned in the substring plus one.

Dividing a String

The split() method, introduced with version 3.0 of Navigator, can be used to divide a string into an array. Once the array is created, methods such as sort() can be used to sort the array elements. Here is a small portion of code that will use the split() method to divide a string into individual words, by using " " as the split character. The sort() method then sorts the elements of the array.

```
var myStr = "here is an interesting string."
var myArray = myStr.split(" ")

myArray.sort()

newString = new String("")

for (var i=0; i < myArray.length; i++) {
   newString += myArray[i] + "<BR>"
}

document.write(newString)
```

If you would like to view the sorted elements of the array, create a string object and use a simple loop to create a sorted string. The output will appear as

```
an
here
interesting
is
string.
```

In this example you might have noticed that the first letter in the string was not capitalized as in previous examples. If the "h" in here had been capitalized, here would have been the first word in the sorted list. Do you know why? This occurs because uppercase letters have lower ASCII values than lowercase letters. When sorting in ascending order, words starting with uppercase letters will always appear before words starting with lowercase letters.

Getting a Character

You can get to an individual character in a string by using an index value. Recall that strings are indexed like arrays with the first character having an index value of zero. In the following portion of code, which character do you think will be returned from the string?

```
var myStr = "Here is an interesting string."

document.write(myStr.charAt(6))
```

If you think the returned character is an "s," you are correct. This is because "H" is at index zero.

Converting Strings to Numbers

Numbers represented as strings can be used in numeric calculations if a little care is exercised. Consider the following portion of code:

```
var myStr1 = "12"
var myStr2 = "45"

Num1 = myStr1 - 0
Num2 = myStr2 - 0

Sum = ((Num1 + Num2) * 2) / 3

document.write(Sum)
```

In this example, the result written to the screen will be the number 38. This result is correct and is based on the fact that the initial addition of 12 + 45 = 57. The string values of "12" and "45" were converted to a numeric 12 and 45 by subtracting a 0 value from each string. JavaScript honors this evaluation and returns a numeric result to Num1 and Num2.

Now, try an experiment. Change the equation to

```
Sum = ((myStr1 + myStr2) * 2) / 3
```

If you print the results of this operation, it will be 830. This is because the "+" operator concatenates the "12" and "45" together, forming a string that equals "1245." When numeric operations are carried out on this string, the 1245 is multiplied by 2 and then divided by 3, returning the numeric 830 as a result.

The best rule of thumb when using this form of data is to make sure it is in numeric form before proceeding with any calculations.

Using parseInt()

JavaScript provides a built-in function, parseInt(), to convert strings to integer numbers. For example, consider the following portion of code:

```
document.write(parseInt("23") + "<BR>")
document.write(parseInt("23.45") + "<BR>")
document.write(parseInt("2A34") + "<BR>")
document.write(parseInt("AB12") + "<BR>")
document.write(parseInt("ABCD") + "<BR>")
document.write(parseInt(23) + "<BR>")
```

The results returned to the screen are

```
23
23
2
NaN
NaN
23
```

When the first two lines of code are executed, the results are predictable. In both cases the integer number 23 is returned. In the third case, the string represents the hexadecimal number 2A34. The parseInt() function converts the initial "2" correctly but stops at the first nonnumeric character. In the fourth line of code, there is no initial numeric value in the hexadecimal number, so a NaN (Not a Number) result is returned. The same occurs when a pure string, such as "ABCD" (which could also be a hexadecimal number, in this case), is used. Finally, the last line of code used an actual integer as the argument, and the function returned an integer 23 as the result.

The parseInt() function allows for an optional argument if you are intent on performing conversions from one numeric base (radix) to another. Simply specify the argument as

```
document.write(parseInt("AB12", 16) + "<BR>")
```

The value returned to the screen will be the decimal equivalent 43794 of the hexadecimal number AB12.

The radix value is usually 2, 8, 10, or 16. The default, with no radix value supplied, is 10.

Using parseFloat()

JavaScript provides a built-in function, parseFloat(), to convert strings to real numbers. For example, consider the following portion of code:

```
document.write(parseFloat("23") + "<BR>")
document.write(parseFloat("23.45") + "<BR>")
document.write(parseFloat("2.A34") + "<BR>")
document.write(parseFloat("AB.12") + "<BR>")
document.write(parseFloat("ABCD") + "<BR>")
document.write(parseFloat(23.45) + "<BR>")
```

The results returned to the screen are

```
23
23.45
2
NaN
NaN
23.45
```

When the first two lines of code are executed, the results are predictable. The parseFloat() function will return an integer result when the argument is an integer and a real number when the argument is a float. In the third case, the string represents the hexadecimal number 2.A34. The parseFloat() function converts the initial "2" correctly but stops at the first nonnumeric character. In the fourth line of code, there is no initial numeric value in the hexadecimal number, so a NaN (Not a Number) result is returned. The same occurs when the string "ABCD" is used. Finally, the last line of code used an actual float value is supplied as the argument, and the function returned the real number 23.45 as the result.

The rule of thumb is to make sure that the argument supplied to the parseFloat() function is a base-10 numeric string representation or float value.

Converting Numbers to Strings

Many times, when programming in JavaScript, you will find it necessary to convert numeric information to string information. JavaScript provides a number of ways this operation can be accomplished.

Using a Concatenation Trick

In the previous section, you learned a trick that JavaScript allows when converting a string to a number. Simply subtract a numeric zero from the string and presto, a numeric value.

There is a similar trick that can be used for converting a numeric value to a string. To perform the conversion, simply concatenate an empty string to the numeric value. Consider this portion of code:

```
var myNum1 = 401
var myNum2 = 401.867
myNum1 += ""
myNum2 += ""

document.write(typeof(myNum1) + "<BR>")
document.write(typeof(myNum2) + "<BR>")
```

In both cases, the results returned to the screen will report that the information is a string.

Using String()

The String() constructor function provides another way numeric information can be converted to a string object. Consider this small portion of code:

```
var myNum = 401.34
var myStr = new String(myNum)

document.write("Here is a string " + myStr)
```

The string object will be concatenated to the string in quotes and the results printed to the screen.

Using toString()

The toString() method is another way numeric information can be converted to a string. The toString() method provides the added benefit of radix conversions when an argument is supplied to the function. Here is a small portion of code that will convert a number to binary, octal, and hexadecimal. Remember, the results printed to the screen are strings.

```
var myNum = 1234

document.write(myNum.toString(2) + " in binary <BR>")
document.write(myNum.toString(8) + " in octal <BR>")
document.write(myNum.toString(16) + " in hexadecimal
<BR>")
```

The results returned to the screen will be

```
10011010010 in binary
2322 in octal
4d2 in hexadecimal
```

If an argument is not supplied to the toString() method, a 10 is used by default.

Testing and Evaluating Expressions

JavaScript provides two methods for testing and evaluating results. If your text string contains an expression that should be evaluated before a specific action is taken, use the eval() method. The isNaN() method can be used to test if a result is a numeric expression or not.

The escape() and unescape() functions are also available for character conversion from ASCII to ISO-8859-1 and back.

Using eval()

In the following portion of code, the user is prompted to enter a group of numbers to perform a mathematical operation. The syntax for operation is numeric value, operation, numeric value, operation. . . . For example, the user could enter 45 + 23 / 2 and then click the OK button on the prompt box.

```
var datain = prompt("Enter Data", "")

document.write("The result of " + datain + " is " +
eval(datain))
```

The eval() function is used to evaluate the user's input and returns the result of the operation to the screen. In this example the result would be

```
The result of 45 + 23 / 2 is 34
```

Try some other number and operator combinations to explore the power of the eval() method.

Using isNaN()

In a previous example, you saw that an operation could return a NaN result. NaN means that the result of the operation is not a number. The isNaN() method can be used to test for NaN results.

Here is a small portion of code that uses the isNaN() function:

```
var myVal = "1234"

if (isNaN(myVal)) {
  alert("This is a number")
} else {
  alert("This is not a number")
}
```

The string "1234" is actually a string of characters and not an actual number so the second alert option is activated in this code segment.

Using escape()

The escape() function can be used to convert a character from ASCII to ISO-8859-1 (Latin −1 character set). It is also used to escape special characters for use in constructing URLs.

Here is a small portion of code that illustrates the escape() function.

```
<HTML>
<HEAD>
<TITLE>Test Program</TITLE>
</HEAD>
<BODY>
<SCRIPT LANGUAGE="JavaScript">

var mystr = "Here is a string."

document.write(escape(mystr))

</SCRIPT>
</BODY>
</HTML>
```

In this example, the string's characters will be returned as they appear. However, the spaces between each word are returned as the ASCII encoding of the space character. The screen's results will be

```
Here%20is%20a%20string.
```

Here %20 represents the hexadecimal value for a space character.

Using unescape()

The unescape() function performs the previous conversion in reverse. Information in ISO-8859-1 form can be converted to its ASCII equivalent. Here is a small portion of code that illustrates this type of operation.

```
var mystr = "%61%62%63%64"

document.write(unescape(mystr))
```

When this portion of code is executed, the characters "abcd" will be printed to the screen. This is because 61 is the hexadecimal equivalent of the letter "a," and so on.

Summary

As you have learned, manipulating string information is very important in any programming language. JavaScript gives you the ability to perform these operations easily. For example, you have learned that

JavaScript handles characters by treating them as one-character length strings. With JavaScript an individual character in a string can be referenced by using an index value. The first character in a string is assigned an index value of zero.

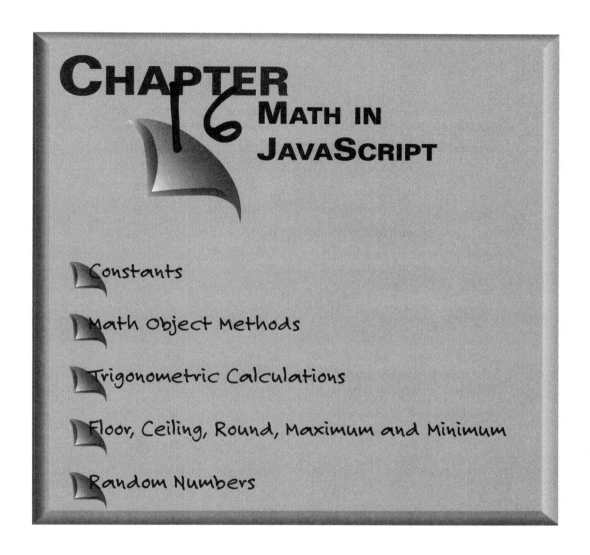

CHAPTER 16 MATH IN JAVASCRIPT

- Constants

- Math Object Methods

- Trigonometric Calculations

- Floor, Ceiling, Round, Maximum and Minimum

- Random Numbers

The Math object in JavaScript gives you the ability to solve mathematical problems that range from simple addition to complex operations involving trigonometric functions, logarithms, exponential calculations, and more. Eight unique constants and 21 mathematical methods provide the computational power for mathematical operations.

This chapter will investigate many of the built-in constants and methods with the use of short program segments. Before you finish, you will understand the strengths and pitfalls of JavaScript math.

Constants and Methods

JavaScript's built-in constants and methods give it computational abilities equal to compiled programming languages such as Visual Basic and C. You'll find that it is easy to bring mathematical operations into any HTML document using JavaScript.

Constants

Table 16.1 lists the eight constants by name and provides a short description of each.

Table 16–1: *Constants Provided by the Math Object*

Name	Description
E	natural number
LN10	natural log of 10
LN2	natural log of 2
LOG10E	log base 10 of E
LOG2E	log base2 of E
PI	numeric value of pi
SQRT1_2	square root of _
SQRT2	square root of 2

Try the JavaScript in this HTML document to find the value for each constant in your browser.

```
<HTML>
<HEAD>
<TITLE>Math Constants</TITLE>
</HEAD>
<BODY>
<SCRIPT LANGUAGE="JavaScript">

document.write("The value of E is " + Math.E +
"<BR>")
```

```
document.write("The value of LN2 is " + Math.LN2 +
"<BR>")
document.write("The value of LN10 is " + Math.LN10 +
"<BR>")
document.write("The value of LOG2E is " + Math.LOG2E
+ "<BR>")
document.write("The value of LOG10E is " +
Math.LOG10E + "<BR>")
document.write("The value of PI is " + Math.PI +
"<BR>")
document.write("The value of SQRT1_2 is " +
Math.SQRT1_2 + "<BR>")
document.write("The value of SQRT2 is " + Math.SQRT2
+ "<BR>")

</SCRIPT>
</BODY>
</HTML>
```

Netscape returned the following values on our computer.

```
The value of E is 2.718281828459045
The value of LN2 is .6931471805599453
The value of LN10 is 2.302585092994046
The value of LOG2E is 1.4426950408889634
The value of LOG10E is .4342944819032518
The value of PI is 3.141592653589793
The value of SQRT1_2 is .7071067811865476
The value of SQRT2 is 1.4142135623730951
```

Math constants can be used directly in a calculation. For example, electrical engineers know that the peak value of a sine wave is the square root of 2 times the rms voltage value. If your wall outlet has a voltage of 120 volts (rms) what is the peak voltage?

```
document.write("The peak voltage is: " +  (120 *
Math.SQRT2) + " volts")
```

Give this example a try. You'll find that the peak voltage is approximately 170 volts.

Methods

Table 16.2 lists 21 methods provided by the Math object and includes a short description of each.

Table 16–2: *Methods Supplied by the Math Object*

Method	Description
abs()	absolute value
acos()	arc cosine
asin()	arc sine
atan()	arc tangent
atan2()	returns the angle of polar coordinate pair for two rectangular coordinates supplied as arguments
ceil()	next integer => than argument
cos()	cosine
eval()	evaluation
exp()	E raised to the argument
floor()	next integer =< than argument
log()	natural logarithm
max()	returns greater of two arguments
min()	returns smaller of two arguments
pow()	raises first argument to the power of the second argument
random()	random number (0 to 1)
round()	rounds to nearest integer
sin()	sine
sqrt()	square root
tan()	tangent
toString()	convert to string
valueOf()	find the value of

You may remember that eval(), toString(), and valueOf() were discussed in the previous chapter dealing with strings. They are repeated here to make the list inclusive.

In the next section we'll investigate the use of several of these methods in interesting examples.

A Table of Sine Values

It is often handy to have a table of trigonometric values handy. The JavaScript code in the following HTML document will print the angle, in degrees, and the sine of the angle for angles between 0 and 45 degrees.

```
<HTML>
<HEAD>
<TITLE>Sine Values</TITLE>
</HEAD>
<BODY>
<SCRIPT LANGUAGE="JavaScript">

document.write("Angle" + "------->" + "Sine" +
"<BR>")

for (var i = 0; i < 46; i++) {
  var radians = i * Math.PI / 180
  document.write(i + "----------->" +
                   Math.sin(radians) + "<BR>")
}

</SCRIPT>
</BODY>
</HTML>
```

Since the angles for trignometric functions are specified in radians, the degree values are converted to radians with the equation

```
radians = degrees * PI / 180
```

To calculate individual sin() values within the **for** loop, just use

```
Math.sin(radians)
```

The output, sent to the screen, is in the format shown below. The listing has been abbreviated to conserve space.

```
Angle------->Sine
0----------->0
1----------->0.01745240643728351
    .
    .
    .
```

```
43----------->.6819983600624985
44----------->.6946583704589973
45----------->.7071067811865475
```

Try experimenting with cos() and tan(), or create a table of values from 0 to 360 degrees in 10-degree increments.

Floor, Ceiling, and Round

The floor() and ceil() methods return the nearest integer value below or above the argument value. The round() method rounds the value up or down to an integer value. Here is a brief example illustrating each method.

```
var num = 123.45678

document.write(Math.floor(num) + "<BR>")
document.write(Math.ceil(num) + "<BR>")
document.write(Math.round(num) + "<BR>")
```

When executed, this JavaScript will produce the following results:

```
123
124
123
```

The floor() method returns a 123 because that is the integer equal to or smaller than the argument 123.45678. The ceil() method returns a 124 because that is the integer equal to or larger than the argument 123.45678. The round() method returns a 123 because the fractional part of the argument is not greater than .5.

Maximum and Minimum

The max() and min() methods return the maximum or minimum, respectively, of the two arguments supplied to each. Here is a short portion of code that illustrates how these methods operate.

```
document.write(Math.max(1234.56, 1234.560001) + "<BR>")
document.write(Math.min(127, 120) + "<BR>")
```

The first line of JavaScript code will return the number 1234.560001 since it is the larger of the two arguments. The second line will return the number 120 since it is the smaller of the two arguments.

Notice that the arguments for max() and min() can be either integers or floats.

Random Numbers

The random() method can be used to return random numbers in the range 0 to 1. If you would like random numbers in the range 0 to 100, simply multiply the results by 100. If you would then like those numbers to be integer values, you can apply the floor(), ceil(), or round() methods.

Here is a small portion of code that illustrates this technique.

```
for (var i = 0; i < 10; i++) {
   document.write(Math.round(Math.random() * 100) +
"<BR>")
}
```

This JavaScript will generate 10 random integer numbers in the range 0 to 100. Here is the output from one sample run.

```
89
71
68
2
17
15
68
93
73
54
```

Are the numbers truly random? Only a good mathematician would know for sure by sampling multiple runs and examining the results. You'll probably find the random() method produces sufficiently random results for most games and calculations that you might create.

Numbers Raised to a Power

The pow() method can be used to raise numbers to a power. The first argument is the number to be raised to the power specified by the second argument.

The JavaScript in the following HTML document illustrates how to raise the number 2 to subsequently higher powers.

```
<HTML>
<HEAD>
<TITLE>To a Power</TITLE>
</HEAD>
<BODY>
<SCRIPT LANGUAGE="JavaScript">

document.write("2 raised to subsequently higher pow-
ers" + "<BR><BR>")

for (var i = 0; i < 20; i++) {
   document.write(Math.pow(2, i) + "<BR>")
}

</SCRIPT>
</BODY>
</HTML>
```

The output from this simple example is shown in the following listing.

```
2 raised to subsequently higher powers

1
2
4
8
16
32
64
128
256
512
1024
2048
4096
8192
16384
32768
65536
131072
```

```
262144
524288
```

Now, try another trick. Alter the original JavaScript code to match the following portion of code and test the program again:

```
document.write("2 raised to subsequently lower pow-
ers" + "<BR><BR>")

for (var i = 0; i < 20; i++) {
   document.write(Math.pow(2, -i) + "<BR>")
}
```

When the table is printed this time, 2 is raised to subsequently lower powers. Examine the output in the following listing:

```
2 raised to subsequently lower powers

1
.5
.25
.125
0.0625
0.03125
0.015625
0.0078125
0.00390625
0.001953125
0.0009765625
0.00048828125
0.000244140625
0.0001220703125
0.00006103515625
0.000030517578125
0.0000152587890625
0.00000762939453125
0.000003814697265625
0.0000019073486328125
```

As a little exercise, alter the JavaScript so that the number 10 is raised or lowered to different powers.

Factorials

Calculating factorials is appropriate in a chapter titled "Math in JavaScript" even if the Math object does not have a built-in method for factorials.

Factorials are easily calculated by using a simple recursion function. Here is a small portion of JavaScript that allows the calculation of any factorial within reason!

```
<HTML>
<HEAD>
<TITLE>Math Constants</TITLE>
</HEAD>
<BODY>
<SCRIPT LANGUAGE="JavaScript">

function factorial(num) {
  if (num == 0)
    return 1

  var result = num * factorial(num - 1)
  document.write(result + "<BR>")
  return result
}

factorial(10)

</SCRIPT>
</BODY>
</HTML>
```

In this example, the factorial of 10 is requested. The JavaScript code will print the intermediate results as each portion of the factorial is calculated. In this case it will be

```
1 * 2 * 3 * 4 * 5 * 6 * 7 * 8 * 9 * 10 = 3628800
```

Here is the output sent to the screen.

```
1
2
6
24
120
720
5040
40320
362880
3628800
```

We started this section by saying that you could calculate any factorial within reason. Okay, so what is reasonable? You'll learn about reasonable limits in the next section.

The Number Object

The Number object is very closely associated with the Math object. With the Number object, you'll be able to discover the upper and lower limits of a number representation in JavaScript.

The Number object has a number of constant properties of interest to us. They include MAX_VALUE, MIN_VALUE, NEGATIVE_INFINITY, and POSITIVE_INFINITY.

Let's find out more about these constants by writing a small piece of JavaScript code that will return information on each of them.

```
document.write(Number.MAX_VALUE + "<BR><BR>")
document.write(Number.MIN_VALUE + "<BR><BR>")
document.write(Number.NEGATIVE_INFINITY + "<BR><BR>")
document.write(Number.POSITIVE_INFINITY + "<BR><BR>")
```

When this code is executed, expect to see results similar to those shown in the following listing:

```
1.7976931348623157e+308

5e-324

-Infinity

Infinity
```

Apparently, we've solved the question of what is reasonable in terms of numeric range. In JavaScript, you can use, calculate, and return any numeric values between

$$5^{-324} \quad <= \quad number <= 1.7976931348623157^{+308}$$

If values go beyond these boundaries, they will be represented as negative and positive infinity.

Summary

In this chapter you learned about JavaScript's math capabilities and how to use them in an HTML document. We're sure you have several projects in mind for using these methods in your own projects

You may want to return to Chapter 15 where several math-related methods were discussed. Specifically, the eval(), isNaN(), parseInt(), parseFloat(), toString(), and ValueOf() were described with the inclusion of simple JavaScript code.

CHAPTER 17 DATE AND TIME

- Date Object Methods

- Working with Dates and Times

- Time Zones

- Year 2000

- Examples

The ability to obtain, use, and set the date and time from an application are fundamental capabilities of any language. In JavaScript, date and time capabilities are obtained by using the Date object. The Date object contains a large variety of methods that allow you, the programmer, to control the date and time information in a variety of different formats. An instance of the Date object can be created very simply:

```
var dateInst = new Date()
```

In this chapter you will learn how to use the Date object to obtain, use, and set date and time information.

Date Object Methods

Date information in JavaScript is stored referencing a starting date, in milliseconds. Ground zero is January 1, 1970. On this date, the hypothetical JavaScript clock started ticking. Time before January 1, 1970 does not exist for Java or JavaScript. That means that JavaScript cannot store reference dates before January 1, 1970 on its internal clock. If you attempt to do so, an error is bound to occur. It does not, however, mean that you can't enter dates such as December 25, 1943 in an application.

To make use of the Date object, JavaScript provides a number of methods that you will see summarized in Table 17.1.

Table 17–1: *Date Object Methods*

Method Name	Description
getDate()	Get the date (1 – 31)
getDay()	Get the day (0 - 6), Sunday = 0
getHours()	Get the hours (0 – 23)
getMinutes()	Get the minutes (0 – 59)
getSeconds()	Get the seconds (0 – 59)
getTime()	Get the time. (in milliseconds)
getTimezoneOffset()	Difference between GMT and local time
getYear()	Get the year (70 to 99 or 2000 +)
parse()	Converts IETF standard format and converts to milliseconds
setDate()	Set the date (1 – 31)
setHours()	Set the hours (0 – 23)
setMinutes()	Set the minutes (0 – 59)
setSeconds()	Set the seconds (0 – 59)
setTime()	Set the time
setYear()	Set the year (70 to 99 or 2000+)

Table 17–1: *Continued*

Method Name	Description
toGMTString()	Date to a GMT string using local offset (Fri, 24 April 1998 06:12:33 GMT)
toLocaleString()	Date to a locale string using local information
UTC()	Converts a comma-delimited format and converts to milliseconds

There are additional methods that are frequently associated with the use of Date object methods. These methods include clearTimeout(), eval(), toString(), setTimeout(), and valueOf(). A number of these methods have already been introduced in the previous chapters.

In the next sections of this chapter, we'll show a variety of techniques for each of the methods listed in Table 17.1. By the end of the chapter, you'll have a good understanding of the use and capabilities of the Date object, and what it can provide for your applications.

Coding Details for Date Object Methods

In this section, we'll examine techniques for writing JavaScript code that uses each of the Date object methods. The portions of sample code are kept as short as possible.

getDate()

The values returned by the getDate() method vary from 1 to 31 and are used to represent a given date in a month.

Here is a complete HTML document showing the portion of JavaScript code that returns the date information to the screen.

```
<HTML>
```

```
<HEAD>
<TITLE>Date & Time</TITLE>
</HEAD>
<BODY>
<SCRIPT LANGUAGE="JavaScript">

var dateInst = new Date()
var date = dateInst.getDate()

document.write("Today's date is: ", date)

</SCRIPT>
</BODY>
</HTML>
```

The date information can be used separately, or combined with information from other methods to build a string of date/time information.

getDay()

The values returned by the getDay() method vary from 0 to 6 and are used to represent a given day of the week. Sunday is represented by the number 0 and Saturday by the number 6.

Here is a complete HTML document showing the portion of JavaScript code that returns the day information to the screen. A simple array named *dayArray[]* is used to convert numeric information to the proper string.

```
<HTML>
<HEAD>
<TITLE>Date & Time</TITLE>
</HEAD>
<BODY>
<SCRIPT LANGUAGE="JavaScript">

var dateInst = new Date()
var day = dateInst.getDay()

dayArray = new Array(7)
dayArray[0] = "Sunday"
dayArray[1] = "Monday"
dayArray[2] = "Tuesday"
dayArray[3] = "Wednesday"
dayArray[4] = "Thursday"
dayArray[5] = "Friday"
dayArray[6] = "Saturday"
```

```
document.write("Today is: ", dayArray[day])

</SCRIPT>
</BODY>
</HTML>
```

The getDay() method is easy to use, as you can see. Did you notice, in Table 17.1, that there is not a corresponding setDay() method provided by the Date object?

getHours()

The values returned by the getHours() method vary from 0 to 23 and are used to represent a military time format. One hour past midnight is 1, but one hour past noon is represented as 13.

Here is a complete HTML document showing the portion of JavaScript code that returns the hour information to the screen in two different formats.

```
<HTML>
<HEAD>
<TITLE>Date & Time</TITLE>
</HEAD>
<BODY>
<SCRIPT LANGUAGE="JavaScript">

var dateInst = new Date()
var hours = dateInst.getHours()

document.write("The number of hours in military for-
mat is: ",
                hours, "<BR>")

if (hours < 12)
  document.write("The number of hours since midnight
is: ",
                hours, "<BR>")
else
  document.write("The number of hours since noon is:
",
                hours - 12, "<BR>")

</SCRIPT>
</BODY>
</HTML>
```

The military time format returns the number of hours that have elapsed since midnight on the given date. The military format can be converted into an AM/PM format or simply used to determine the number of hours that have elapsed since midnight or noon on a given day. In this example, simply subtracting 12 from the military format and using a simple **if** statement will return the latter.

getMinutes()

The values returned by the getMinutes() method vary from 0 to 59 and are used to represent the number of minutes that have elapsed since the start of the hour.

Here is the JavaScript code that returns the minute information to the screen:

```
var dateInst = new Date()
var minutes = dateInst.getMinutes()

document.write("Minutes from start of hour: ",
               minutes, "<BR>")
```

As you can see, most Date object methods are straightforward in their use.

getSeconds()

The values returned by the getSeconds() method vary from 0 to 59 and are used to represent the number of seconds that have elapsed since the start of the minute.

Here is the JavaScript code that returns the second information to the screen:

```
var dateInst = new Date()
var seconds = dateInst.getSeconds()

document.write("Seconds from start of minute: ",
               seconds, "<BR>")
```

For a little variation, let's combine the getHour(), getMinute(), and getSecond() methods in a different type of example. Here is a com-

plete HTML document showing the portion of JavaScript code that
returns the hour, minute, and second information to an alert box.

```
<HTML>
<HEAD>
<TITLE>Date & Time</TITLE>
</HEAD>
<BODY>
<SCRIPT LANGUAGE="JavaScript">

var dateInst = new Date()
var hours = dateInst.getHours()
var minutes = dateInst.getMinutes()
var seconds = dateInst.getSeconds()

if (minutes < 10)
  minutes = "0" + minutes

if (seconds < 10)
  seconds = "0" + seconds

alert("It's " + hours + ":" + minutes + ":" + sec-
onds +
      " Is it time for a Java break?")

</SCRIPT>
</BODY>
</HTML>
```

The getHours(), getMinutes(), and getSeconds() methods return
information to the *hours*, *minutes*, and *seconds* variables. Since we
will be printing in the (hh:mm:ss) format, we will need to correct the
value in *minutes* and *seconds* to concatenate a leading zero onto the
string for values less than 10. This is easy to do with a simple **if** statement.

The information used with alert() is just a string formed by text and
the variable data.

getTime()

The values returned by the getTime() method represent the number of
milliseconds that have elapsed since 1/1/1970.

Here is an HTML document containing JavaScript code that
returns this information in seconds, minutes, hours, days, and years:

```
<HTML>
<HEAD>
<TITLE>Date & Time</TITLE>
</HEAD>
<BODY>
<SCRIPT LANGUAGE="JavaScript">

var time = new Date()
var seconds = time.getTime()/1000

document.write("According to your computer's clock
<BR>")
document.write("the following time has transpired")
document.write(" since 1/1/1970 <BR> <BR>")
document.write(seconds, " seconds <BR> or ")
document.write(seconds/60, " minutes <BR> or ")
document.write(seconds/3600, " hours <BR> or ")
document.write(seconds/86400, " days <BR> or approxi-
mately ")
document.write(seconds/31536000, " years <BR>")

</SCRIPT>
</BODY>
</HTML>
```

The accuracy of the getTime() method is, of course, related to the accuracy of your computer's internal clock. The use of the getTime() method is also a useful way of comparing dates.

getTimezoneOffset()

The getTimezoneOffset() method returns the offset in minutes measured from Greenwich Mean Time. The number of minutes is converted to hours by dividing it by 60.

```
var time = new Date()
var offset = time.getTimezoneOffset()/60

document.write("According to your system's clock
<BR>")
document.write("your GMT offset is ", offset, " hours")
```

If you live in the United States, the offset will be 5 hours for EST and 8 hours for PST. Corrections are made for daylight savings time. The offset is determined from your original settings for your time zone when you installed Windows.

getYear() and the Year 2000

The value returned by the getYear() method will be an integer varying from 70 to 99 or 2000+. Microsoft, in Windows 98, has corrected the year 2000 problem. The system clock, via the getYear() method, will return integers from 70 to 99 representing years in the twentieth century. However, when the year 2000 arrives, the getYear() method will start returning integers starting at 2000.

Here is a HTML document containing JavaScript code that correctly reports the current year well past the turn of the century when running under Netscape:

```
<HTML>
<HEAD>
<TITLE>Date & Time</TITLE>
</HEAD>
<BODY>
<SCRIPT LANGUAGE="JavaScript">

var dateInst = new Date()
var years = dateInst.getYear()

document.write("This application returns the correct
year<BR>")
document.write("correcting for the year 2000!
<BR><BR>")
if (years > 99)
  document.write("This is ", years)
  else
    document.write("This is 19", years)

</SCRIPT>
</BODY>
</HTML>
```

If you want to test this application, set your system clock to the year 2002. Presto—the correct date. Oh, if it was just this easy for the rest of the world!

parse()

The parse() method converts date and time information in the following format:

```
day, date month year hours:minutes:seconds timezone
```

The returned information is given in milliseconds as the difference between the test date and 1/1/1970. For example, you could use Wed, 25 Mar 1998 22:21:20 GMT. Notice that both the day and month are abbreviated.

Here is a small portion of JavaScript code that will convert the date 10 May 1983 to the number of seconds that has elapsed between that date and 1/1/1970.

```
var dateInst = new Date()
var testdate = "10 May 1983"

document.write("This application uses the parse()
method<BR>")
document.write("to convert a month-day-year format
and return<BR>")
document.write("the difference between 1/1/1970 and
this date<BR>")
document.write("in days.<BR><BR>")

document.write("The difference is: ")
document.write(Date.parse(testdate)/86400000, " days")
```

When using the parse() method, it is very important to use a proper time zone designator. In the United States, you can use designators such as EST, CST, and so on. When in doubt, use the getTimezoneOffset() method discussed earlier to help determine the proper zone.

setDate()

The setDate() method accepts integer values from 1 to 31 as an argument. These values are used to represent a given date in a month.

Here is a complete HTML document showing the portion of JavaScript code that sets the date and then displays the new information on the screen.

```
<HTML>
<HEAD>
<TITLE>Date & Time</TITLE>
</HEAD>
<BODY>
<SCRIPT LANGUAGE="JavaScript">

var dateInst = new Date()
dateInst.setDate(24)

document.write("The new date is: ",
dateInst.getDate())

</SCRIPT>
</BODY>
</HTML>
```

You'll find most of the setXXX() methods are as straightforward as the setDate() method.

setHours()

The setHours() method argument accepts values from 0 to 23. These values represent a military time format. Two hours past midnight is 2, but two hours past noon is represented as 14.

See getHours() for an example using the "get" version of this method. The setDate() method also contains a useful application illustrating how to test "set" methods.

setMinutes()

The setMinutes() method argument accepts values from 0 to 59. These values represent the number of minutes past the hour.

See getMinutes() for an example using the "get" version of this method. The setDate() method also contains a useful application illustrating how to test "set" methods.

setSeconds()

The setSeconds() method argument accepts values from 0 to 59. These values represent the number of seconds past the minute.

See getSeconds() for an example using the "get" version of this method. The setDate() method also contains a useful application illustrating how to test "set" methods.

setTime()

The argument supplied to the setTime() method represents the number of milliseconds that have elapsed since 1/1/1970.

Here is an HTML document containing JavaScript code that returns this information in seconds, minutes, hours, days, and years:

```
<HTML>
<HEAD>
<TITLE>Date & Time</TITLE>
</HEAD>
<BODY>
<SCRIPT LANGUAGE="JavaScript">

var time = new Date()
var seconds = time.getTime()/1000

document.write("According to your computer's clock
<BR>")
document.write("the following time has transpired")
document.write(" since 1/1/1970 <BR> <BR>")
document.write(seconds, " seconds <BR> or ")
document.write(seconds/60, " minutes <BR> or ")
document.write(seconds/3600, " hours <BR> or ")
document.write(seconds/86400, " days <BR> or approxi-
mately ")
document.write(seconds/31536000, " years <BR>")

</SCRIPT>
</BODY>
</HTML>
```

The accuracy of the getTime() method is, of course, related to the accuracy of your computer's internal clock.

setYear()

The argument value accepted by the getYear() method is an integer starting in 1970 and continuing past the turn of the century.

```
<HTML>
<HEAD>
<TITLE>Date & Time</TITLE>
</HEAD>
<BODY>
<SCRIPT LANGUAGE="JavaScript">

var dateInst = new Date()
dateInst.setYear(2003)
var years = dateInst.getYear()

document.write("Well, it must be ")

if (years > 99)
  document.write(years)
  else
    document.write("19", years)

</SCRIPT>
</BODY>
</HTML>
```

Notice that while the setYear() argument can use years such as 1970, 1998, 2003, the getYear() method returns values between 70 and 99 for the current century and values from 2000 + for the next century. This application corrects the returned value for this situation.

toGMTString()

The toGMTString() method will use the settings on your system's internal clock and then form a GMT string in the following format:

```
day, date month year hours:minutes:seconds timezone
```

For example, a string might be returned with this date and time information: Wed, 25 Mar 1998 22:21:20 GMT. Notice that both the day and month are abbreviated.

Here is a small portion of JavaScript code that will return a string in this format.

```
var dateInst = new Date()
var datestr = dateInst.toGMTString()

document.write("The GMT formatted string is: ", dat-
estr)
```

toLocaleString()

The toLocaleString() method will use the settings on your system's internal clock and then form a date and time string using the following format:

```
Month/Day/Year hours:minutes:seconds
```

For example, a string might be returned with this date and time information 03/14/1998 10:21:31.

Here is a small portion of JavaScript code that will return a string in this format.

```
var dateInst = new Date()
var datestr = dateInst.toLocaleString()

document.write("The Locale formatted string is: ", dat-
estr)
```

UTC()

The UTC() method uses a list of date/time information separated by commas to create and return the difference, in milliseconds, between the specified date and 1/1/1970. The method assumes a GMT time format.

In the following HTML document a GMT date of November 6, 2001 is used with a time of 13:20:21.

```
<HTML>
```

```
<HEAD>
<TITLE>Date & Time</TITLE>
</HEAD>
<BODY>
<SCRIPT LANGUAGE="JavaScript">

var datelist = Date.UTC(2001, 10, 6, 13, 20, 21)
var dateInst = new Date(datelist)

document.write("Here are the number of
milliseconds<BR>")
document.write("since 1/1/1970 and the given
date:<BR>")
document.write(datelist,"<BR><BR>")

document.write("Or, the format can be converted
and<BR>")
document.write("returned in this manner:<BR>")
document.write(dateInst,"<BR><BR>")

</SCRIPT>
</BODY>
</HTML>
```

The output sent to the screen by the JavaScript code is shown next.

```
Here are the number of milliseconds
since 1/1/1970 and the given date:
1005052821000

Or, the format can be converted and
returned in this manner:
Tue Nov 06 08:20:21 Eastern Standard Time 2001
```

In the first portion of the program's output, the millisecond difference is determined and displayed. Note in the second portion that our formatting has returned the information formatted for our locale, the east coast of the United States. The military time of 13 hours has been corrected for the offset of 5 hours between EST and GMT.

Summary

You have learned how to use several methods in this chapter for formatting and returning time and date information. You also learned that JavaScript is capable of correcting for the year 2000 problem when used in conjunction with Windows 98. Continue experimenting with these methods. You'll see that they are easy to incorporate in your JavaScript code and add real programming power to your HTML documents.

PART FOUR

HTML and JavaScript

Chapters 18–23 take you beyond the fundamentals of HTML 4.0 and JavaScript. Here you'll look at the integration of HTML and JavaScript concepts involving frames and layers, cookies, history lists, and various JavaScript objects. In the final chapter, you'll even learn how to create a custom JavaScript object. When you master the material in this section, you will have a complete understanding of JavaScript object-oriented concepts.

CHAPTER 18
FRAMES, OBJECTS, AND LAYERS

Frames

Objects

Layers and Layering

Examples

The concepts of HTML frames, objects, and layers can be used to bolster your Web applications and increase control of the view area. While these topics are independent of JavaScript, JavaScript can be used as a programming tool in many areas. In the section dealing with layers, JavaScript code is used to move a shape about on the screen. This crude animation example can be used for the foundation for more complex animation projects you might have in mind.

Use the JavaScript concepts you have learned in the previous chapters to build more robust applications using frames, objects, and layers.

Frames

Frames can be used to create imaginative document views by allowing the viewing area to be divided into multiple sections. Once divided, each section can be treated independently from the others with some serving as navigation frames while others serve as content frames. For example, imagine the viewing area as being represented by a picture window. Frames added to the document viewing area are comparable to adding windowpanes to the picture window. Now, instead of one big screen, your viewing area can be neatly divided and organized. For example, consider this situation: A viewing area is divided into three frames. One frame holds an image of a college campus. Another frame holds a navigation menu, allowing the user to make choices as to what information they will view. The third frame is used to allowing scrolling through text material related to the previous navigation menu selection.

HTML 4.0 officially recognizes in-line frames. In-line frames allow developers to insert a frame within a block of text. In-line frames are no longer restricted to just the borders of HTML documents. The only restriction of in-line frames, when compared with standard frames, is that they cannot be resized.

You will find that the material discussed in this section will work with Netscape Communicator (version 4.0 and later) and the Microsoft Internet Explorer (version 4.0 and later). However, not all browsers support frames so precautions must be taken for those cases.

In the following sections you will learn how to create frames, specify the number of frames in a viewing area, set their size, resizing and scrolling capabilities, borders, and margins. You'll see that frames are easy to create and use and should be a part of a well-defined display. Frames can make it easy for your users to navigate your site.

Using the <FRAMESET> Tag

Documents incorporating frames use the <FRAMESET> tag to define the layout of all views in the window. The <FRAMESET> element is used in place of the <BODY> element. Elements, normally placed in the <BODY> element, cannot be placed before the first <FRAMESET> element.

The syntax for using the complete container is straightforward:

```
<FRAMESET frameset_attributes>
   .
   .
   .
</FRAMESET>
```

The HTML 4.0 attributes for <FRAMESET> include cols and rows. Table 18.1 names and describes <FRAMESET> attributes.

Table 18–1: *<FRAMESET> Attributes Used in HTML 4.0*

Attribute	Description
cols	Layout of vertical frames. Length of each frame is expresses in a physical unit (pixels, integer) or as a percentage of the actual viewing area.
rows	Layout of horizontal frames. Length of each frame is expressed in a physical unit (pixels, integer) or as a percentage of the actual viewing area.

Here is an example showing how <FRAMESET> can be used to create three vertical frames of approximately the same value:

```
<FRAMESET cols="33%,33%,34%">
```

Another example illustrates how four horizontal rows could be created:

```
<FRAMESET rows="20%,20%,30%,30%">
```

A grid can be constructed by specifying both the number of columns and rows. Here is the code necessary to create a grid with four columns and three rows:

```
<FRAMESET cols="20%,20%,30%,30%"  rows="33%,33%,34%">
```

Figure 18.1 shows this layout in a screen show produced with the following HTML code.

```
<HTML>
<HEAD>
<TITLE>Experimenting with Frames</TITLE>
</HEAD>

<FRAMESET cols="20%,20%,30%,30%" rows="33%,33%,34%">
```

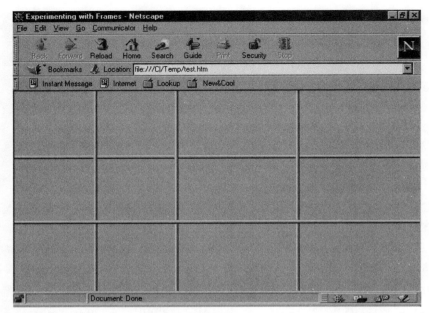

Figure 18–1:   *<FRAMESET> is used to create a grid in the viewing area.*

```
    <FRAME src="c1r1.html">
    <FRAME src="c2r1.html">
    <FRAME src="c3r1.html">
    <FRAME src="c4r1.html">
    <FRAME src="c1r2.html">
    <FRAME src="c2r2.html">
    <FRAME src="c3r2.html">
    <FRAME src="c4r2.html">
    <FRAME src="c1r3.html">
    <FRAME src="c2r3.html">
    <FRAME src="c3r3.html">
    <FRAME src="c4r3.html">
</FRAMESET>

</HTML>
```

Frame sets can also be nested. For example,

```
<FRAMESET cols="20%,20%,30%,30%">
  <FRAMESET rows="33%,33%,34%">
```

As you have probably figured out, if the cols attribute is not specified, each row will extend the entire width of the window. Likewise, if the rows attribute is not specified, each column will extend the entire length of the window. Views are divided from left to right for columns and top to bottom for rows.

The length and height values are given as percentages (using %), pixels, or a relative integer length (using *).

Consider the following example:

```
<FRAMESET cols="2*, 220,3*">
```

In this case, three columns are created. The second column is set to 220 pixels. The first and third frames divide the remaining space proportionally. The first frame will receive 40 percent and the third frame 60 percent of the remaining space. The default always adds to 100 percent.

When percentages are used, it is left to the browser to correctly adjust for under- and overspecifications of percentages.

Using the <FRAME> Tag

The <FRAMESET> element is used to define the layout of all views within a window. <FRAME> tags defining the contents and appearance of each individual view follow the <FRAMESET> tag.

The syntax for the <FRAME element> within the <FRAMESET> container is

```
<FRAMESET frameset_attributes>
  <FRAME frame_attributes>
  <FRAME frame_attributes>
  <FRAME frame_attributes>
   .
   .
   .
</FRAMESET>
```

There are several attributes that can be used with the <FRAME> element. These include frameborder, marginheight, marginwidth, name, noresize, scrolling, and src. Table 18.2 names and describes various <FRAME> attributes.

Table 18–2: *HTML 4.0 <FRAME> Attributes*

Attribute	Description
frameborder	A border is drawn between adjacent frames. Use a value of 1 (default). A value of 0 specifies no border.

Table 18–2: HTML 4.0 <FRAME> Attributes (Continued)

Attribute	Description
longdesc	Provides a link to a long description of the frame. Useful for nonvisual user agents.
marginheight	Space between frame contents and top and bottom margins. Value must be > 1 pixel. Default value determined by browser.
marginwidth	Space between frame contents and the left and right margins. Value must be > 1 pixel. Default value determined by browser.
name	Assigns a name to the current frame.
noresize	When this attribute is present, the frame cannot be resized.
scrolling	Set to auto|yes|no. The default is auto and provides scrolling when necessary. A yes value always provides scrolling capabilities. A no value never provides scrolling capabilities.
src	Specifies the URL location of the document to be contained by the frame.

Nesting can also be achieved using <FRAME> and <FRAMESET> elements. Here is another example illustrating nesting:

```
<HTML>
<HEAD>
<TITLE>More Frames</TITLE>
</HEAD>

<FRAMESET cols="150,*,*">
  <FRAMESET rows="150,*">
    <FRAME src="image1.gif">
    <FRAME src="doc2.html">
  </FRAMESET>
  <FRAME src="doc3.html">
  <FRAME src="doc4.html">
</FRAMESET>

</HTML>
```

In this case, an image (approximately 150 x 150 pixels) is placed in the upper-left corner of the viewing area. This location represents the first frame. Two additional columns are specified, each to occupy one-half of the remaining horizontal viewing area. These will hold documents three and four, respectively. A second row will be inserted under the first column and will occupy the remaining column length. This frame will hold the contents of document 2. Figure 18.2 shows the resulting screen.

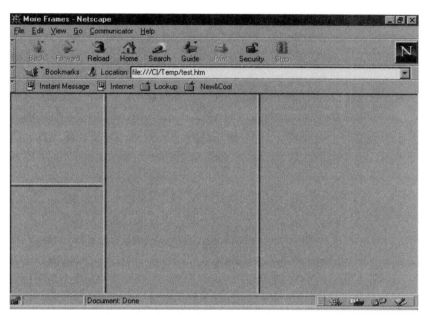

Figure 18–2:   *Multiple frames within a viewing area.*

Examine the screen and the previous listing to see if you can determine how this layout was achieved.

Using the <NOFRAMES> Tag

In cases where frames are not supported, use the <NOFRAMES> tag to identify content that is to be viewed when frames are not displayed. The <NOFRAMES> element, also known as an *alternate context* tag, can be used in the <FRAMESET> container or in the <BODY> of a document used within a frameset.

Here is an example where the document specifies a frameset with two identical rows, each occupying one-half of the viewing area each. Create this example and name the document master.html.

```
<HTML>
<HEAD>
<TITLE>A problem if frames aren't displayed</TITLE>
</HEAD>
<FRAMESET rows="50%,50%">
   <FRAME src="main.html">
<FRAME src="document.html">
   </FRAMESET>
</HTML>
```

In this example the first frame will incorporate a main.html document and the second frame will use document.html. If the browser is not displaying frames, the user will not see anything since there is no <BODY> element in the previous listing. A better way to write this would be to restructure the master.html and main.html documents. Here is the new and better master.html.

```
<HTML>
<HEAD>
<TITLE>NOFRAMES to the rescue</TITLE>
</HEAD>
<FRAMESET rows="50%,50%">
   <FRAME src="main.html">
<FRAME src="document.html">
   <NOFRAMES>
   <A href="main.html">
   </A>
   </NOFRAMES>
</FRAMESET>
</HTML>
```

Here is the new main.html.

```
<HTML>
<BODY>
<NOFRAMES>
   (place the document.html contents here)
</NOFRAMES>
   (remainder of the main.html document goes here)
</BODY>
</HTML>
```

In this example the document.html contents are included at the top of the main.html document within a <NOFRAMES> container. The main.html and master.html are then linked when frames are not displayed.

Using the <IFRAME> Tag

The <IFRAME> tag can be used to insert frames within a block of text. This element allows the frame to be inserted, aligned, and so on. The syntax for <IFRAME> is similar to that of the <FRAME> element. The src attribute refers to the information to be inserted in-line. A frame created with <IFRAME> cannot be resized, so the resize attribute is nonfunctional.

Here is an example, named Iframe.htm:

```
<HTML>
<HEAD>
<TITLE>An IFRAME Example</TITLE>
</HEAD>

<BODY>
<H1>An in-line frame example!</H1>
<HR>

<P>
This is a regular HTML document that contains simple
<BR>
text to view.  An in-line frame will be inserted <BR>
under this text to illustrate how this can be done.
</P>

<IFRAME src="data.htm" width="200"
  height="175" scrolling="yes">
</IFRAME>

<P>
You will find that a small in-line frame is ideal for
providing instant detail <BR>
for text that the user encounters within the main
document.
</P>

</BODY>
</HTML>
```

In this example a normal HTML document is created first. If frames are displayed, a paragraph of text will be displayed. Next, an in-line frame with additional text will be inserted. Finally, another paragraph of regular text will follow. Figure18.3 shows the resulting screen for this example.

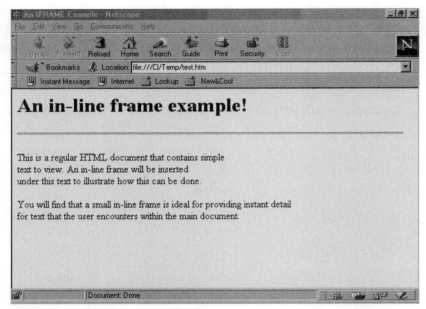

Figure 18–3: *Inserting an in-line frame is easy to do.*

Referencing the Target Frame

Developers can reference the frame as a target of links defined by other elements when a name is assigned to a frame using the name attribute. The target attribute can be set for elements that create links (<A> and <LINK>), image maps (<AREA>), and forms (<FORM>).

Here is an example named Target.html that will illustrate this concept.

```
<HTML>
<HEAD>
<TITLE>Illustrating the target attribute</TITLE>
</HEAD>

<FRAMESET rows="15%,25%,60%">
  <FRAME name="top" src="top.html">
  <FRAME name="middle" src="middle.html">
  <FRAME name="bottom" src="bottom.html">
</FRAMESET>

</HTML>
```

The <FRAMESET> element is used to create three frames. The first row occupies the top 15 percent of the viewing area, the second frame, 25 percent, and the final frame 60 percent. The frames are named top, middle, and bottom, respectively. Their contents will be top.html, middle.html, and bottom.html, respectively. Let's examine the individual document contents next.

The contents of the first document, named top.html, are shown next.

```
<HTML>
<BODY bgcolor="#00FFFF">

<P>
This portion of text will remain fixed in the first
frame.<BR>
Use the second frame to experiment with the target
attribute by<BR>
making a selection that "targets" the third frame.
</P>

</BODY>
</HTML>
```

This document will set the background color of the frame to light blue and then print some text in the frame. The contents of this frame are fixed and will not change.

The second frame sets the background color to yellow and then identifies the bottom frame as the target. Depending on the selection, the admin.html, dept.html, or stud.html documents will replace the contents of the bottom.html. This document is named middle.html.

```
<HTML>
<BODY>
<BODY bgcolor="#FFFF00">

<A href="admin.html" target="bottom">Administrative
Structure</A>
<BR>
<A href="dept.html" target="bottom">Department
Structure</A>
<BR>
<A href="stud.html" target="bottom">Student
Structure</A>

</BODY>
</HTML>
```

The third frame uses an empty document named bottom.html.

```
<HTML>
```

```
<BODY>


</BODY>
</HTML>
```

As selections are made within the second frame, various documents will "target" the bottom frame and replace its contents.

If the Administrative Structure is selected, admin.html will replace the contents of the bottom.html frame. The following listing represents the contents of the admin.html file:

```
<HTML>
<BODY>

<P>
At this college we have:<BR>
   One President<BR>
   Three Vice Presidents<BR>
   Three Division Deans<BR>
</P>

</BODY>
</HTML>
```

If the Department Structure is selected, dept.html will replace the contents of the bottom.html frame. The following listing represents the contents of the dept.html file:

```
<HTML>
<BODY>

<P>
Within a department we have:<BR>
   One department chair<BR>
   Several full-time faculty<BR>
   Several full and part-time adjunct faculty<BR>
   One Technical Assistant
</P>

</BODY>
</HTML>
```

Finally, if the Student Structure is selected, stud.html will replace the contents of the bottom.html frame. The following listing represents the contents of the stud.html file:

```
<HTML>
<BODY>

<P>
```

```
Among the student body, we have:<BR>
   Full time students<BR>
   Part time students
</P>

</BODY>
</HTML>
```

Figure 18.4 shows the initial viewing area.

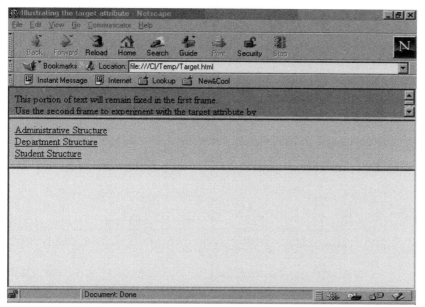

Figure 18–4:   The initial viewing area of the target example.

Figure 18.5 shows the viewing area and the updated contents of the third frame when the Department Structure is selected in the middle frame.

The contents of the bottom frame are changed because they are targeted by items in the second frame.

There are four special target names that can be used in place of a specific target: _blank, _parent, _self, and _top. Table 18.3 names and describes these special target names.

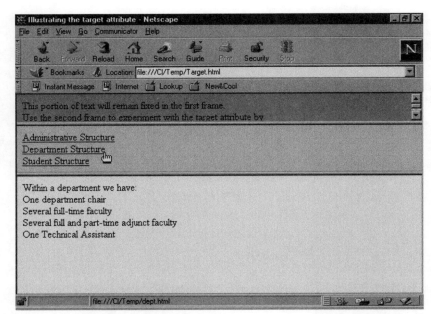

Figure 18–5: *The new contents of the bottom frame.*

Table 18–3: *Special Target Names*

Target Name	Description
_blank	Displays contents in a new, empty window that replaces the framed windows. This window has no name. Selecting the browser's "Back" button returns the user to the frame windows.
_parent	Displays contents in the immediate <FRAME-SET> parent of the document. If the frame has no parent, then this behaves like _self.
_self	Displays contents in the same frame where the link is located. _self is typically the default.
_top	Displays contents in a new, full-sized viewing area.

In the previous example, if the contents of this portion of the middle.html document were changed from

```
<A href="dept.html" target="bottom">Department
Structure</A>
<BR>
```

to

```
<A href="dept.html" target="_self">Department
Structure</A>
<BR>
```

the results of this change would be as shown in Figure 18.6.

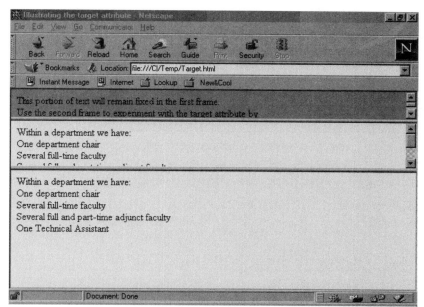

Figure 18–6: *Example HTML document viewed in the Netscape browser*

As you can see, the contents of the middle frame are replaced, since _self identifies the target as the frame containing the link.

Objects

A weakness of HTML is the fact that the number of tags and containers has been fixed from one version to another. This means that developers desiring extended HTML capabilities have had no means of extending HTML outside proprietary elements. As you have already learned, proprietary elements usually mean chaos for developers trying to implement applications for multiple browsers even when the choice is limited to just the Microsoft Internet Explorer or the Netscape Navigator.

The <OBJECT> container in HTML 4.0 has solved this problem. The <OBJECT> tag was officially introduced by the World Wide Web Consortium (W3C) with HTML 4.0. The <OBJECT> container is a first, and good, attempt at making HTML extensible. When a browser encounters an <OBJECT> container in an HTML document, it knows that it is about to deal with an image, applet, another HTML document, and so on. Previously defined containers can also handle many of the types handled by <OBJECT> containers. This includes <IMG>, <IFRAME>, <MAP>, and so on. These containers can still be used. The <OBJECT> container also handles applets. As a matter of fact, the <APPLET> container itself has been depreciated in favor of the <OBJECT> container.

The use of the <OBJECT> container will be investigated in this section. You'll also learn the syntax and parameters associated with the <OBJECT> and <PARAM> elements and investigate how they relate to other familiar containers. Additional work with HTML and JavaScript objects will be discussed in Chapters 21, 22, and 23.

Using the <OBJECT> Tag

The <OBJECT> tag is presented by HTML 4.0 as a generic solution to object inclusion for new and old media types. The use of the <OBJECT> element usually involves specifying source code, initial values, and any necessary runtime data. Images, for example, may include hyperlinks.

The <OBJECT> element uses a large number of attributes. Table 18.4 lists and describes the attributes associated with the <OBJECT> element.

Table 18–4: *<OBJECT> Element Attributes*

Attribute	Description
Align	Specifics the object's location in the viewing area. Use *bottom* to align the bottom of the element with the current baseline. Bottom is the default. Use *middle* to vertically align the center of the object with the current baseline. Use *top* to vertically align the object with the top of the current text line. Use *left* or *right* to align the image with the current left or right margin, respectively.

Table 18–4: *Continued*

387

Attribute	Description
Archive	Specifies a space-separated archive list.
Border	Specifies the border width placed around the object. The browser sets the default.
Class	Specifies a documentwide identifier.
Classid	Specifies the location of an object's implementation with a URL.
Codebase	Specifies the base path used to resolve a relative URL given by *classid*. The default is the base URL of the current document.
Codetype	Specifies the Internet media type of data used by the object specified by *classid*. The default value is that specified by the *type* attribute. The use of *codetype* avoids loading information for unnecessary media types.
Data	Specifies a URL for the location of the object's data.
Declare	A Boolean attribute used to make the <OBJECT> definition a declaration only. This requires that the object be instantiated by another <OBJECT> definition that refers to this declaration.
Dir	Specifies text direction.
Export	Specifies export shapes to parent.
Height	Specifies the height of an object in pixels.
Hspace	Specifies the amount of space to the left and right of an object. No default is specified.
Id	Specifies the object for the viewing area. It can also be used to locate other objects or hyperlinks.
Lang	Specifies language information.
Name	This attribute is used with forms. The name identifies objects in a <FORM> container to be submitted.
Onclick	Specifies an action relating to a mouse click (push/release).

Table 18–4: *<OBJECT> Element Attributes (Continued)*

Attribute	Description
Ondblclick	Specifies an action relating to a mouse double-click (push/release).
Onkeydown	Specifies an action relating to a key down event.
Onkeypress	Specifies an action relating to a key press (down/release) event.
Onkeyup	Specifies an action relating to a key release event.
Onmousedown	Specifies an action relating to a mouse button push.
Onmousemove	Specifies an action relating to the movement of the mouse.
Onmouseout	Specifies an action related to moving the mouse out of the area.
Onmouseover	Specifies an action related to moving the mouse into the area.
Onmouseup	Specifies an action relating to a mouse button release.
Shapes	Used with client-side image maps. For example, <OBJECT data="my.jpg" shapes> <A href=myshape.html shape=rect coords="0,0,150,150"> </OBJECT>
Standby	Specifies a message that a browser may display while loading the object's implementation and data. For example, standby="loading file" or standby="please wait!"
Style	Specifies in-line style information.
Tabindex	Specifies keyboard tabbing navigation.
Title	Specifies element titles.

Table 18–4: *Continued*

389

Attribute	Description
Type	Specifies the Internet media type of data used by the object specified by *data*. The use of *type* avoids loading information for unnecessary media types. If no value is specified, the browser must attempt to identify the media type. For example, type="image/gif" or type="video/avi"
Usemap	Specifies a URL used with a client-side image map.
Vspace	Specifies the amount of space above and below an object. No default is specified.
Width	Specifies the width of an object in pixels.

The browser provides mechanisms for rendering the most common data types. These data types may include, but are not limited to, avi, gif, html, jpeg, mov, mpeg, plain, and wav. If the data type isn't supported, the browser can seek an external application for support. The <OBJECT> element is used to render an object internally, externally, or by a program identified by the developer.

The <OBJECT> element depends upon three pieces of information:

- Initial values, where applicable, for the object's use at runtime. This is typically done via the <PARAM> element.
- The data to be rendered. For example, if the object renders color data, the location of that data must be indicated.
- The object's implementation. In other words, what is the location of the object's code.

Browsers interpret an <OBJECT> element by either rendering the object or rendering the object's contents.

For example, here is a portion of code that attempts to load a Java applet:

```
<OBJECT codetype="application/octet-stream"
  classid="java:program.start" width="450"
  height="350">
Click mouse here to view images in a Java applet
```

```
</OBJECT>
```

Here a Java applet is rendered in the viewing area with a width of 450 pixels and a height of 350 pixels.

It is also possible to bring an ActiveX object to the viewing area:

```
<OBJECT classid="clsid:884C8FEF-iEF8-11CE-A4DC-
080072E12601"
   data="http://www.hereitis.com/ole/myobject.stm">
   This object is not currently supported
</OBJECT>
```

It is also possible for <OBJECT> containers to be nested. The following example first attempts to lead a Perl application. If the Perl application cannot be rendered, a JPEG image, on the local hard disk, will be rendered in its place:

```
<OBJECT title="Great shapes"
   classid="http://www.mysite.pic/myprogram.pl">
     <!-- Otherwise, try this image -->
   <OBJECT data="rectangle.jpg">
     <!-- Otherwise, display this text -->
     An rectangle shape.
   </OBJECT>
</OBJECT>
```

In this example, a browser will attempt to render the first <OBJECT> element possible. The first attempt will be to execute *myprogram.pl*. If this is not possible, an attempt will then be made to display an image of a rectangle (rectangle.jpg).

In this example, the first <OBJECT> element specifies a program that has no data or initial values. The second <OBJECT> element will rely on the browser to handle the image type since no location is defined. Alternative text is provided for situations where both <OBJECTS> fail to be rendered.

Consider a complete example that will attempt to load a GIF satellite weather image from a specific location.

```
<HTML>
<HEAD>
<TITLE>Viewing GIF Weather Images</TITLE>
</HEAD>
<BODY>

<OBJECT
   data="http://www.atmos.washington.edu/cgi-bin/lat-
est.cgi?ir16km"
   type="image/gif" align=center
```

```
        standby="Weather image loading"
        height="400" width="400" title="Weather">

      <!-- If not, try this one -->
      <OBJECT data="c:\temp\9803311200.gif"
        type="image/jpeg" align=center
        standby="Alternate weather image loading"
        height="400" width="400" title="earth">
      </OBJECT>
    </OBJECT>

  </BODY>
</HTML>
```

In this example, if the first object cannot be rendered, an attempt will be made to load the same GIF image previously stored on the local hard disk. Figure 18.7 shows the viewing area for one attempt.

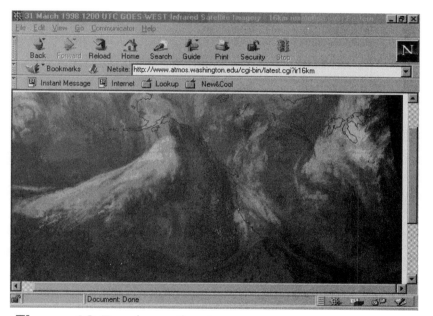

Figure 18-7:   *A weather image.*

In this case, the original object is rendered, so the GIF's image from the hard disk is not accessed. It is also possible for data to be supplied in-line or from an external source. In-line sources are typically faster but limited in the amount of data. External sources are slower but offer vast resources of data.

Working with Multiple Instantiations

Often a document can contain more than one instance of the same object. This is called multiple instantiation. It is possible to separate the object declaration from its instantiations. The advantage of this is that a single retrieval of an object is made even when it is reused several times.

When the declare attribute is set in the <OBJECT> element, the object will not be executed when read by the browser. The use of the declare attribute requires that the ID attribute also be set to a unique value. All future instantiations will refer to this ID attribute value.

Here is a complete example that makes use of the previous weather satellite application to show the syntax for multiple instantiation.

```
<HTML>
<HEAD>
<TITLE>Multiple Instantiations</TITLE>
</HEAD>
<BODY>

<OBJECT declare
  id="gif-image"
  data="c:\temp\9803311200.gif"
  type="image/gif"
  standby="Please Wait - Loading GIF Image"
  height="400" width="400" title="Earth">
  An Earth picture from a weather satellite.
</OBJECT>

A weather disturbance off the <A href="#gif-image">
  Pacific Coast.</A>

</BODY>
</HTML>
```

Figure 18.8 shows the image that is rendered when the HTML document is loaded.

Multiple mouse clicks on the "Pacific Coast" text produce multiple instantiations. Notice the address shown in Figure 18.9 as compared to Figure 18.8.

If a browser doesn't support the declare attribute, it must render the contents of the <OBJECT> declaration.

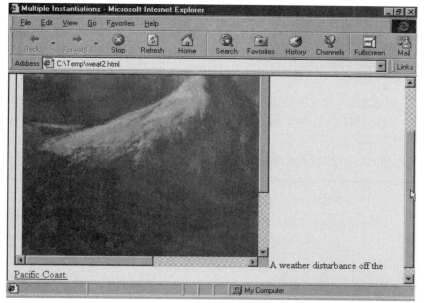

Figure 18–8:   The original image object is loaded.

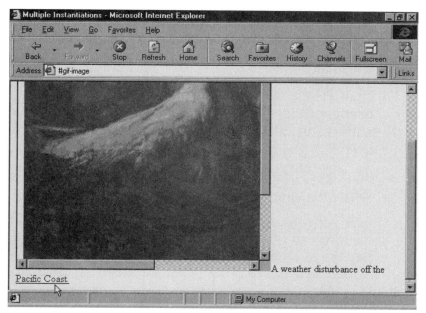

Figure 18–9:   An instantiation of the original object.

Using the <PARAM> Tag

Initial values to be used by an object at runtime are specified with the use of the <PARAM> tag in conjunction with the <OBJECT> tag. Multiple <PARAM> tags may follow an <OBJECT> tag. Names and values are passed to the object on its standard input. The <PARAM> tag uses the attributes listed and described in Table 18.5.

Table 18–5: *<PARAM> Element Attributes*

Attribute	Description
id	Specifies a documentwide ID.
name	Specifies the runtime parameter name. The object must know the parameter name.
type	Specifies the Internet media type of data used by the object specified by *value* attribute when *valuetype* is set to "ref." This specifies the type of values found at the URL.
value	Specifies the value of a runtime parameter specified by *name*. The object determines the meaning of the value.
valuetype	Specifies the value type as data, ref, or object.
	data: Passes the specified *value* to the object's implementation as a string. Embedded character and/or numeric character entities are resolved. This is the default.
	ref: Passes the URL specified by *value* where runtime values are stored.
	object: Passes a fragment URL specified by *value* that identifies an object declaration in the same document. Use the *id* attribute.

Examine the following portion of code to illustrate the use of the <PARAM> element. Here the <PARAM> tags specify initial values, and the height and width of the rendered object.

.
.
.

```
<OBJECT
   classid="http://www.mylocation.com/jpgviewer"
   standby="Loading a mountain">
<PARAM name="init_values"
    value="./Shel09_1.jpg"
    valuetype="ref">
<PARAM name="height" value="220">
<PARAM name="width" value="180">
</OBJECT>
```

.
.
.

The standby attribute is set here to warn the user of a possible delay in seeing the rendered object.

Using the <IMG> or <OBJECT> Tag

In Chapter 4 you learned how to use the <IMG> tag to render a graphics image in the viewing area. The syntax is fairly simple. For example,

```
<IMG src="ftp://explorer.arc.nasa.gov/pub/Weather/
         GOES-8/jpg/vis/4km/9711211644.jpg">
```

An equivalent example, using the <OBJECT> element, takes on this form:

```
<OBJECT data="ftp://explorer.arc.nasa.gov/pub/Weather/
             GOES-8/jpg/vis/4km/9711211644.jpg"
         type="image/jpg">
```

You may be asking, "Why use <OBJECT> when rendering images with <IMG> requires less code?" The answer is that all file types, even if they are not HTML file types, can be treated as objects.

You'll also find that the use of <OBJECT> in place of <IMG> eliminates the dialog that occurs when you attempt to link to a file type not known by the system. The system does not have to deal with the returned MIME type. The burden rests with the browser and associated helper applications.

Using the \<IFRAME\> or \<OBJECT\> Tag

Earlier in this chapter the use of the \<IFRAME\> tag was investigated. HTML 4.0 actually allows you to accomplish the same feats with the \<OBJECT\> element. Here is a sample \<IFRAME\> example.

```
<HTML>
<HEAD>
<TITLE>An IFRAME Example</TITLE>
</HEAD>

<BODY>
<H1>An in-line frame example!</H1>
<HR>

<P>
This is a regular HTML document that contains simple
<BR>
text to view.  An in-line frame will be inserted <BR>
under this text to illustrate how this can be done.
</P>

<IFRAME src="data.htm" width="200"
  height="175" scrolling="yes">
</IFRAME>

<P>
You will find that a small in-line frame is ideal for
providing instant detail <BR>
for text that the user encounters within the main
document.
</P>

</BODY>
</HTML>
```

Remember that the \<IFRAME\> element allows a document to be inserted into another document. The inserted document, named data.html, will remain independent of the initial document.

Here is the same application modified to use the \<OBJECT\> tag. The following listing shows the necessary changes:

```
<HTML>
<HEAD>
<TITLE>An OBJECT tag replaces the IFRAME tag</TITLE>
</HEAD>

<BODY>
<H1>An in-line frame example!</H1>
<HR>
```

```
<P>
This is a regular HTML document that contains simple
<BR>
text to view.  An in-line frame will be inserted <BR>
under this text to illustrate how this can be done.
</P>

<OBJECT data="c:\data.html" width="200"
  height="175" scrolling="yes">
</OBJECT>

<P>
You will find that a small in-line frame is ideal for
providing instant detail <BR>
for text that the user encounters within the main
document.
</P>

</BODY>
</HTML>
```

Figure 18.10 shows the object as rendered to the viewing area.

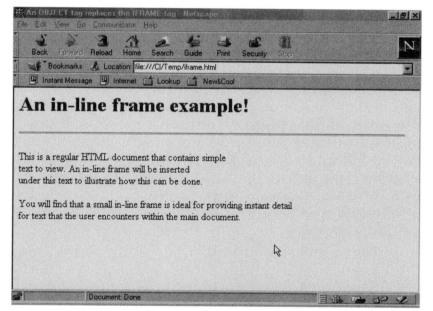

Figure 18–10:   *A document can be embedded within another by using <IFRAME> or <OBJECT>.*

The embedded document using <OBJECT> is rendered within another document but remains independent of that document. This is similar to using the <IFRAME> element.

Revisiting Image Maps

Recall that you learned how to build both client-side and server-side image maps in Chapter 6. The image was rendered with the <IMG> element and the map was identified with the <MAP> element. Then each area of the map was set using the <AREA> element.

The <OBJECT> container can also be used to specify a client-side image map. Server-side maps are specified in the conventional manner presented in Chapter 6.

To use a client-side map specified with the <OBJECT> container, the shape attribute must be set and the image map defined within the container.

Here is an application, from Chapter 6, that builds a client-side image map in the conventional manner.

```
<HTML>

<HEAD>
<TITLE>Client-side imagemap</TITLE>
</HEAD>
<BODY>

<IMG src="ImgMap1.jpg" usemap="#firstmap">
<P>You want to go where today?<BR>
<MAP name="firstmap">
<AREA href="http://www.microsoft.com/office/"
   shape="rect"
   coords="0, 0, 210, 137">
<AREA href="http://www.microsoft.com/word/"
   shape="rect"
   coords="211, 0, 420, 137">
<AREA href="http://www.microsoft.com/excel/"
   shape="rect"
   coords="0, 138, 210, 275">
<AREA href="http://www.microsoft.com/access/"
   shape="rect"
   coords="211, 138, 420, 275">
</MAP>

</BODY>
</HTML>
```

Figure 18.11 shows how this client-side map is rendered.

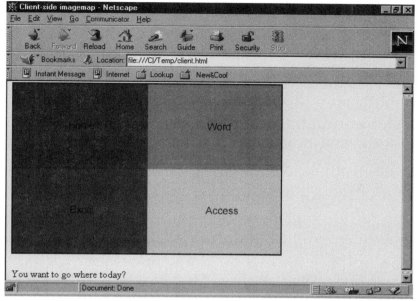

Figure 18–11:   *A client-side image map using <IMG>, <MAP>, and <AREA> elements.*

The previous example can be modified to use the <OBJECT> tag. The following listing shows the necessary changes.

```
<HTML>

<HEAD>
<TITLE>Client-side imagemap with OBJECT</TITLE>
</HEAD>

<BODY>
<OBJECT data="ImgMap1.jpg" firstmap>
<P>You want to go where today?<BR>
<A href="http://www.microsoft.com/office/" shape="rect"
   coords="0, 0, 210, 137"></A>
<A href="http://www.microsoft.com/word/" shape="rect"
   coords="211, 0, 420, 137"></A>
<A href="http://www.microsoft.com/excel/"
shape="rect"
   coords="0, 138, 210, 275"></A>
<A href="http://www.microsoft.com/access/" shape="rect"
   coords="211, 138, 420, 275"></A>
</OBJECT>

</BODY>
```

```
</HTML>
```

The shape attribute notifies the <OBJECT> element that an image map is to be defined. The image map is defined within the <OBJECT> container with each region of the map being specified using the <A> container. Each <A> element then uses the shape attribute to specify the unique region.

As of this writing, neither Internet Explorer (version 4.71) nor Netscape Communicator (version 4.04) fully supported client-side maps included in this manner. This may be a temporary problem that will be addressed with the release of HTML 4.0 by the W3C standards committee.

Layers and Layering

The formal use of the <LAYER> and <ILAYER> containers was first introduced by Netscape. At this writing, layers have not been included by the W3C group and are not a part of the proposed HTML 4.0 standard. The concept and capabilities of layers, however, demand they be introduced in almost any HTML book.

There are differences between the concept of layering and the <LAYER> container. Layering, as a concept, means placing one thing over another. We layer clothes in the winter to stay warm: undergarments, regular clothes, and coats. The concept is simple enough. All browsers permit some degree of layering, as you will see in this chapter. When used in this context, <LAYER> and </LAYER> represent the top and bottom of the garments—undergarments and the coat.

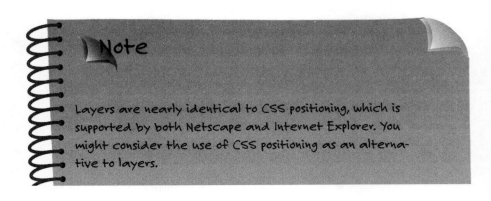

Note

Layers are nearly identical to CSS positioning, which is supported by both Netscape and Internet Explorer. You might consider the use of CSS positioning as an alternative to layers.

The <LAYER> container is currently supported by Netscape Communicator, versions 4.0 and later. As of this writing, Microsoft Internet Explorer version 4.72 does not support the <LAYER> container. If the W3C group doesn't endorse it, it will probably be exclusively Netscape's tag.

Portions of the viewing area can be controlled with the <LAYER> container. If multiple layers are used, some may show their contents while others may choose to hide theirs. Using the left, top, width, and height attributes, you can precisely specify each layer's position.

In this section, we'll first look at some layering concepts and then investigate the use of the <LAYER> container and a close relative, the <ILAYER> container. You'll learn that you are already familiar with many "layering" concepts.

Layering with the <DIV> Tag

Text and images can be layered in a very simple fashion. Here is an example that uses the <DIV> container to place two portions of text in the viewing area. One portion of text is drawn in red and the other portion of text in blue.

Here is the code for this example, named Layer1.html.

```
<HTML>
<HEAD>
<TITLE>zIndex with text</TITLE>
<STYLE type="text/css">
  H2 {border: 4pt double; text-align: center;
      font: 60pt arial}
</STYLE>
</HEAD>
<BODY>
<H1><CENTER>Text zIndex Demo</CENTER></H1>

<DIV id="text1" style="position: absolute; top:
120px;
  left: 60px; color: red; z-index: 2">
<H2>The Text1 box</H2>
</DIV>
<DIV id="text2" style="position: absolute; top:
160px;
  left: 100px; color: blue; z-index: 1">
<H2>The Text2 box</H2>
</DIV>
```

```
</BODY>
</HTML>
```

In this example, notice that styling concepts from Chapter 8 have been used to set the <H2> border style, text alignment, and font size.

The <DIV> tag allows the document to be divided into a number of divisions, with each division containing, for example, its own text. The style attribute sets the absolute position for the *top* and *left* of the text as well as for the font color and size.

The text was made to overlap to illustrate the concept of layering. As a matter of fact, by using the z-index attribute, you can decide which layer appears on top. As you face the viewing area, the y-axis of the screen is represented by the vertical coordinate of the viewing area while the x-axis of the screen is represented by the horizontal coordinate of the viewing area. The z-axis, is an imaginary line starting at the viewing area and moving toward your eyes. Positions on the z-axis with low values appear closer to the screen. Positions on the z-axis with high values appear closer to your eyes. Thus, in this previous example, the red text is closer to the screen than the blue text. When you view the figure, the red text will overlap the blue text. In other words, the red text layer is on top of the blue text layer. You can experiment and change the z-order around and place the red text on top of the blue text simply by changing the z-index value.

The use of z-indexing adds the concept of 3D to the viewing area, but it does not correct for perspective. Regardless of the z-order numbers, the text or image will always be drawn to the same size. If you want to give a proper perspective to the shape of text, you will have to adjust the size of the text or image yourself.

Figure 18.12 shows the viewing area for this example.

In the next example, we'll use the <IMG> container to place three images in the viewing area. The images in this example are simply rectangles filled with specific colors. However, you can chose to use artwork or photographs if you desire.

The code for this example is named Layer2.html.

```
<HTML>
<HEAD>
<TITLE>zIndex with shapes</TITLE>
</HEAD>
<BODY>
<H1><CENTER>Image zIndex Demo</CENTER></H1>
```

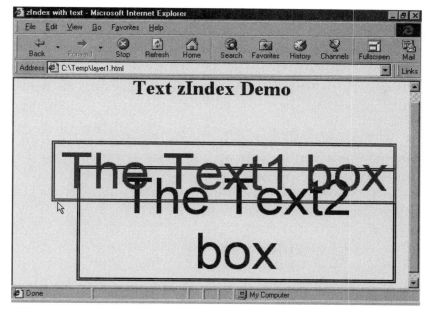

Figure 18–12: *Layering is achieved with the <DIV> container and z-indexing.*

```
<IMG src="ybox.jpg" id=yellowshape
  style="container: positioned;
  position: absolute; top: 50;
  left: 50; height:100; width:200;
  z-index: 2">
<IMG src="bbox.jpg" id=blueshape
  style="container: positioned;
  position: absolute; top: 80;
  left: 80; height:100; width:200;
  z-index: 1">
<IMG src="rbox.jpg" id=redshape
  style="container: positioned;
  position: absolute; top: 110;
  left: 110; height:100; width:200;
  z-index: 3">

</BODY>
</HTML>
```

In this example, the <IMG> tag allows three images to be placed in the viewing area. The images were created and saved in the JPEG files format with the Microsoft Image Composer.

Examine the code and note that the style attribute is used to set the absolute position of the image by specifying the *top*, *left*, *height*, and *width* values. Also notice that the *z*-index value has been set for each shape.

Based on the knowledge of *z*-ordering, you can predict which shape will be in the top, middle, and bottom positions. For this example, the red shape will be on top, closest to your eye, and the blue shape will be one the bottom, nearest the screen. Remember that higher *z*-orders move the shape closer to your eye while lower *z*-orders move the shape closer to the screen.

Figure 18.13 shows the screen's viewing area for this example.

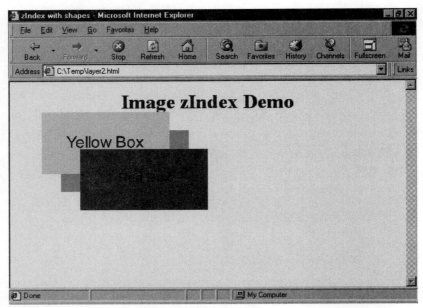

Figure 18–13: *Layering is achieved with the <IMG> tag and z-ordering.*

When we tried this example using Microsoft Internet Explorer, we found that it rendered its documents' contents correctly. However, Netscape Navigator did not produce correct results.

Both of the previous examples illustrate that it is possible to work with layers within a normal document using familiar tags. In the remaining sections of this chapter, we'll investigate how the <LAYER> and <ILAYER> containers provide a new dimension to Web page design.

Using the <LAYER> and <ILAYER> Tags

The <LAYER> and <ILAYER> tags allow a number of attributes to be set for each layer created.

Table 18.6 lists the attributes, properties, and a short description of
<LAYER> and <ILAYER>. These values are identical for both
<LAYER> and <ILAYER> elements except where noted.

Table 18–6: *<LAYER> and <ILAYER> Element Attributes*

Attribute	Properties	Description
above	Use name of any layer.	Specifies that the present layer is above the given layer name.
background	Use any desired URL.	Specifies a background image to be displayed.
below	Use name of any layer.	Specifies that the present layer is below the given layer name.
bgcolor	Use the hexadecimal format #RRGGBB.	Specifies the background color for the layer.
clip	Use: clip.left, clip.right, clip.top, clip.bottom, clip.height, and clip.width.	Specifies a clip rectangle with left, right, top, and bottom values. Values in pixels are the default. Information within the clip rectangle in a given layer is visible in the viewing area.
left	Specify an integer value representing the distance.	For <LAYER> this value specifies the layer's left edge measured from the left edge of the viewing area. Units measured in pixels are the default. For <ILAYER> this value specifies the left offset from the last tag or text.
name	Use any valid string.	Specifies a name that is referenced by a script language such as JavaScript or VBScript.
parentLayer	Use any valid string.	Specifies the layer in which the named layer is contained.
siblingAbove	Use any valid string.	Specifies that the current layer is above the given layer.

Table 18–6: *<LAYER> and <ILAYER> Element Attributes (Continued)*

Attribute	Properties	Description
siblingBelow	Use any valid string.	Specifies that the current layer is below the given layer.
src	SRC="URL"	SRC is a URL that the layer is pointing to. The contents of the HTML file will be the layer.
top	Specify an integer value representing the distance.	For <LAYER> this value specifies the layer's top edge measured from the top edge of the viewing area. Unit defaults are pixels. For <ILAYER> this value specifies the top offset from the last tag or text.
visibility	Use show, hide, or inherit.	Specifies if the layer is visible using *show*, *hide*, or *inherit*. Inherit uses the visibility attribute of the parent.
width	Specify an integer value representing the width.	Specifies the width of the layer. Widths specified in pixels are the default.
zindex	Specify an integer value representing the z-index.	Specifies the z-index value of layer display. Using an imaginary line from the viewing area to the user's eye, higher values place the layer closer to the user while lower numbers place the layer closer to the viewing area.

In addition to the attributes and properties, certain methods (functions) are available for each layer. Table 18.7 provides a list and short description of these methods.

Table 18–7: *<LAYER> and <ILAYER> Methods*

Method	Parameter	Description
visibility()	Use "show," "hide," or "inherit."	Specifies the layer's visibility.
offset()	Use any integer value to specify the *x,y* offset.	Specifics the layer's left and top offsets. Pixels values are the default. Offset can be to the left (negative numbers), to the right (positive numbers), up (negative numbers), or down (positive numbers).
moveAbove()	Use any valid string for the layer name.	Specifies that the present layer is to be placed above the identified layer.
moveBelow()	Use any valid string for the layer name.	Specifies that the present layer is to be placed below the identified layer.
moveTo()	Use any integer value to specify the *x,y* position.	Specifies the position to place a layer by using the upper-left starting position of the layer.
resize()	Use any integer value to specify the width and height values.	Specifies the new size of a resized layer. The width and height values are given in pixels by default.

In the previous programming example we layered three different color rectangles using the <IMG> tag. In the following example, we'll create a similar (but not identical) example using the <LAYER> element. This example is named Layer3.html.

```
<HTML>
<HEAD>
<TITLE>z-Indexing with layers</TITLE>
</HEAD>
<BODY>
<H1><CENTER>z-Index with Layers Demo</CENTER></H1>

<LAYER name="red" left=50 top=50 width=200 height=100
  visibility=show bgcolor="#FF0000" z-index=1>
```

```
</LAYER>
<LAYER name="green" left=80 top=80 width=200
height=100
  visibility=show bgcolor="#00FF00" z-index=3>
</LAYER>
<LAYER name="blue" left=110 top=110 width=200
height=100
  visibility=show bgcolor="#0000FF" z-index=2>
</LAYER>

</BODY>
</HTML>
```

In this example, the <LAYER> element is used to create three identically sized colored rectangles. The first rectangle is set at a position starting at a viewing position of 50, 50 pixels. The second rectangle is started at 80, 80 and the third at 110, 110. The visibility attribute of each rectangle is set to *show*. If z-ordering weren't used, the rectangles would be layered in the order they are specified: red, green, and blue. However, z-index numbers rearrange this ordering to green, blue, and red. Figure 18.14 is a screen shot of the viewing area. The green rectangle is the top layer in this figure.

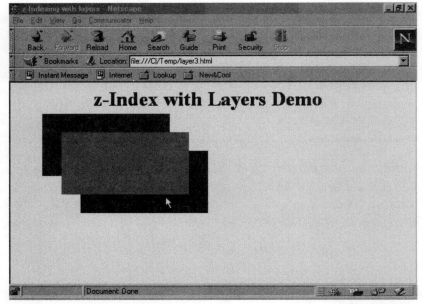

Figure 18–14: *The <LAYER> element is used to create three distinctive layers.*

To further your understanding of <LAYER> and <ILAYER> attributes, why not take the time to modify the visibility and *z*-index attributes. It is always fun to try and predict results before you execute new code.

Simple Animation Using JavaScript and Layers

Layers lend themselves to animation techniques because they can be sized to almost any shape and because they can be placed precisely in any viewing area. In the following example, we'll create a small red rectangular layer and then move it about in a 640 x 480 pixel viewing area. This example is named Layer4.html.

```
<HTML>
<HEAD>
<TITLE>Bouncing Shape Demo</TITLE>
</HEAD>
<BODY rgcolor="#FFFF00">
<H1><CENTER>Layer Animation</CENTER></H1>

<LAYER name="shape" top=240 left=320 height=15
  width=15 bgcolor=#FF0000></LAYER>
<SCRIPT language="JavaScript">
function motion() {
  yPos=yPos+yStep;
  xPos=xPos+xStep;
  if (xPos>640) {xStep=-xStep}
  if (xPos<0) {xStep=-xStep}
  if (yPos>480) {yStep=-yStep}
  if (yPos<0) {yStep=-yStep}
  document.layers["shape"].top=yPos;
  document.layers["shape"].left=xPos;
  setTimeout ("motion()", 5);
}

xStep=2;
yStep=2;
xPos=320;
yPos=240;
motion();
</SCRIPT>

</BODY>
</HTML>
```

This example starts by creating a simple layer with the following code.

```
<LAYER name="shape" top=240 left=320 height=15
  width=15 bgcolor=#FF0000></LAYER>
```

The layer is named *shape* and is simply a red 15 x 15 pixel rectangle initially located at a viewing position of 320 x 240 pixels. JavaScript is used as the scripting language to create the motion() function.

```
<SCRIPT language="JavaScript">
function motion() {
  yPos=yPos+yStep;
  xPos=xPos+xStep;
  if (xPos>640) {xStep=-xStep}
  if (xPos<0) {xStep=-xStep}
  if (yPos>480) {yStep=-yStep}
  if (yPos<0) {yStep=-yStep}
    .
    .
    .
```

The layer (object) will bounce about in a viewing area set to the size of a VGA 640 x 480 screen. If the object approaches a left-right or top-bottom boundary, the step position is reversed to send the object in the opposite direction. Each time the function is executed, the position of the layer is changed by specifying new *top* and *left* positions.

```
    .
    .
    .
  document.layers["shape"].top=yPos;
  document.layers["shape"].left=xPos;
  setTimeout ("motion()", 5);
}
```

The JavaScript setTimeout() function is used to pace the movement of the object. The time interval is set to 5 milliseconds. Experiment with this value to speed up or slow down the movement.

The final portion of code shows how the initial values for the layer are set.

```
xStep=2;
yStep=2;
xPos=320;
yPos=240;
motion();
</SCRIPT>
```

The initial object position agrees with the position the object was drawn at using the <LAYER> element. The step size is set to 2 for both the horizontal and vertical increments. If this value is increased, the motion will appear to speed up, but the movement will be more coarse or jerky. If the value is decreased to 1, the motion will appear to slow down, but the movement will be smoother.

Figure 18.15 shows a screen shot of the layer shortly after the motion began.

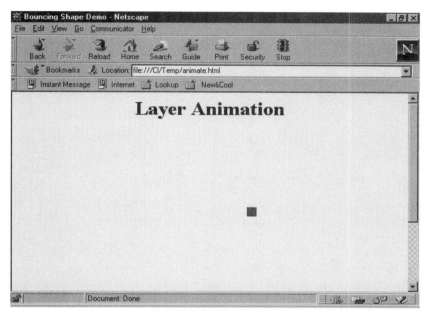

Figure 18–15: *Layers can be moved about in the viewing area producing simple animation.*

Now, it is your turn. Why not replace the animated rectangle with an image? Use a graphics editor to create an image of a dog, plane, boat, or flying toaster. Now insert the image in place of the colored rectangle. Wow!

Clipping and Relative Positioning

The final example will demonstrate how to create a clipping rectangle using the <LAYER> element and then show how <ILAYER> positions layers relative to the last text or image displayed.

Examine the following code, named Layer5.html.

```
<HTML>
<HEAD>
<TITLE>Using LAYER and ILAYER together</TITLE>
</HEAD>
<BODY>
<H1><CENTER>LAYER and ILAYER Demo</CENTER></H1>

More than one LAYER or ILAYER can be used in a
document to create dramatic effects.

<LAYER name="gray" left=50 top=250 width=200
height=50
   visibility=show bgcolor="#C0C0C0" clip="0, 0, 100,
60">
   Such as the text enclosed in this clipping rectan-
gle.
</LAYER>

As you know with ILAYER, positioning is relative
to the last text or image in the viewing area.

<ILAYER name="yellow" width=50 height=20
   visibility=show bgcolor="#FFFF00">
   Use this type of layering to produce dramatic
effects.
</ILAYER>

There is no limit to what you can do with layers!

</BODY>
</HTML>
```

Here, a layer is created with the <LAYER> element and positioned so that its upper-left corner is at a viewing position of 50, 250 pixels. The width of the layer is set to 200 pixels and the height to 100 pixels.

```
<LAYER name="gray" left=50 top=250 width=200 height=100
   visibility=show bgcolor="#C0C0C0" clip="0, 0, 100,
60">
   Such as the text enclosed in this clipping rectan-
gle.
</LAYER>
```

A clipping rectangle is created with the dimensions shown in the previous portion of code. As you view Figure 18.16, you'll notice that not all of the text is displayed. The clipping rectangle only displays that portion of text within the clipping area.

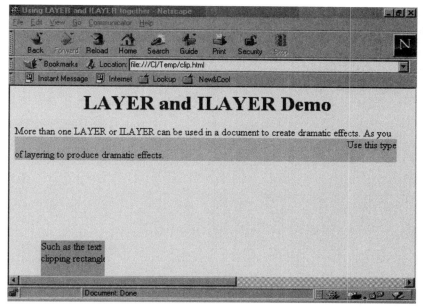

Figure 18–16: *The grayed box (lower portion of the screen) shows text in the visible clipping region.*

The <ILAYER> element places layers relative to the last text or image that was displayed. The following portion of code creates a yellow layer and places it immediately after the previous text.

```
<ILAYER name="yellow" width=50 height=20
   visibility=show bgcolor="#FFFF00">
   Use this type of layering to produce dramatic
effects.
</ILAYER>
```

The text contained within the <ILAYER> container will appear within the yellow layer. Examine Figure 18.16 again to see how this layer is placed within the viewing area.

Summary

In this chapter you learned how to work with HTML frames, objects, and layers. During our investigation of these concepts you have seen how they can be used to enhance Web applications. Additionally, you learned that JavaScript can be used as a programming tool in many areas, such as in the example illustrating animation. You also learned that life is not perfect. Many of the layer concepts that work so well under the Internet Explorer do not work under Netscape. In those situations, cascading style sheets are your best alternative (see Chapter 8 for more details).

CHAPTER 19 COOKIES

- Cookie Details

- Attributes

- Request Header

- Examples

You learned how to create simple forms in Chapter 7 and then investigated the server-side use of CGI scripts in Chapter 9. In this chapter we'll investigate the use of the cookie property, its purpose, and how it can be used to access information stored in a cookie file.

By definition, cookies are a means by which CGI scripts in server-side applications and JavaScripts in client-side applications can be used to store and retrieve information. This information is typically stored on the client side in a text file, such as cookies.txt. The term cookies was first used by Netscape and later adopted by other browsers. The name cookie has no significance so we'll resist applying the names sugar, peanut butter, ginger snap, and so on to the examples in this chapter.

Netscape provides a detailed source of information regarding cookies at http://www.netscape.com/newsref/std/cookie_spec.html. You should check this location for current cookie information. Much of the information in this chapter was developed from this site.

Cookie Details

A server can send a piece of state information, which the client will store, when an HTTP object is returned to the client. Typically, the state object will contain a description of the range of URLs for which the state is valid. Additional HTTP requests falling in the range will include information regarding the current value of the state object as sent from the client to the server.

According to Netscape, "this simple mechanism provides a powerful new tool which enables a host of new types of applications to be written for Web-based environments." For example, a shopping cart application can store information about the items selected for a specific shopping trip. Fee services, such as stock market and reference information providers, can return registration information to the client and free them from having to enter user ID information for each connection.

Cookie Access

A cookie is accessible to the client when a Set-Cookie header is part of an HTTP response. This is usually provided by a CGI script file.

The syntax used by a CGI script takes the following form:

```
Set-Cookie: NAME=VALUE; expires=DATE;
path=PATH; domain=DOMAIN_NAME; secure
```

This script allows access to new data that will be stored by the client for later retrieval and use.

When using JavaScript you can access values with the assignment operator. Use this syntax:

```
document.cookie = "NAME=VALUE      // VALUE as a string
[; expires=DATE]                   // DATE as GMT
format string
[; path=PATH]                          // Path name
[; domain=DOMAIN-NAME]             // Domain name
[; secure]                             // Secure
```

In the following sections we'll examine each of these attributes.

The NAME=VALUE Attribute

The NAME=VALUE string is a sequence of characters and is the only required attribute for the Set-Cookie header. Excluded from this sequence are commas, semicolons, and whitespace.

Here are a few valid name=value pairs that can be used for this attribute:

```
NAME1=Tango_Murray
NAME2=Tia_Pappas
CITY=Wilmington
```

If commas, semicolons, or whitespace must be placed in the string, then an encoding method must be used. For example, the URL style %XX encoding can be used.

The expires=DATE Attribute

The expires=DATE attribute uses a string that gives the valid lifetime of the cookie. When the expiration date has been reached, the cookie will no longer be stored and will not be retrievable.

The string containing the date information is formatted as

```
Weekday, DD-Mon-YYYY HH:MM:SS GMT
```

This formatting is based on RFC 822, 850, 1036, and 1123. The only legal time zone is GMT. The separators between the elements of the date must be dashes and those between the elements of the time must be colons. This is an optional attribute. If expires is not specified, the cookie automatically expires at the end of the current session.

The path=PATH Attribute

On versions of Netscape Navigator 1.1 and earlier, the cookie path must be explicitly set to "/" in order to be saved properly when using the expires attribute.

The path=PATH attribute is used to provide a subset of URLs in a domain where the cookie is valid. When a cookie has passed domain matching, the path name of the URL is compared with the path attribute. If a match occurs, the cookie is treated as valid and sent with the URL request.

The path "/" is the most general path. However, if the path is set to "/foo," a match would also occur for "/foohere," "/foo/here.html," and so on.

When a path is not given, the default assumption is that it is the same path as the document that contains the cookie.

The domain=DOMAIN_NAME Attribute

The domain=DOMAIN_NAME attribute is used when searching the cookie list for valid cookies. A comparison is made of the domain attributes of the cookie with the Internet domain name of the host from where the URL will be retrieved. When a tail match occurs, the cookie then goes through path matching to determine if it can be sent. Tail matching matches the domain attribute against the tail of a fully qualified domain name of a host. For example, the domain attribute "tester.com" would match the host names "circuit.tester.com" and "electrical.circuit.tester.com."

Netscape warns that only hosts within a specified domain can set a cookie for the domain. In addition, domains falling into the COM, EDU, NET, ORG, GOV, MIL, and INT categories must have at least two periods. All other domains must incorporate three periods in them.

If a domain is not specified, the default value is assumed to be the host name of the server that generated the cookie response.

The secure Attribute

The secure attribute is used to mark the cookie as secure. When the cookie is marked in this manner, it will be transmitted only if the communication channel with the host is a secure one. An HTTPS (HTTP over SSL) server is considered secure. If secure is not used, the cookie will be sent over unsecured channels.

The Cookie HTTP Request Header

When a URL is requested from an HTTP server, the browser attempts to match the URL against all cookies. If a match is found, a line containing the name/value pairs of all matching cookies is included in the HTTP request. For example,

```
Cookie: NAME1=STRING1; NAME2=STRING2; NAME3=STRING3...
```

Special Netscape Notes

The following series of notes is provided by Netscape (see previously provided URL) for HTTP cookies.

It is possible to issue multiple Set-Cookie headers in a single server response.

Multiple instances of the same path and name will overwrite each other. The latest instance takes precedence. Instances using the same path but with different names add additional mappings.

If the path is set to a higher-level value it does not override other more specific path mappings. When there are multiple matches for a given cookie name, involving separate paths, all the matching cookies will be sent.

The expires header informs the client when it is safe to purge the mapping. The client may also delete a cookie before its expiration date arrives when the number of cookies exceeds its internal limits.

All cookies sent to a server with a more specific path mapping should be sent before cookies with less specific path mappings are sent. For example, a cookie "name1=foo1" with a path mapping of "/" should be sent after a cookie "name2=foo2" with a path mapping of "/test" when they are both to be sent.

A client is restricted in the number of cookies it can store. Here are the specifications:

300 cookies total.

4 kilobytes per cookie.

20 cookies per server or domain.

When the 300 cookie limit or the 20 cookie per server limit is met, clients should delete the least recently used cookie. Likewise, when a cookie is larger than 4 kilobytes it should be trimmed to fit. The cookie name should remain intact as long as it is less than 4 kilobytes.

When a CGI script attempts to delete a cookie, it can do it by returning a cookie with the same name, and an expires time which is set in the past. The path and name must match exactly in order for the expiring cookie to replace the valid cookie.

The Set-cookie response header should never be cached.

When a proxy server receives a response that contains a Set-cookie header, it should propagate the Set-cookie header to the client. Likewise, if a client request contains a cookie header, it should be forwarded through a proxy.

Examples

Let's look at a few examples which will show us how exchanges take place with the use of cookies. Then we'll examine a complete JavaScript example that will illustrate how to create a cookie.

CASE 1: FIRST TRANSACTION SEQUENCE

In this CGI example the client requests a document and receives the following response:

```
Set-Cookie: CUSTOMER=GEORGE_WASHINGTON; path=/;
expires=Sunday, 11-Oct-98 07:22:34 GMT
```

Then, if the client requests a URL in path "/", it sends the following on this server:

```
Cookie: CUSTOMER=GEORGE_WASHINGTON
```

If the client requests a document and receives in the response

```
Set-Cookie: CATALOG_NUMBER=CHERRY_TREE_SEEDS_0001;
path=/
```

then, if the client requests a URL in path "/", it sends the following on this server:

```
Cookie: CUSTOMER=GEORGE_WASHINGTON;
  CATALOG_NUMBER=CHERRY_TREE_SEEDS_0001
```

If the client receives

```
Set-Cookie: DELIVERY=PONY_EXPRESS; path=/foo
```

then, if the client requests a URL in path "/", it sends the following on this server:

```
Cookie: CUSTOMER=GEORGE_WASHINGTON;
  CATALOG_NUMBER=CHERRY_TREE_SEEDS_0001
```

And, if the client requests a URL in path "/foo", it sends the following on this server:

```
Cookie: CUSTOMER=GEORGE_WASHINGTON;
  CATALOG_NUMBER=CHERRY_TREE_SEEDS_0001;
  DELIVERY=PONY_EXPRESS
```

Case 2: Second Transaction Sequence

First, let's start by assuming that all CGI mappings from case 1 have been cleared. Now, if the client receives

```
Set-Cookie: CATALOG_NUMBER=CHERRY_TREE_SEEDS_0001;
path=/
```

then, if the client requests a URL in path "/", it sends the following on this server:

```
Cookie: CATALOG_NUMBER=CHERRY_TREE_SEEDS_0001
```

If the client receives

```
Set-Cookie: CATALOG_NUMBER=SHOVEL_0014; path=/tools
```

then, if the client requests a URL in path "/tools", it sends the following on this server:

```
Cookie: CATALOG_NUMBER=SHOVEL_0014;
   CATALOG_NUMBER=CHERRY_TREE_SEEDS_0001
```

Notice that there are two name/value pairs named "CATALOG_NUMBER." This is because of the inheritance of the "/" mapping in addition to the "/tools" mapping.

CASE 3: CREATING A COOKIE

The following HTML document uses two simple JavaScript functions. The first function creates a simple cookie with the name "George_Washington." The second JavaScript function is called from within the first function to open, write, and close the document.

```
<HTML>
<HEAD>
<TITLE>Creating a cookie</TITLE>
<SCRIPT LANGUAGE="JavaScript">

function createcookie() {
   document.cookie="name = George_Washington"
   showcookie()
}

function showcookie() {
   document.open()
   document.write(document.cookie)
   document.close()
}

</SCRIPT>
</HEAD>

<BODY onLoad ="createcookie()">
</BODY>
</HTML>
```

Notice in Figure 19.1 that the spaces are not included when the name/value pair is written.

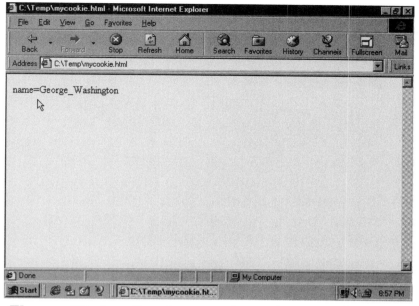

Figure 19-1: *Creating a cookie with a name/value pair.*

If a cookie of this name already exists, the browser will replace the contents of the original cookie with that of this cookie. Note: This application is currently supported by Microsoft's Internet Explorer versions 4.0 and later but not by Netscape.

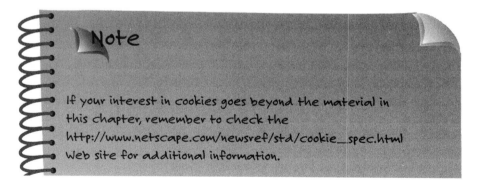

Note

If your interest in cookies goes beyond the material in this chapter, remember to check the http://www.netscape.com/newsref/std/cookie_spec.html Web site for additional information.

Summary

In this chapter you learned about the cookie property, its purpose, and how it is used to access information stored in a cookie file.

A lot of controversy concerning cookies has arisen because cookies are used by CGI scripts in server-side applications and JavaScripts in client-side applications to store and retrieve information. As you learned, this information is usually stored on the client side in a text file, such as cookies.txt.

With a little searching, you should be able to determine what user information has been stored in your computer's cookie file.

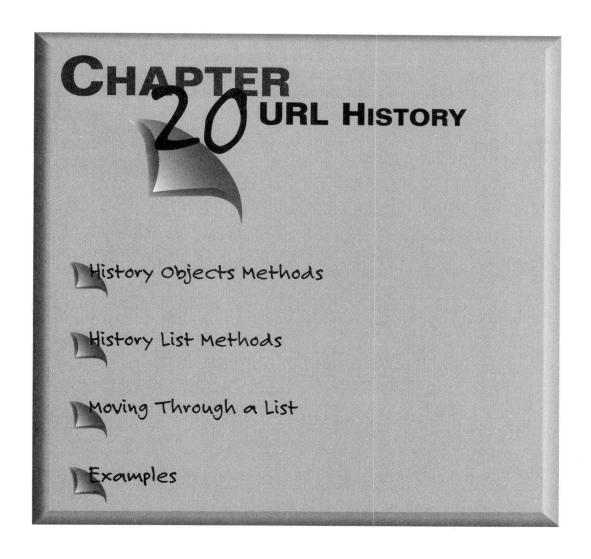

CHAPTER 20 URL HISTORY

- History Objects Methods

- History List Methods

- Moving Through a List

- Examples

Many products, such as Windows or the browser you are using, maintain history lists. A history list is simply a list of recently used applications, or, in the case of your Web browser, recently visited URL locations. A user can access the URL history by using the Go and Bookmark menus. If you click on the Go menu in either Netscape or Internet Explorer, you will see a list of the recent URLs for the current session. Figure 20.1 shows the URLs for a typical session.

By using simple JavaScript code in an application, you can direct the user to any location contained in the history list. You'll find methods, such as forward and backward, that will allow you to accomplish

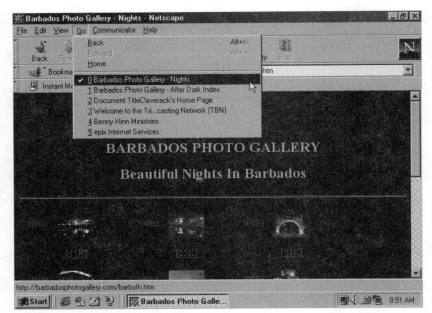

Figure 20–1: *The history list can be accessed via the Go menu for the current session.*

the same actions with software as the Forward and Back buttons on your browser.

In this chapter you will learn how to access and manipulate the history list with the use of the history object.

History Object Methods

History list information can be manipulated with JavaScript by using a number of methods. It is important to note that only the history list can be manipulated, not the URL contents of the list itself. To make use of the History object, JavaScript provides the methods shown in Table 20.1.

Table 20-1: *History Object Methods*

Method Name	Description
back()	Loads the most recent entry in the history list. This entry has an index of –1.
forward()	Loads the entry from the history list with an index value of +1.
go()	Loads the entry from the history list into the browser window.

The length property can be used to identify the number of entries in the history list. New versions of browsers also support current, next, and previous properties if data tainting is enabled on the browser.

In the next sections of this chapter, we'll examine each of the methods listed in Table 20.1 in more detail and create some simple examples. By the end of the chapter, you'll have a good understanding of the use and capabilities of the History object.

Moving through a List

History lists are created in a unique manner. Imagine a line representing positive and negative integer values, as shown in Figure 20.2.

On the line, shown in Figure 20.2, the number zero (0) represents the currently loaded document. The previously loaded document has an index of minus one (-1). Any documents loaded before that document have increasingly higher negative values. If a document is loaded after the current document, it will have an index of plus one (+1).

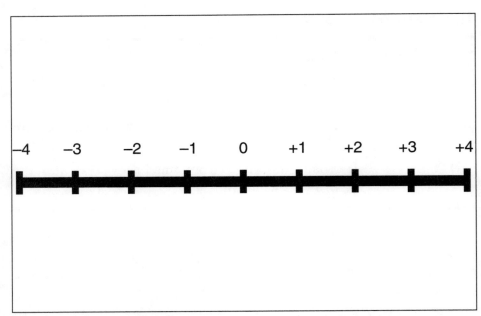

−4   −3   −2   −1   0   +1   +2   +3   +4

Figure 20–2: *History list indexing uses positive and negative integers.*

You must realize that if the current document has an index of zero (0), the history list must dynamically allocate index numbers as URL locations are changed. The index allocation is handled automatically.

Examples Using Methods and Properties

The examples in this section highlight how the history list can be manipulated with the various methods and properties.

History List Length

If you click the mouse on the Go menu, you can easily count the number of items in the current history list. Sometimes it might be helpful to determine it with a short piece of JavaScript code. The following

HTML document, named Length.html, and associated JavaScript code will display the current length of the history list.

```
<HTML>
<HEAD>
<TITLE> Length of History List </TITLE>
<SCRIPT LANGUAGE = "JavaScript">

function findlength() {
var his_str = ""

his_str = "History List Length"
his_str += " = " + history.length
alert(his_str)
}

</SCRIPT>
</HEAD>

<BODY>
<P> Click on button to view history
list length. </P>
<FORM>
<INPUT TYPE = "button" VALUE="Get Length"
onClick = "findlength()">
</FORM>

</BODY>
</HTML>
```

Figure 20.3 shows the execution of the program and a view of the current history list. Notice that the entries in the history list are not listed by index number.

Using the back() Method

To investigate the back() method, make sure your history list contains several URL locations. You can use the Back button in your browser to move backward in this history. The following HTML document, named Back.html, and associated JavaScript code will move backward in the history list via software control.

```
<HTML>
<HEAD>
<TITLE> Back up in the History List </TITLE>
<SCRIPT LANGUAGE = "JavaScript">
</SCRIPT>
```

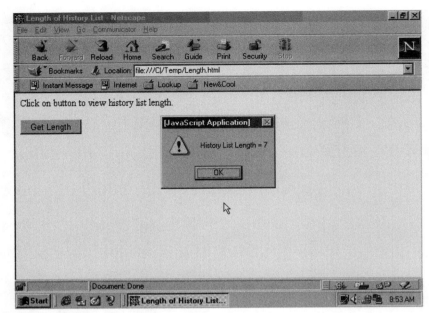

Figure 20–3: *An Alert box displays the current history list length.*

```
</HEAD>

<BODY>
<P> Click on button to back up in the
history list. </P>
<FORM>
<INPUT TYPE = "button" VALUE="Back up!"
onClick = "history.back()">
</FORM>

</BODY>
</HTML>
```

Figure 20.4 shows the Back.html document just prior to clicking the button.

Since the Back.html document has been loaded into the browser, it is the current entry. When the button is clicked, the browser will display the URL that was displayed just prior to loading this document, as shown in Figure 20.5.

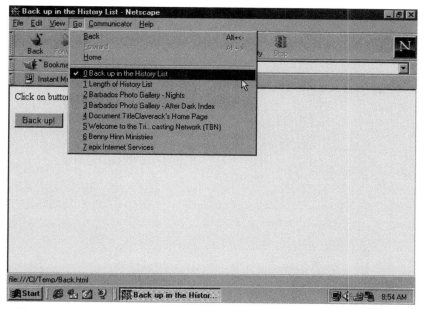

Figure 20–4:   The Back.html application is the current entry
in the history list.

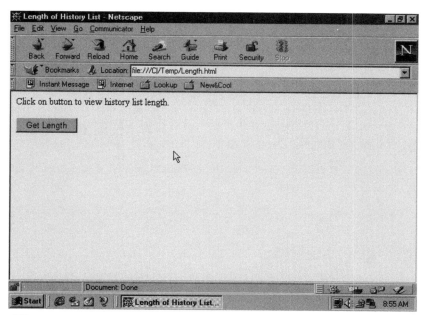

Figure 20–5:   By clicking the button, the previously loaded
URL is displayed.

Using the forward() Method

Actually, without doing some additional work, the forward method will do nothing in this example. Do you know why? Let's suppose the user developed a document, named Forward.html, similar to the following listing:

```
<HTML>
<HEAD>
<TITLE> Forward in the History List </TITLE>
<SCRIPT LANGUAGE = "JavaScript">
</SCRIPT>
</HEAD>

<BODY>
<P> Click on button to move forward in the
history list. </P>
<FORM>
<INPUT TYPE = "button" VALUE="Move Forward!"
onClick = "history.forward()">
</FORM>

</BODY>
</HTML>
```

The code looks similar enough to the back.html application in the previous application. If that application worked, why shouldn't this application work? Actually, you have probably figured this out. Since the document was loaded as the current or topmost entry, there is no place to move! Click all you want—you just sit at the current position in the history list. You have to load additional URLs and then back up to this document to test it. Then and only then will it work.

It is for this reason that the forward() method is not used nearly as frequently as the back() method.

Using the go() Method

To investigate the go() method, make sure your history list contains several URL locations. You can use the Back button in your browser to move backward in this history by clicking it once each time you wish to move backward. The following HTML document, named Go.html, and associated JavaScript code will move several steps backward in the history list via software control.

```
<HTML>
<HEAD>
<TITLE> Go Somewhere in the History List </TITLE>
<SCRIPT LANGUAGE = "JavaScript">
</SCRIPT>
</HEAD>

<BODY>
<P> Click on button to go backward in the
history list. </P>
<FORM>
<INPUT TYPE = "button" VALUE="Go Backward!"
onClick = "history.go(-3)">
</FORM>

</BODY>
</HTML>
```

Figure 20.6 shows the Go.html document just prior to clicking the button.

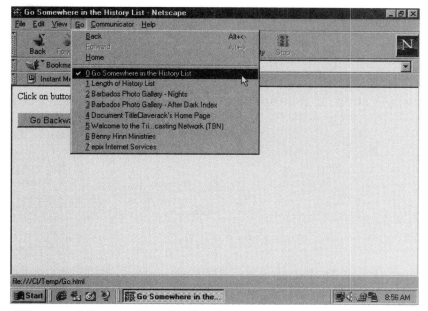

Figure 20–6:   _The Go.html application is the current entry in the history list._

Since the Go.html document has been loaded into the browser, it is the current entry. When the button is clicked, the browser will back up three URL entries, counting the current entry as the first. Figure 20.7 shows where we landed on our computer.

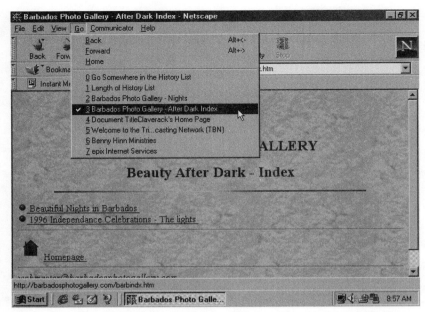

Figure 20–7: *By clicking the button, the go() method backs up several entries in the history list.*

If you are still trying to figure out how we got here, refer to Figure 20.3 which showed the history list for the current session.

Moving in Both Directions

Now that you've learned how to use the forward() and back() methods, let's combine them in one HTML document to create an HTML document with a little more versatility. You can still use the Back and Forward buttons in your browser to move backward or forward in the history. The following HTML document, named Both.html, and associated JavaScript code will give you the same results under software control.

```
<HTML>
<HEAD>
<TITLE> Have it both ways </TITLE>
<SCRIPT LANGUAGE = "JavaScript">

function goforward() {
  history.forward()
}
```

```
function gobackward() {
  history.back()
}

</SCRIPT>
</HEAD>

<BODY>
<P> Click on button to view history list
properties. </P>
<FORM>
<INPUT TYPE = "button" VALUE="Forward"
onClick = "goforward()">
<INPUT TYPE = "button" VALUE="Backward"
onClick = "gobackward()">
</FORM>

</BODY>
</HTML>
```

Figure 20.8 shows the Both.html document and the current history list just prior to clicking either the Forward or Backward button.

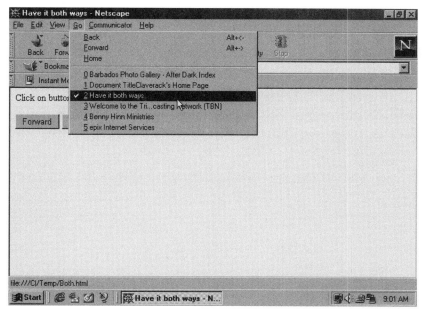

Figure 20–8: *The Both.html application is the current entry in the history list.*

If you load several URLs before and after loading the Both.html document, you can click either button and see a change in the window. Figure 20.9 shows the results of clicking the Forward button.

Figure 20–9: *By clicking the Forward button, the next URL is displayed.*

Summary

In this chapter you learned how your browser, and even Windows, use and maintain history lists. By maintaining a set of recently visited URL locations, or applications in the case of Windows, a user can access this list by using the Go and Bookmark menus.

History lists make it easy to revisit popular URL locations that you have found interesting.

CHAPTER 21
THE NAVIGATOR OBJECT

Navigator Object Properties

Examples

Often it is important to be able to detect, with software, user-specific information. The Navigator object will allow us to find information on the browser name, version, code name, and agent.

When this information is available, it is possible to create HTML documents that operate correctly regardless of whether the user is using Netscape, Internet Explorer, or some other browser.

The Navigator object is similar to the Math object in that instances of the object do not need to be created before its use. To use the Navigator object, use the various object properties to return specific values.

In this chapter you will learn how to detect and view various Navigator object properties. With this information in hand you can develop more robust HTML documents that will work effectively on any browser.

Navigator Object Properties

The Navigator object supports a number of properties, as you can see in Table 21.1.

Table 21–1: *Navigator Object Properties*

Property Name	Description
AppName	Browser name.
AppVersion	Browser version number.
AppCodeName	Browser code name.
MimeTypes	Obtains an array of available mimetypes.
Plugins	Obtains an array of available plug-ins.
UserAgent	Browser user agent.

In the next sections of this chapter, we'll examine each of the Navigator properties listed in Table 21.1, with the exception of mimeTypes and plugins. The properties of mimeTypes and plugins will be examined in Chapter 22. By the end of the chapter, you'll have a good understanding of the use and capabilities of the Navigator object.

Examples Using Methods and Properties

The examples in this section are straightforward and highlight how the various properties of the Navigator object can be read and manipulated with simple JavaScript code.

The appName Property

The following simple HTML document, named Name.html, will return the name of the browser being used.

```
<HTML>
<HEAD>
<TITLE> Navigator Object </TITLE>
</HEAD>
<BODY>
<SCRIPT LANGUAGE = "JavaScript">

var browser_str = ""

browser_str = "Name = " + navigator.appName

document.open()
document.write(browser_str)
document.close()

</SCRIPT>
</BODY>
</HTML>
```

Figure 21.1 shows the execution of the program and displays the browser being used for this example.

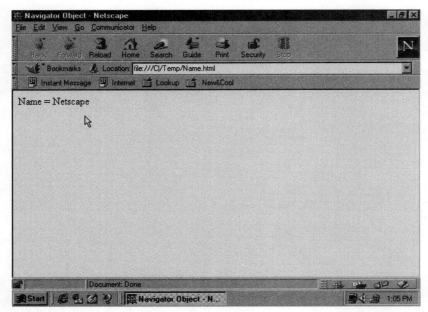

Figure 21–1:   *The current browser's name is displayed.*

The appVersion Property

Sometimes it might be desirable to know the version of the browser being used to determine if certain tags will be valid. The following HTML document, named Version.html, will return the version of the browser.

```
<HTML>
<HEAD>
<TITLE> Navigator Object </TITLE>
</HEAD>
<BODY>
<SCRIPT LANGUAGE = "JavaScript">

var browser_str = ""

browser_str = "Version = " + navigator.appVersion

document.open()
document.write(browser_str)
document.close()

</SCRIPT>
</BODY>
</HTML>
```

Figure 21.2 shows the current version when Netscape is being used as the browser.

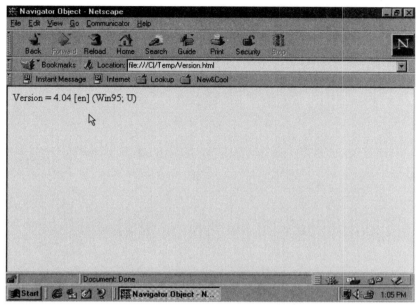

Figure 21–2: *Netscape's current version number for this application.*

The string information returned by appVersion uses the following format:

```
version number (additional information)
```

In the example shown in Figure 21.2, the Netscape version number is 4.04. The platform is incorrectly identified as Win95 since we are using a Windows 98 Beta. The "U" indicates a domestic version of Navigator that uses strong encryption techniques. An "I" in this position means an international version.

Figure 21.3 shows the current version for Microsoft's Internet Explorer.

In the example shown in Figure 21.3, the Internet Explorer major version number is 4.0. The additional comments tell us that it is compatible with a minor version number (4.01) and is operating in a Windows 98 environment.

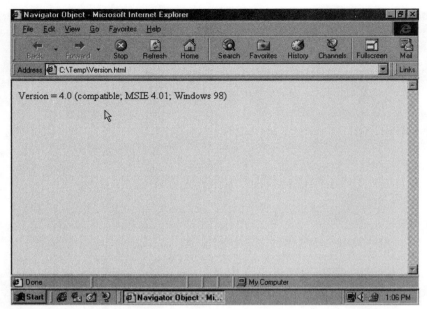

Figure 21–3: *The current version number for Microsoft Internet Explorer.*

Using the appCodeName Property

Without doing a lot of additional work, the previous HTML document can be modified to return the code name with the appCodeName property.

```
<HTML>
<HEAD>
<TITLE> Navigator Object </TITLE>
</HEAD>
<BODY>
<SCRIPT LANGUAGE = "JavaScript">

var browser_str = ""

browser_str = " Code Name = " + navigator.appCodeName

document.open()
document.write(browser_str)
document.close()

</SCRIPT>
</BODY>
</HTML>
```

Figure 21.4 shows the code name "Mozilla" is returned when run under Netscape. Actually, the same code name is returned from the Internet Explorer.

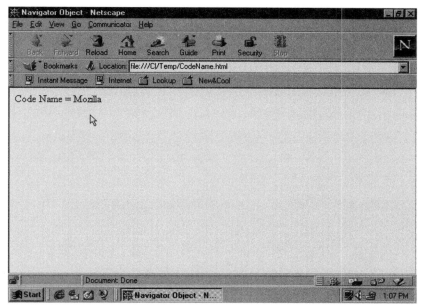

Figure 21–4: *The code name is determined with the appCodeName property.*

If Mozilla is returned as the code name, you are using either Netscape or Internet Explorer. Other browsers are likely to return different code names.

Using the userAgent Property

The userAgent property actually combines the information of the appCodeName and appVersion properties. The information is separated, in the string, by a "/". The following HTML document, named User.html, returns the string information from the user agent.

```
<HTML>
<HEAD>
<TITLE> Navigator Object </TITLE>
</HEAD>
<BODY>
```

```
<SCRIPT LANGUAGE = "JavaScript">

var browser_str = ""

browser_str = " userAgent = " + navigator.userAgent

document.open()
document.write(browser_str)
document.close()

</SCRIPT>
</BODY>
</HTML>
```

Figure 21.5 shows the code name "Mozilla" is returned when run under Netscape with the version number and platform version (incorrectly) attached to the string.

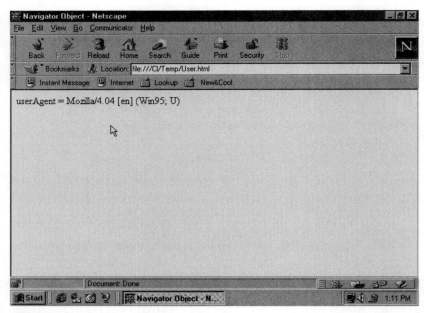

Figure 21–5: *The userAgent property combines the information provided by the appCodeName and appVersion properties for Netscape.*

Figure 21.6 shows the information rendered by the document under Microsoft's Internet Explorer.

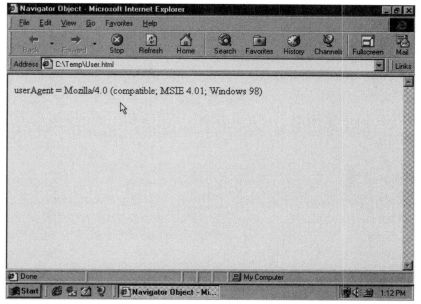

Figure 21–6: *The userAgent property combines the information provided by the appCodeName and appVersion properties for Internet Explorer.*

Browser- and Version-Specific Documents

The information returned by the various Navigator object properties allows us to test the browser platform to insure compatibility with the current document. The following application checks to see if the current browser is either Netscape or Internet Explorer. A simple alert is used to report the browser name.

```
<HTML>
<HEAD>
<TITLE> Navigator Object </TITLE>
<SCRIPT LANGUAGE = "JavaScript">

function decision() {

  var Browser_str = ""

  Browser_str = navigator.appName

  if (Browser_str == "Netscape")
    alert("Your browser is Netscape!")
  else {
```

```
      if (navigator.appName == "Microsoft Internet
Explorer")
        alert("Your browser is the Internet
Explorer!")
      else {
        alert("This browser is not Netscape or
Internet Explorer!")
      }
    }
}

</SCRIPT>
</HEAD>
</BODY>
<FORM>

<INPUT TYPE = "button" VALUE="What Browser is this?"
  onClick="decision()">

</FORM>
</BODY>
</HTML>
```

You can use code similar to this in a more robust application if you need to avoid HTML tags that are browser specific.

In a similar manner you can check the version number of the browser and make a similar decision. Here is a short HTML document with JavaScript code that will branch to two different locations dependent upon whether the version number of the browser is 4.0 or above.

```
<HTML>
<HEAD>
<TITLE> Navigator Object </TITLE>
<SCRIPT LANGUAGE = "JavaScript">

function decision() {

  var Browser_str = ""

  Browser_str = parseInt(navigator.appVersion)

  if (Browser_str >= 4)
```

```
    alert("Your browser is version 4 or greater!")
  else {
    alert("Your browser is not the latest version!")
  }
}

</SCRIPT>
</HEAD>
</BODY>
<FORM>

<INPUT TYPE = "button" VALUE="What Version is this?"
  onClick="decision()">

</FORM>
</BODY>
</HTML>
```

This code might be important for HTML documents designed to take advantage of certain dynamic HTML features.

Summary

In this chapter you learned how the Navigator object allows us to find information on the browser name, version, code name, and agent. This information helps create universal applications that operate correctly whether the user is using Netscape, Internet Explorer, or some other browser.

You have learned that the Navigator object is similar to the Math object in that instances of the object do not need to be created before its use. This chapter also investigated various Navigator object properties.

CHAPTER 22

THE PLUGIN AND MIMETYPE OBJECTS

- Plugin Object Properties

- MimeType Object Properties

- Examples

In the previous chapter you learned that the Navigator object provided two properties that weren't discussed in that chapter. These properties were the mimeTypes[] and the plugins[]. We postponed a discussion of these properties until this chapter in order to discuss two additional objects: the Plugin and MimeType objects.

Browsers use plug-ins to enhance their overall capability. For example, plug-ins can add sound and video capabilities simply and efficiently. Their *transparent* use makes them easy to implement, and in most cases, you won't even know they have been loaded. A browser will call a specific plug-in to process data that is referenced in an HTML document.

Plug-ins can be added at startup time or anytime during the browser session. Netscape and Internet Explorer have directories set aside just for plug-ins.

Using the <EMBED> Tag

The <EMBED> tag is used in an HTML document to reference data that will be handled by a plug-in. Here is a simple example:

```
<P> Add this AVI clip </P>
<EMBED SRC = "EARTHSML.AVI"
        WIDTH = 320
        HEIGHT = 240
        PLAY_LOOP = 5>
```

Here the SRC refers to the URL source for the data to be used by the plug-in. The WIDTH parameter gives the width, in pixels, for the image to be rendered. The HEIGHT parameter gives the height, in pixels, for the image to be rendered. In this example, the image will be displayed in an area 320 x 240 pixels. The PLAY_LOOP parameter designates how many times the AVI clip will be repeated.

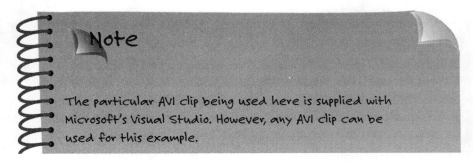

Note

The particular AVI clip being used here is supplied with Microsoft's Visual Studio. However, any AVI clip can be used for this example.

Now, using the previous portion of code to <EMBED> data, let's create an HTML document with a small portion of JavaScript code that will use the plug-in's parameter for the Navigator object to determine if the AVI plug-in is available. The Navigator object was discussed in the previous chapter. This document is named Plugins.html.

```
<HTML>
<HEAD>
<TITLE> Navigator Object </TITLE>
<SCRIPT LANGUAGE = "JavaScript">
```

```
function showit() {
  if (navigator.plugins["video/msvideo"])
    alert("You found it")
}

</SCRIPT>
</HEAD>
<BODY>

<P> Add this AVI clip </P>
<EMBED SRC = "EARTHSML.AVI"
    WIDTH = 320 HEIGHT = 240 PLAY_LOOP = 5>

<FORM>
<INPUT TYPE = "button" Name = "plugin"
  VALUE = "Display plugin info"
  onClick = showit()>
</FORM>

</BODY>
</HTML>
```

In this example, the AVI clip's data is made available to the plug-in using the <EMBED> tag. A user can click on the button to activate a simple JavaScript function named showit(). The showit() function uses the following code to determine if the AVI plug-in is available.

```
function showit() {
  if (navigator.plugins["video/msvideo"])
    alert("You found it")
}
```

The Plugin object is an array containing the names and descriptions of all plug-ins installed on the system. Here we simply check to see if "video/msvideo" is found in the array. If it is, the alert() function notifies the user of their success. The key here is to know that AVI files are associated with "video/msvideo." In the next sections, you'll learn how to determine that information concerning plug-ins installed on your system.

Plugin Object's Properties

The Plugin object supports a number of properties as you can see in Table 22.1.

Table 22-1: *Plugin Object's Properties*

Property Name	Description
name	plug-in name.
filename	plug-in file name.
description	a plug-in supplied description.
length	number of array elements.
type	array of mimeTypes

In the following example, we'll investigate several of these properties. By the end of this section, you'll have a good understanding of the use and capabilities of the Plugin object and its associated properties.

```
<HTML>
<HEAD>
<TITLE> Plugins </TITLE>
</HEAD>
<BODY>
<SCRIPT LANGUAGE = "JavaScript">

function showit() {
  var i

  document.writeln("<TABLE><TR VALIGN = TOP>")
  for(i = 0; i < navigator.plugins.length; i++) {
    document.writeln("<TR VALIGN = TOP>" + "<TD>" +
    navigator.plugins[i].name + "<TD>" +
    navigator.plugins[i].description + "</TR>")
  }
  document.writeln("</TABLE>")
}
</SCRIPT>

<P> Add this AVI clip </P>
<EMBED SRC="EARTHSML.AVI"
   WIDTH= 320 HEIGHT=240 PLAY_LOOP=5>

<FORM>
<INPUT TYPE = "button" Name="plugin"
  VALUE="Display plugin info"
  onClick=showit()>
</FORM>
```

```
</BODY>
</HTML>
```

Plug-in information is stored in an array. To access any array element, simply use the parameter name, filename, description, or length. In this example, a simple table will be created that will display the name and description of each plug-in. The array starts at an index value of 0. The array's length is reported by the length parameter.

```
function showit() {
  var i

  document.writeln("<TABLE><TR VALIGN = TOP>")
  for(i = 0; i < navigator.plugins.length; i++) {
    document.writeln("<TR VALIGN = TOP>" + "<TD>" +
    navigator.plugins[i].name + "<TD>" +
    navigator.plugins[i].description + "</TR>")
  }
  document.writeln("</TABLE>")
}
```

Figure 22.1 shows the document just prior to pushing the button. You can see a picture of the video clip even if you can't see the globe rotating.

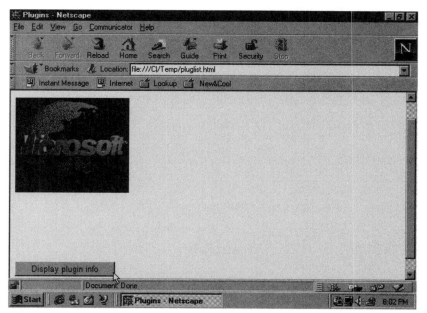

Figure 22–1: *A picture of the video clip before pushing the button.*

When the button is pushed, the plug-in information for this computer will be returned. Figure 22.2 shows the name and description for each installed plug-in.

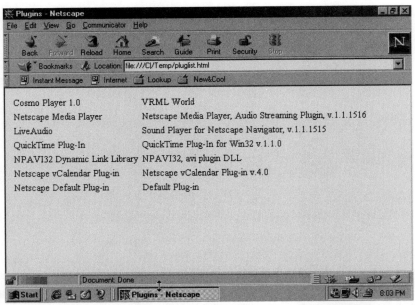

Figure 22–2: *A list of the plug-ins available on this computer.*

You can continue this example by creating a fancier table or by including a request for the file name of each plug-in.

If you want to use the type property, you will have to create a two-dimensional array, since the Plugin object is accessed as an array and each mimeType is then accessed as an array. Here is a simple example:

```
document.write(navigator.plugins[i][j].type)
```

MimeType Object's Properties

The MimeType object supports a number of properties, as you can see in Table 22.2.

Table 22–2: *MimeType Object's Properties*

Property Name	Description
type	MIME name.
description	a MIME-supplied description.
enabledPlugin	plug-in object for MIME type.
length	number of array elements.
suffixes	permitted file name extensions

The name MIME is derived from Multipurpose Internet Mail Extension. As you might guess by the name, it was created to allow attachments to be made for e-mail messages.

In the following example, we'll investigate several of these properties listed in Table 22.2 and learn what MIME types are available on this system. By the end of this section, you'll have a good understanding of the use and capabilities of the MimeType object and its associated properties.

```
<HTML>
<HEAD>
<TITLE> Multipurpose Internet Mail Extension </TITLE>
</HEAD>
<BODY>
<SCRIPT LANGUAGE = "JavaScript">

function showit() {
  var i

  document.writeln("<TABLE><TR VALIGN = TOP>")
  for(i = 0; i < navigator.mimeTypes.length; i++) {
    document.writeln("<TR VALIGN = TOP>" + "<TD>" +
    navigator.mimeTypes[i].description + "<TD>" +
    navigator.mimeTypes[i].type + "<TD>" +
    navigator.mimeTypes[i].suffixes + "</TR>")
  }
  document.writeln("</TABLE>")
}
</SCRIPT>

<P> Add this AVI clip </P>
<EMBED SRC="EARTHSML.AVI"
   WIDTH= 320 HEIGHT=240 PLAY_LOOP=5>

<FORM>
```

```
<INPUT TYPE = "button" Name="plugin"
  VALUE="Display plugin info"
  onClick=showit()>
</FORM>

</BODY>
</HTML>
```

Information on MIME types is stored in an array. To access any array element, simply use the parameters—type, description, enablePlugin, length, or suffixes.

In this example, the globe will continue to turn! In addition, a simple table will be created that will display the description, type, and suffixes of each array entry. The array starts at an index value of 0. The array's length is reported by the length parameter.

When the button is pushed, the MIME type information for this computer will be returned. Figure 22.3 shows the requested information for each MIME type.

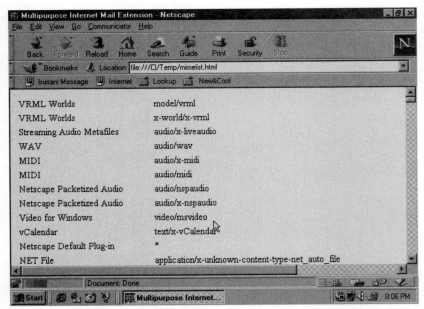

Figure 22–3: A list of the MIME types available on this computer.

Now, while looking at Figure 22.3, flip back in the book to the first example in this chapter named Plugins.html. That example set about to determine if a particular AVI plug-in had been installed. We checked to see if the following statement was true:

```
if (navigator.plugins["video/msvideo"])
```

You might have questioned how we knew to look for "video/msvideo" to check for an AVI plug-in. The answer is that we had the information from the MIME array. Can you find "video/msvideo" in the list of Figure 22.3?

Summary

In this chapter you learned about two additional Navigator object properties: mimeTypes[] and plugins[]. These properties closely parallel the Plugin and MimeType objects.

By using these Navigator object properties, you learned, for example, that plug-ins can add sound and video capabilities to an HTML document. Now you have tools that will add a professional touch to your documents.

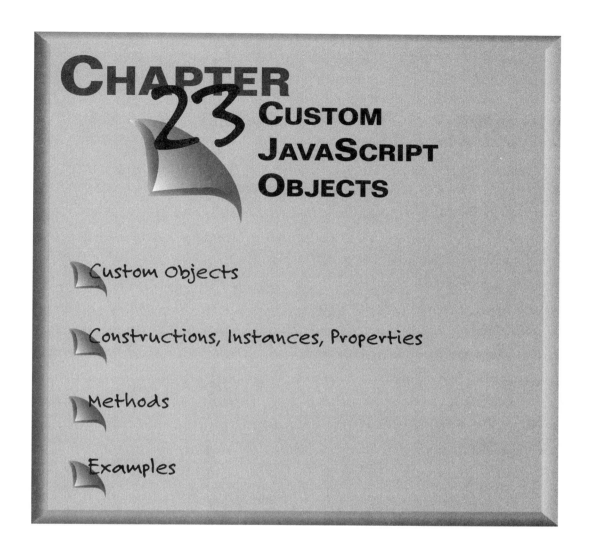

CHAPTER 23 CUSTOM JAVASCRIPT OBJECTS

- Custom Objects

- Constructions, Instances, Properties

- Methods

- Examples

In this chapter we'll investigate the techniques involved with creating custom JavaScript objects. In the previous chapters we have worked with various JavaScript objects such as Math, Navigator, Plugins, and MimeType. As you know from the previous chapters these objects often include properties, methods, and events that enhance their performance and make the supplied object more versatile.

If you have programmed in object-oriented C++, you know the value of good object libraries such as the Microsoft Foundation Class (MFC) library. Well-developed libraries save the developer design time, debugging time, and ensure a common interface when developing application code. JavaScript objects, developed alone in an application or in a group and saved in a library, offer the same advantages.

In this chapter you will learn how to create simple custom objects that include their own properties and methods.

Custom Object Makeup

You will find that developing custom JavaScript objects does not differ that much from writing JavaScript functions. While there are commercial products that JavaScript objects use almost automatically, there is nothing mysterious about creating your own objects with the tools you have already learned about throughout this book.

Most custom JavaScript objects involve the creation of a constructor, definition of object properties, methods, and events and possibly the use of prototype methods. We'll investigate each of these components in the following sections.

Constructors

Custom JavaScript objects are defined with a special class of function called a constructor. Here is a simple constructor that will be used to define a custom automobile object.

```
function automobile(autoname, automanuf, automodel,
                    autocolor, autobody) {

    // properties
    this.name = autoname
    this.manuf = automanuf
    this.model = automodel
    this.color = autocolor
    this.body = autobody


    // methods
    this.showit = showit
}
```

As you can see, the constructor takes on the familiar form of an object that you learned how to create in Chapter 11 and uses the **function** keyword. In this example, the constructor accepts five parameters (autoname...autobody). The self-referential keyword **this** is used so that the Automobile object can be referenced from other parts of the HTML document. This object uses one method, showit(), that is defined external to the object.

Instances

When you learned to create objects in Chapter 11, you also learned that instances of an object are created with the *new* statement. You have also learned that before using built-in JavaScript objects, you'll need to create an instance of the object with the *new* statement. There are a few exceptions to this rule, such as the Math object, which really serves as a simple container object.

If an instance of the previously created object is desired, it could take on this form.

```
SportUtility = new automobile("Jeep", "Chrysler",
"Wrangler",

                                "Green", "Soft Top")
```

More than one instance of the object is possible, so the following instantiation is also possible.

```
SportCar = new automobile("ZX2", "Ford", "Escort",
                        "Red", "Sedan")
```

In both cases, the *new* statement is used to create a unique instance of the Automobile object.

Properties

Properties can be referenced in custom objects just as they are in regular objects, with the use of the dot (.) member operator. Using our previous examples, the following properties of individual objects could be returned using the dot (.) member operator.

```
SportCar.manuf
SportUtility.color
```

```
SportUtility.body
SportCar.name
```

The same form can be used to set object properties. For example, you might see JavaScript code similar to the following:

```
SportUtility.color = "black"
SportCar.manuf = "GM"
```

Methods

Methods are referenced in the same manner as properties. The dot (.) member operator uses the same syntax as with regular objects. Again, from our previous examples, the object method could be referenced as shown in the following examples:

```
SportCar.showit()
SportUtility.showit()
```

Prototype Methods

A special type of custom object method is called the prototype method. When instances of the custom object are created using the new operator, prototype methods will apply to all instances of the object.

For example, it is often useful to add methods that can be used to print results to the screen. For example, the syntax for a prototype method using strings takes on the following form:

```
this.toWrite = new Function("return this.name + \
                            ', ' + this.manuf +
\
                            ', ' + this.model +
\
                            ', ' + this.color +
\
                            ', ' + this.body")
```

In this section we'll investigate three example applications that will illustrate many of the uses for custom objects and prototype methods.

A Custom Automobile Object

In the first example, we'll combine the bits and pieces of code shown in this chapter up to this point. The completed HTML document, named CustObj.html, will contain the custom Automobile object and two instantiations of the object: SportUtility and SportCar.

```
<HTML>
<HEAD>
<TITLE> A Custom Object </TITLE>
<SCRIPT LANGUAGE = "JavaScript">

function showit() {
  with (document) {
    open()
    write(this.name + ", ")
    write(this.manuf + ", ")
    write(this.model + ", ")
    write(this.color + ", ")
    write(this.body)
    close()
  }
}

function automobile(autoname, automanuf, automodel,
                    autocolor, autobody) {
  // properties
  this.name = autoname
  this.manuf = automanuf
  this.model = automodel
  this.color = autocolor
  this.body = autobody

  // methods
  this.showit = showit
}
```

```
var SportUtility
var SportCar

SportUtility = new automobile("Jeep", "Chrysler",
"Wrangler",
                                "Green", "Soft Top")
SportCar = new automobile("ZX2", "Ford", "Escort",
                            "Red", "Sedan")
</SCRIPT>
</HEAD>

<BODY>

<P>Click on the appropriate button to view specific
properties of a unique custom object.</P>

<FORM>
<INPUT TYPE = "button" Name="SU"
  VALUE="Sport Utility"
  onClick="SportUtility.showit()">
<INPUT TYPE = "button" Name="SC"
  VALUE="Sport Car"
  onClick="SportCar.showit()">
</FORM>

</BODY>
</HTML>
```

Figure 23.1 shows the initial screen after loading the CustObj.html document.

Two instantiations of the custom object are accessible. If you click either button, the showit() function will print details of the particular instantiation's member variables to the window. Figure 23.2 shows the output for the SportUtility instantiation.

A Custom Automobile Object with Prototype Method

In the second example, named ProtoStr.html, we'll simply modify the previous example to include a prototype method. The HTML document will contain the custom Automobile object and two instantiations of the object: SportUtility and SportCar. In addition, you'll see how the prototype method is added to the custom object. Here is the complete HTML document.

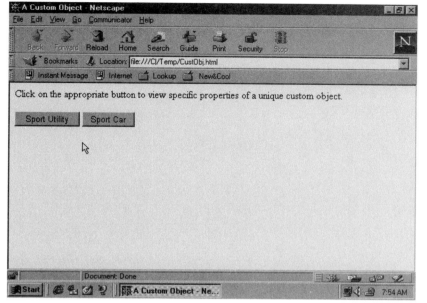

Figure 23–1:   The initial screen of the HTML document containing a custom object.

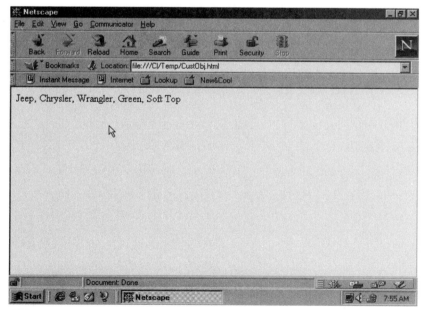

Figure 23–2:   The SportUtility instantiation's member variable information is displayed.

```
<HTML>
<HEAD>
<TITLE> A Custom Object with Prototype Method
</TITLE>
<SCRIPT LANGUAGE = "JavaScript">

function showit(mydata) {
  with (document) {
    open()
    write(mydata)
    close()
  }
}

function automobile(autoname, automanuf, automodel,
                    autocolor, autobody) {
  // properties
  this.name = autoname
  this.manuf = automanuf
  this.model = automodel
  this.color = autocolor
  this.body = autobody
}

var SportUtility
var SportCar

SportUtility = new automobile("Jeep", "Chrysler",
"Wrangler",
                              "Green", "Soft Top")
SportCar = new automobile("ZX2", "Ford", "Escort",
                          "Red", "Sedan")
// prototype method
automobile.prototype.toWrite = new Function("return
this.name + \
                                             ', '
+ this.manuf + \
                                             ', '
+ this.model + \
                                             ', '
+ this.color + \
                                             ', '
+ this.body")
</SCRIPT>
</HEAD>

<BODY>
<P>Click on the appropriate button to view specific
properties of a unique custom object.</P>

<FORM>
<INPUT TYPE = "button" Name="SU"
```

```
VALUE="Sport Utility"
  onClick=showit(SportUtility.toWrite())>
<INPUT TYPE = "button" Name="SC"
  VALUE="Sport Car"
  onClick=showit(SportCar.toWrite())>
</FORM>

</BODY>
</HTML>
```

In this example, the prototype method is defined outside the custom Automobile object using the **prototype** keyword.

```
// prototype method
automobile.prototype.toWrite = new Function("return
this.name + \
                                             ', '
+ this.manuf + \
                                             ', '
+ this.model + \
                                             ', '
+ this.color + \
                                             ', ' +
this.body")
```

The prototype method returns a string built of the custom object's properties. Examine the complete HTML document and note that the showit() function is not a part of the custom object as it was in the first example.

Thus, when information is to be displayed for a particular instance of the custom object, the onClick parameter for the pushbutton must also be changed.

```
<INPUT TYPE = "button" Name="SC"
  VALUE="Sport Car"
  onClick=showit(SportCar.toWrite())>
```

Figure 23.3 shows the output from this application when the Sport Car button is selected.

A Custom Object with Prototype Method

In the third example, named ProtoVal.html, we'll modify the previous example to allow us to make numeric calculations and return a result. The custom object named Hypotenuse includes a prototype method. Here is the complete HTML document.

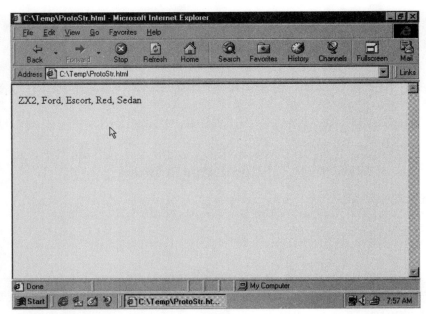

Figure 23–3: *The prototype method returns string information to the showit() function.*

```
<HTML>
<HEAD>
<TITLE> A Custom Object with Prototype Method
</TITLE>
<SCRIPT LANGUAGE = "JavaScript">

function showit(mydata) {
  with (document) {
    open()
    write(mydata)
    close()
  }
}

function hypotenuse(n1, n2) {
  // properties
  this.num1 = n1
  this.num2 = n2
  this.thevalue = Math.sqrt(this.num1 * this.num1
                            + this.num2 *
this.num2)
}

var gethypot

gethypot = new hypotenuse(100, 200)

// prototype method
```

```
hypotenuse.prototype.toWrite = new Function("return
'<BR>' \
                                    + 'The base is = '\
                                    + this.num1 +
'<BR>'\
                                    + 'The height is =
'\
                                    + this.num2\
                                    + '<BR><BR>'\
                                    + 'The hypotenuse
is = '\
                                    + this.thevalue")
</SCRIPT>
</HEAD>

<BODY>
<P>Click on the button to view the
sides and hypotenuse of a right triangle.</P>

<FORM>
<INPUT TYPE = "button" Name="hypot"
   VALUE="Calculate Hypotenuse"
   onClick=showit(gethypot.toWrite())>
</FORM>

</BODY>
</HTML>
```

This example is particularly interesting because it shows that an object can be called within a custom object. Examine the following portion of code:

```
function hypotenuse(n1, n2) {
   // properties
   this.num1 = n1
   this.num2 = n2
   this.thevalue = Math.sqrt(this.num1 * this.num1
                                    + this.num2 *
this.num2)
}
```

Notice that the Math object is used to calculate the square root of the sum of the squared triangular sides. The prototype method, toWrite(), returns the numeric results to the screen in a formatted form.

```
// prototype method
hypotenuse.prototype.toWrite = new Function("return
'<BR>' \
                                    + 'The base is = '\
                                    + this.num1 +
'<BR>'\
```

```
                                           +  'The height is =
 '\
                                           +  this.num2\
                                           +  '<BR><BR>'\
                                           +  'The hypotenuse
is = '\
                                           +  this.thevalue")
```

Figure 23.4 shows the output from this application when the button is selected.

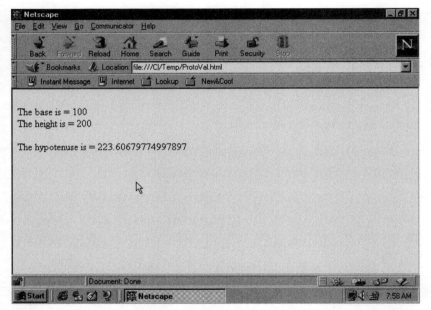

Figure 23–4: *The sides and hypotenuse of a right triangle are returned.*

Summary

In this chapter you learned some of the newest concepts dealing with JavaScript and creating custom objects. If this topic interests you, we recommend you continue your development by checking out Netscape's Web location. Here you will learn the latest developments in this exciting and ever-changing field.

You may have reached the end of this book, but you have not reached the end of what there is to learn. We're *not* finished either! See you on the Web!

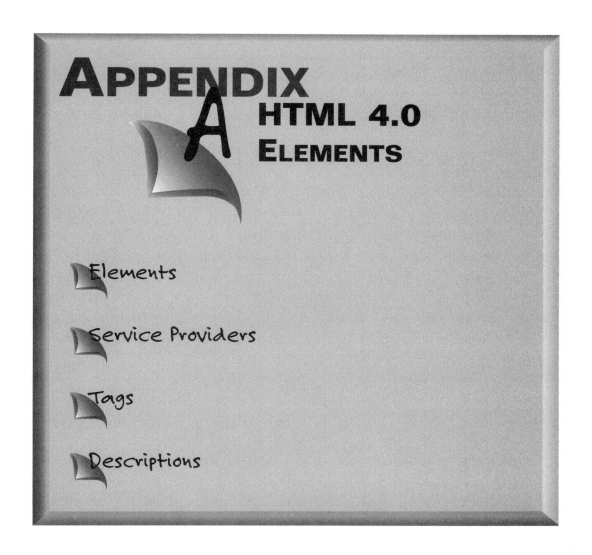

APPENDIX A
HTML 4.0 ELEMENTS

- Elements
- Service Providers
- Tags
- Descriptions

Table A.1 contains the elements approved for HTML 4.0. You will also find information reflecting the elements supported by Microsoft Internet Explorer and Netscape.

Table A–1: *HTML 4.0 Elements*

Element	Internet Explorer	Netscape	Start Tag	End Tag	Description
A	yes	yes	yes	yes	Anchor
ACRONYM	yes	yes	yes	yes	Acronym

471

Table A-1: HTML 4.0 Elements (Continued)

Element	Internet Explorer	Netscape	Start Tag	End Tag	Description
ADDRESS	yes	yes	yes	yes	Author information
APPLET	yes	yes	yes	yes	Java applet
AREA	yes	yes	yes	no	Client-side image map area
B	yes	yes	yes	yes	Bold font
BASE	yes	yes	yes	no	Document-based URL
BASEFONT	yes	yes	yes	no	Font size
BDO	yes	yes	yes	yes	BiDi override
BIG	yes	yes	yes	yes	Large text style
BLOCKQUOTE		yes	yes	yes	yes (Block quotation)
BODY	yes	yes	optional	optional	Document body
BR	yes	yes	yes	no	Line break
BUTTON	yes	yes	yes	yes	Pushbutton
CAPTION	yes	yes	yes	yes	Table caption
CENTER	yes	yes	yes	yes	Alignment (center)
CITE	yes	yes	yes	yes	Citation
CODE	yes	yes	yes	yes	Code fragment
COL	yes	no	yes	no	Table column

Element	Internet Explorer	Netscape	Start Tag	End Tag	Description
COLGROUP	yes	no	yes	optional	Table column (group)
DD	yes	yes	yes	optional	Definition description
DEL	yes	yes	yes	yes	Deleted text
DFN	yes	yes	yes	yes	Instance definition
DIR	yes	yes	yes	yes	Directory
DIV	yes	yes	yes	yes	Generic language or style container
DL	yes	yes	yes	yes	Definition list
DT	yes	yes	yes	optional	Definition term
EM	yes	yes	yes	yes	Emphasis (similar to bold)
FIELDSET	yes	yes	yes	yes	Form control group
FONT	yes	yes	yes	yes	Font (local)
FORM	yes	yes	yes	yes	Form (interactive)
FRAME	yes	yes	yes	no	Frame (subwindow)
FRAMESET	yes	yes	yes	yes	Subdivision of window
H1	yes	yes	yes	yes	Heading (style 1)

Table A–1: *HTML 4.0 Elements (Continued)*

Element	Internet Explorer	Netscape	Start Tag	End Tag	Description
H2	yes	yes	yes	yes	Heading (style 2)
H3	yes	yes	yes	yes	Heading (style 3)
H4	yes	yes	yes	yes	Heading (style 4)
H5	yes	yes	yes	yes	Heading (style 5)
H6	yes	yes	yes	yes	Heading (style 6)
HEAD	yes	yes	optional	optional	Document head
HR	yes	yes	yes	no	Horizontal rule
HTML	yes	yes	optional	optional	Document root element
I	yes	yes	yes	yes	Italic font style
IFRAME	yes	yes	yes	yes	In-line sub-window
IMG	yes	no	yes	no	Embedded image
INPUT	yes	yes	yes	no	Form control
INS	yes	yes	yes	yes	Inserted text
ISINDEX	yes	yes	yes	no	Single-line prompt

Element	Internet Explorer	Netscape	Start Tag	End Tag	Description
KBD	yes	yes	yes	yes	User entered text
LABEL	yes	yes	yes	yes	Field label text
LEGEND	yes	yes	yes	yes	Fieldset legend
LI	yes	yes	yes	optional	List item
LINK	yes	no	yes	no	Link
MAP	yes	yes	yes	yes	Client-side image map
MENU	yes	yes	yes	yes	Menu list
META	yes	yes	yes	no	Meta information
NOFRAMES	yes	yes	yes	yes	Container for non-frame-based rendering
NOSCRIPT	yes	no	yes	yes	Container for non-script-based rendering
OBJECT	yes	yes	yes	yes	Embedded object
OL	yes	yes	yes	yes	Ordered list
OPTION	yes	no	yes	optional	Selectable choice
P	yes	yes	yes	optional	Paragraph
PARAM	yes	yes	yes	no	Property value

Table A–1: HTML 4.0 Elements (Continued)

Element	Internet Explorer	Netscape	Start Tag	End Tag	Description
PRE	yes	yes	yes	yes	Preformatted text
Q	yes	yes	yes	yes	In-line quote
S	yes	yes	yes	yes	Strike-through (text style)
SAMP	yes	yes	yes	yes	Program output, scripts, and so on.
SCRIPT	yes	yes	yes	yes	Script statement
SELECT	yes	yes	yes	yes	Option selector
SMALL	yes	yes	yes	yes	Small text style
SPAN	yes	no	yes	yes	Generic language or style container
STRIKE	yes	yes	yes	yes	Strike-through text
STRONG	yes	yes	yes	yes	Strong emphasis
STYLE	yes	no	yes	yes	Style information
SUB	yes	yes	yes	yes	Subscript
SUP	yes	yes	yes	yes	Superscript
TABLE	yes	yes	yes	yes	Table

Element	Internet Explorer	Netscape	Start Tag	End Tag	Description
TBODY	yes	no	optional	optional	Table body
TD	yes	yes	yes	optional	Table data cell
TEXTAREA	yes	yes	yes	yes	Text field (multiline)
TFOOT	yes	no	yes	optional	Table footer
TH	yes	yes	yes	optional	Table header cell
THEAD	yes	no	yes	optional	Table header
TITLE	yes	yes	yes	yes	Document title
TR	yes	yes	yes	optional	Table row
TT	yes	yes	yes	yes	Mono-spaced font style (teletype)
U	yes	yes	yes	yes	Underlined text style
\UL	yes	yes	yes	yes	Unordered list
VAR	yes	yes	yes	yes	Instance of a variable or program argument

Additional information on tags, elements, and containers can be found in each chapter of this book.

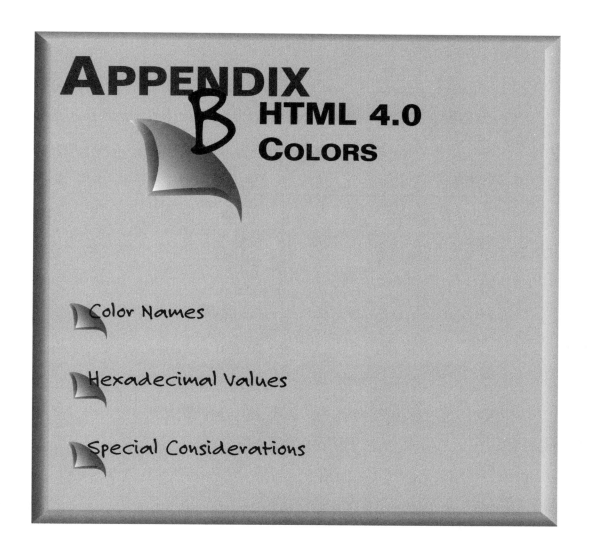

APPENDIX B

HTML 4.0 COLORS

- Color Names
- Hexadecimal Values
- Special Considerations

Document colors can often be specified by name or by a hexadecimal number giving the Red, Green, and Blue (RGB) mix. The attribute value type "color" (%Color) also refers to color definitions as specified in RGB.

For example, the color red can be specified by name or by the hexadecimal number #FF0000. Likewise, green can be specified by name or by the hexadecimal number #00FF00. Altering the RGB values can create color mixes. For example, fuchsia can be formed by name or by the hexadecimal number #FF00FF.

Each RGB color is represented by a hexadecimal number that varies from 00 to FF or from 0 to 255 decimal. That means that there are 256 x 256 x 256 = 16,777,216 possible color combinations that can be used if your equipment is capable of rendering those colors.

Table B.1 shows a list of standard HTML color names and their equivalent hexadecimal values.

Table B–1: *Color Names and Hexadecimal Values*

Color Name	Hexadecimal Values
Aqua	"#00FFFF"
Black	"#000000"
Blue	#0000FF"
Fuchsia	"#FF00FF"
Gray	"808080"
Green	#008000
Lime	"#00FF00"
Maroon	"#800000"
Navy	"#000080"
Olive	#808000"
Purple	"#800080"
Red	"#FF0000"
Silver	"#C0C0C0"
Teal	"#008080"
White	"#FFFFFF"
Yellow	"FFFF00"

The W3C suggests that even though colors add significant amounts of information to documents and make them more readable, they should be used with caution. The use of HTML elements and attributes for color has been deprecated in favor of style sheets.

Problems related to the use of colors include

- Colors can vary from one computer platform to another.
- Users who are color challenged cannot view or read certain combinations of colors.
- Background and foreground colors that are not well chosen add confusion to document readability.

Also, when practical, adopt common conventions to minimize user confusion. In addition, if you use a background image or set the background color, then be sure to set the various text colors as well.

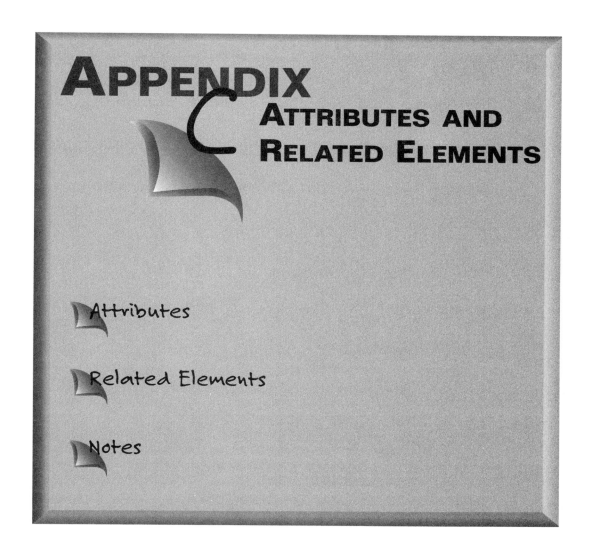

APPENDIX C
ATTRIBUTES AND RELATED ELEMENTS

- Attributes

- Related Elements

- Notes

Most elements use or require several attributes. Many of these attributes are shared in common between elements. The W3C's information on the relationship between parameters and elements is shown in Table C.1.

Table C–1: *Attribute and Element Relationships*

Attribute Name	Related Elements	Note
abbr	TD TH	Abbreviation used for header.

Table C–1: *Attribute and Element Relationships (Continued)*

Attribute Name	Related Elements	Note
accept-charset	FORM	Character sets that are supported.
accept	INPUT	MIME types available for file uploading.
accesskey	A AREA BUTTON INPUT LABEL LEGEND	Key character accessibility.
action	FORM	Provides information for the server-aside form handler.
align	CAPTION	Alignment is relative to the table.
	APPLET IFRAME IMG INPUT OBJECT	Horizontal or vertical alignment.
	LEGEND	Alignment is relative to fieldset.
	TABLE	Aligns table position relative to window.
	DIV H1 H2 H3 H4 H5 H6 P	Provides text or general alignment information.
	COL COLGROUP TBODY	

Table C–1: *Continued*

485

Attribute Name	Related Elements	Note
	TD	
	TFOOT	
	TH	
	THEAD	
	TR	
	HR	
alink	BODY	Use with bgcolor, text, link, vlink, and alink.
alt	APPLET	Provides alt information.
	INPUT	
	AREA	
	IMG	
archive	OBJECT	Archive list separated with spaces.
axes	TD	Header cell's ID list.
	TH	
axis	TD	List of groups of related headers.
	TH	
background	BODY	Document background (texture tile).
bgcolor	TABLE	Cell background color.
	TR	Row background color.
	TD	Cell background color.
	TH	
	BODY	Background color.
border	OBJECT	Link border width.
	IMG	
	TABLE	Sets frame width for table.
cellpadding	TABLE	Spacing within a cell.
cellspacing	TABLE	Spacing between cells.

Table C–1: *Attribute and Element Relationships (Continued)*

Attribute Name	Related Elements	Note
char	COL	Indicates the alignment char. For example, char='*'.
	COLGROUP TBODY TD TFOOT TH THEAD TR	
charoff	COL COLGROUP TBODY TD TFOOT TH THEAD TR	Provides the offset for the alignment character.
charset	A DIV LINK SCRIPT SPAN	Provides character encoding of a linked resource.
checked	INPUT	Used by radio buttons and checkboxes.
cite	BLOCKQUOTE Q	The URL for the source document.
	DEL INS	Provides information for the reason for the change.
class	Excluded elements: BASE BASEFONT FRAME FRAMESET HEAD	Provides a list of classes separated by spaces.

Table C–1: *Continued*

487

Attribute Name	Related Elements	Note
	HTML	
	IFRAME	
	META	
	PARAM	
	SCRIPT	
	STYLE	
	TITLE	
classid	OBJECT	Provides the implementation ID.
clear	BR	Indicates the text flow control.
code	APPLET	The class file for applet.
codebase	APPLET	Provides the base URL for applet (optional).
	OBJECT	Provides an additional URL when required by some systems.
codetype	OBJECT	Provides the code for Internet content type.
color	BASEFONT FONT	Provides an RGB color value in hexadecimal. For example, green is #00FF00."
cols	FRAMESET	When not specified, defaults to one column.
	TABLE	Used for immediate display mode.
	TEXTAREA	Provides compact information.
colspan	TD TH	Specifies the number of columns spanned by a cell.
compact	DIR MENU	Provides compact information.

Table C–1: *Attribute and Element Relationships (Continued)*

Attribute Name	Related Elements	Note
	DL OL UL	Indicates the reduced interitem spacing.
content	META	Related information.
coords	AREA	Provides a list of values separated by commas.
	A	Used with OBJECT SHAPES.
data	OBJECT	References an object's data.
datetime	DEL INS	Indicates an ISO date format (when changed).
declare	OBJECT	Declares but doesn't instantiate the flag.
defer	SCRIPT	UA may defer execution of script.
dir	Excluded elements: APPLET BASE BASEFONT BDO BR FONT FRAME FRAMESET HR IFRAME PARAM SCRIPT	Indicates the direction for text.
	BDO	Provides directionality.
disabled	BUTTON INPUT LABEL OPTGROUP	Indicates that the control is not available in this context.

Table C-1: *Continued*

489

Attribute Name	Related Elements	Note
	OPTION SELECT TEXTAREA	
enctype	FORM	Provides form enctype information.
face	BASEFONT FONT	Provides a list of font names separated by commas.
For	LABEL	Used to match field ID values.
Frame	TABLE	Specifies which part of a table frame to include.
Frameborder	FRAME IFRAME	Allows frame borders to be requested.
headers	TD TH, and so on	IDs for header cells.
Height	IFRAME OBJECT	Provides the height value.
	TD TH	Indicates cell height.
	IMG	Provides the height (in pixels).
	APPLET	
Href	A LINK	The URL for a linked resource.
	AREA	Acts as a hypertext link.
	BASE	Provides Href information.
hreflang	A DIV LINK SPAN	Language code.

Table C–1: *Attribute and Element Relationships (Continued)*

Attribute Name	Related Elements	Note
Hspace	OBJECT	Provides the horizontal gutter.
	APPLET IMG	
http-equiv	META	Indicates a HTTP response header name.
Id	Excluded elements: BASE HEAD HTML META SCRIPT STYLE TITLE	Provides a unique documentwide ID.
Ismap	IMG	Used with server-side image maps.
label	OPTION OPTGROUP	Used for hierarchical menus.
Lang	Excluded elements: APPLET BASE BASEFONT BR FONT FRAME FRAMESET HR IFRAME PARAM SCRIPT	Provides a language value.
Language	SCRIPT	Indicates the script language name (predefined).
link	BODY	Provides link information.

Table C–1: *Continued*

491

Attribute Name	Related Elements	Note
longdesc	IMG	Used as a link to a long description.
	FRAME	
	IFRAME	
marginheight	FRAME IFRAME	Provides margin heights (pixels).
marginwidth	FRAME IFRAME	Providesmargin widths (pixels)
maxlength	INPUT	Indicates the maximum characters for text fields.
media	STYLE	Use with the given media.
	DIV LINK SPAN	Use when rendering on the given media.
method	FORM	Indicates the method used to submit the form.
multiple	SELECT	The default is a single selection.
name	MAP TEXTAREA	Provides name information.
	APPLET	Allows multiple applets to locate each other.
	SELECT	Provides the field name.
	BUTTON	Allows a submit button for scripting or forms.
	FRAME IFRAME	Identifies the name of the frame for targeting.
	A	Indicates a link end.
	INPUT OBJECT	Allows submission as part of a form.

JavaScript and HTML 4.0 User's Resource

Table C–1: *Attribute and Element Relationships (Continued)*

Attribute Name	Related Elements	Note
	PARAM	Used to identify the property's name.
	META	Used to identify the meta information name.
nohref	AREA	The region has no action associated with it.
noresize	FRAME	Permits frames to be resized by the user.
noshade	HR	Indicates no shade.
nowrap	TD TH	Turns off word wrapping.
object	APPLET	Identifies a serialized applet file.
Onblur	A AREA BUTTON INPUT LABEL SELECT TEXTAREA	The identified element has lost the focus.
Onchange	INPUT SELECT TEXTAREA	The element's value was changed.
Onclick	Excluded elements: APPLET BASE BASEFONT BDO BR FONT FRAME FRAMESET HEAD HTML	Indicates that a mouse (pointer) button was clicked.

Table C–1: *Continued*

Attribute Name	Related Elements	Note
	IFRAME ISINDEX META PARAM SCRIPT STYLE TITLE	
ondblclick	Excluded elements: APPLET BASE BASEFONT BDO BR FONT FRAME FRAMESET HEAD HTML IFRAME ISINDEX META PARAM SCRIPT STYLE TITLE	Indicates that a mouse (pointer) button was double-clicked.
onfocus	A AREA BUTTON INPUT LABEL SELECT TEXTAREA	Indicates that the element has the focus.
onkeydown	Excluded elements: APPLET BASE BASEFONT	Indicates that a key (keyboard) was depressed.

Table C–1: *Attribute and Element Relationships (Continued)*

Attribute Name	Related Elements	Note
	BDO BR FONT FRAME FRAMESET HEAD HTML IFRAME ISINDEX META PARAM SCRIPT STYLE TITLE	
onkeypress	Excluded elements: APPLET BASE BASEFONT BDO BR FONT FRAME FRAMESET HEAD HTML IFRAME ISINDEX META PARAM SCRIPT STYLE TITLE	Indicates that a key (key board) was depressed and released.

Table C–1: *Continued*

495

Attribute Name	Related Elements	Note
onkeyup	Excluded elements: APPLET BASE BASEFONT BDO BR FONT FRAME FRAMESET HEAD HTML IFRAME ISINDEX META PARAM SCRIPT STYLE TITLE	Indicates that a depressed key (keyboard) was released.
onload	FRAMESET	Indicates that all the frames have been loaded.
	BODY	Indicates that the document has been loaded.
onmousedown	Excluded elements: APPLET BASE BASEFONT BDO BR FONT FRAME FRAMESET HEAD HTML IFRAME ISINDEX META	Indicates that a mouse (pointer) button was depressed.

Table C–1: *Attribute and Element Relationships (Continued)*

Attribute Name	Related Elements	Note
	PARAM SCRIPT STYLE TITLE	
onmousemove	Excluded elements: APPLET BASE BASEFONT BDO BR FONT FRAME FRAMESET HEAD HTML IFRAME ISINDEX META PARAM SCRIPT STYLE TITLE	Indicates that the mouse (pointer) was moved within the given area.
onmouseout	Excluded elements: APPLET BASE BASEFONT BDO BR FONT FRAME FRAMESET HEAD HTML IFRAME ISINDEX META PARAM	Indicates that the mouse (pointer) was moved away from the given area.

Table C–1: *Continued*

497

Attribute Name	Related Elements	Note
	SCRIPT STYLE TITLE	
onmouseover	Excluded elements: APPLET BASE BASEFONT BDO BR FONT FRAME FRAMESET HEAD HTML IFRAME ISINDEX META PARAM SCRIPT STYLE TITLE	Indicates that a mouse (pointer) was moved onto the given area.
onmouseup	Excluded elements: APPLET BASE BASEFONT BDO BR FONT FRAME FRAMESET HEAD HTML IFRAME ISINDEX META PARAM SCRIPT	Indicates that a depressed mouse (pointer) button was released.

Table C–1: *Attribute and Element Relationships (Continued)*

Attribute Name	Related Elements	Note
	STYLE	
	TITLE	
onreset	FORM	Indicates that the form has been reset.
onselect	INPUT	Indicates that text has been selected.
	TEXTAREA	
onsubmit	FORM	Indicates that the form has been submitted.
onunload	FRAMESET	Indicates that all frames have been removed.
	BODY	Indicates that the document has been removed.
profile	HEAD	Indicates the dictionary of meta information.
prompt	ISINDEX	Gives a prompt message.
readonly	TEXTAREA	Provides text area information.
	INPUT	Used for both text and passwords.
rel	A	Indicates forward link types.
	LINK	
rev	A	Indicates reverse link types.
	DIV	
	LINK	
	SPAN	
rows	FRAMESET	When not specified, the default is one row.
	TEXTAREA	Provides text area information.
rowspan	TD	Indicates the number of rows spanned by a ell.
	TH	

Table C-1: *Continued*

499

Attribute Name	Related Elements	Note
rules	TABLE	Indicates the number of rulings between rows and columns.
scheme	META	Allows the selection of the form of content.
scope	TD TH, etc.	Scope covered by header cells.
scrolling	FRAME IFRAME	Allows the inclusion of a scroll bar.
selected	OPTION	Provides selection information.
shape	AREA	Used to control the interpretation of coordinates.
	A	Used with OBJECT SHAPES.
shapes	OBJECT	Indicates that the object has shaped hypertext links.
size	HR	
	FONT	Specified size. For example, size="+2" or size=6.
	INPUT	Indicates input specific to each type of field.
	BASEFONT	Indicates the base font size.
	SELECT	Indicates that rows are visible.
span	COLGROUP	Specifies the default number of columns in a group.
	COL	Specifies the number of columns spanned by a group.

Table C–1: *Attribute and Element Relationships (Continued)*

Attribute Name	Related Elements	Note
src	SCRIPT	The URL for an external script.
	INPUT	Used for fields containing images.
	FRAME IFRAME	Indicates the source of the frame's content.
standby	OBJECT	The message that will be displayed during loading.
start	OL	Indicates the starting sequence number.
style	Excluded items: BASE BASEFONT FRAME FRAMESET HEAD HTML IFRAME META PARAM SCRIPT STYLE TITLE	Indicates the style information.
summary	TABLE	Gives the purpose or structure for output.
tabindex	A AREA BUTTON INPUT OBJECT SELECT TEXTAREA	Indicates the tabbing order position.

Table C–1: *Continued*

501

Attribute Name	Related Elements	Note
target	AREA BASE LINK	Indicates the location of the rendered linked resource.
	A	Indicates where to render a resource.
	DIV FORM SPAN	Indicates where to render the result.
text	BODY	Text information for the body of the document.
title	STYLE	Provides an advisory title.
	FRAME FRAMESET IFRAME META PARAM SCRIPT STYLE TITLE	Provides an advisory title (anchors).
type	OBJECT	Indicates the Internet content type for data.
	LINK	Provides the advisory Internet content type.
	INPUT	Indicates what type of control is needed.
	LI	Indicates a list item style.
	OL	Indicates the numbering style.
	UL	Indicates a bullet style.
	BUTTON	Indicates use as a form's Submit or Reset button.

Table C–1: *Attribute and Element Relationships (Continued)*

Attribute Name	Related Elements	Note
	SCRIPT	Indicates the content type for the script language.
	PARAM	Provides the media type information.
	A DIV STYLE SPAN	Indicates the content type for the style language.
usemap	OBJECT	Provided the image map reference.
	IMG INPUT	Indicates the use of a client-side image map.
valign	COL COLGROUP TBODY TD TROOT TH THEAD TR	Provides information for vertical alignment in cells.
value	OPTION	Indicates the default will be to element content.
	BUTTON	Indicates that information is passed to the server when submitted.
	PARAM	.Provides the property value.
	INPUT	Required by radio buttons and checkboxes.
	LI	Provides a reset to the sequence number.
valuetype	PARAM	Indicates how a value is to be interpreted.

Table C–1: *Continued*

503

Attribute Name	Related Elements	Note
version	HTML	Provides a constant value.
vlink	BODY	Provides link information.
vspace	OBJECT	Indicates the vertical gutter.
	APPLET IMG	
width	HR	Provides width information.
	IFRAME OBJECT	Provides the width information.
	TD TH	Width for a given cell.
	IMG	Provides the width information (pixels).
	APPLET	
	COL	Provides the width information for columns.
	COLGROUP	Provides the default width for enclosed columns.
	TABLE	Provides the table width relative to the window.
	PRE	Provides width information.

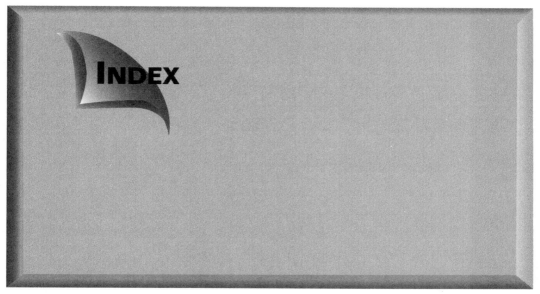

INDEX

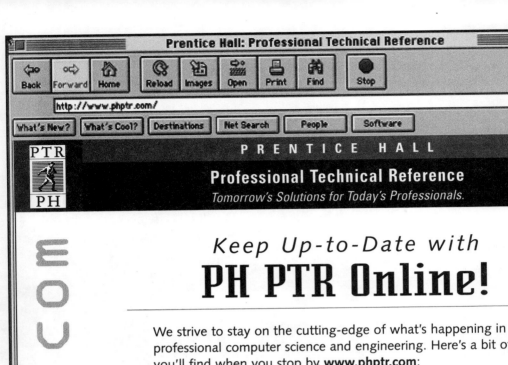